One, Holy, Catholic, and Apostolic

Tome 2

The Mercersburg Theology Study Series
Volume 7

The Mercersburg Theology Study Series presents attractive, readable, scholarly modern editions of the key writings of the nineteenth-century theological movement led by Philip Schaff and John Nevin. It aims to introduce the academic community and the broader public more fully to Mercersburg's unique blend of American and European, Reformed and Catholic theology.

Founding Editor
W. Bradford Littlejohn

Series Editors
Lee Barrett
David W. Layman

Published Volumes
1. *The Mystical Presence and the Doctrine of the Reformed Church on the Lord's Supper*
Edited by Linden J. DeBie
2. *Coena Mystica: Debating Reformed Eucharistic Theology*
Edited by Linden J. DeBie
3. *The Development of the Church*
Edited by David R. Bains and Theodore Louis Trost
4. *The Incarnate Word: Selected Writings on Christology*
Edited by William B. Evans
6. *Born of Water and the Spirit: Essays on the Sacraments and Christian Formation*
Edited by David W. Layman

One, Holy, Catholic, and Apostolic

Tome 2

John Nevin's Writings on Ecclesiology (1851–1858)

By
JOHN WILLIAMSON NEVIN

Edited by
Sam Hamstra Jr.

General Editor
David W. Layman

WIPF & STOCK · Eugene, Oregon

ONE, HOLY, CATHOLIC, AND APOSTOLIC, TOME 2
John Nevin's Writings on Ecclesiology (1851–1858)

Mercersburg Theology Study Series 7

Copyright © 2017 Wipf and Stock. All rights reserved. Except for brief quotations in critical publications or reviews, no part of this book may be reproduced in any manner without prior written permission from the publisher. Write: Permissions, Wipf and Stock Publishers, 199 W. 8th Ave., Suite 3, Eugene, OR 97401.

Wipf & Stock
An Imprint of Wipf and Stock Publishers
199 W. 8th Ave., Suite 3
Eugene, OR 97401

www.wipfandstock.com

PAPERBACK ISBN: 978-1-5326-1962-5
HARDCOVER ISBN: 978-1-4982-4603-3
EBOOK ISBN: 978-1-4982-4602-6

Manufactured in the U.S.A.   AUGUST 9, 2017

Contents

Contributors | vii
Editorial Approach and Acknowledgments | ix

General Editor's Introduction to *Tome 2* | 1

Document 1: "Catholicism" (1851)

    Editor's Introduction | 9
    Catholicism | 11

Document 2: "The Christian Ministry" (1854)

    Editor's Introduction | 35
    The Christian Ministry | 38

Document 3: "Hodge on the Ephesians" (1857)

    Editor's Introduction | 59
    Hodge on the Ephesians [First Article] | 62
    Hodge on the Ephesians: Second Article | 88

Document 4: "Thoughts on the Church" (1858)

    Editor's Introduction | 129
    Thoughts on the Church [First Article] | 131
    Thoughts on the Church: Second Article | 153

Bibliography | 173
Subject and Author Index | 181

Contributors

Sam Hamstra Jr. is the Affiliate Professor of Church History and Worship at Northern Seminary, as well as the Founder and President of ChapterNext, a church consultancy. He is the editor of several studies, most recently *The Reformed Pastor: Lectures on Pastoral Theology by John Williamson Nevin,* and has authored several works on worship, most recently *What's Love Got to Do With It?: How the Heart of God Shapes Worship.*

David W. Layman earned his Ph. D. in Religion from Temple University in 1994. Since then, he has been a lecturer in religious studies and philosophy at schools in south-central Pennsylvania. He is editor for volume 6 of the Mercersburg Theology Study Series, *Born of Water and the Spirit: Essays on the Sacraments and Christian Formation.*

John Williamson Nevin (1803–86), professor successively at Western Theological Seminary, the Theological Seminary of the German Reformed Church at Mercersburg, and Franklin and Marshall College. He was a leading nineteenth-century theologian and founding editor of *Mercersburg Review.*

Editorial Approach and Acknowledgments

The purpose of this series is to reprint the key writings of the Mercersburg theologians in a way that is both fully faithful to the original and yet easily accessible to non-specialist modern readers. These twin goals, often in conflict, have determined our editorial approach throughout. We have sought to do justice to both by being very hesitant to make any alterations to the original, but being very free with additions to the original in the form of annotations.

We have decided to leave spelling, capitalization, and emphasis exactly as in the original, except in cases of clear typographical errors, which have been silently corrected. We have, however, taken a few liberties in altering punctuation—primarily comma usage, which is occasionally quite idiosyncratic and awkward in the original texts, but also other punctuation conventions which are nonstandard and potentially confusing today. In several articles the volume editor has added quotation marks to the original author's quotes as required by modern conventions. We have also adopted standard modern conventions such as the italicization of book titles and foreign-language words. The entirety of the text has been re-typeset and re-formatted to render it as clear and accessible as possible; pagination, of course, has accordingly been changed. Original section headings have been retained; in articles which lacked any section headings in the original, we have added headings of our own in brackets.

Original footnotes are retained, though for ease of typesetting, they have been subsumed within the series of numbered footnotes which includes the annotations we have added to this edition. Our own annotations and additions, which comprise the majority of the footnotes, are wholly enclosed in brackets, whether that be within a footnote that was original, or around an entire footnote when it is one that we have added.

Source citations in the original have been retained in their original form, but where necessary, we have provided expanded citation information in brackets or numerated footnotes, and have sought to direct the reader toward modern editions of these works, where they exist. Where citations are lacking in the original, we have tried as much as possible to provide them in our footnotes.

In the annotations we have added (generally in the footnotes, though very occasionally in the form of brackets in the body text), we have attempted to be comprehensive without becoming cumbersome. In addition to offering citations for works referenced in the original, these additions fall under four further headings:

1. Translation
2. Unfamiliar terms and historical figures
3. Additional source material
4. Commentary

We have attempted to be comprehensive in providing translations of any untranslated foreign-language quotations in these works, and have wherever possible made use of existing translations in standard modern editions, to which the reader is referred.

Additional annotations serve to elucidate any unfamiliar words, concepts, or (especially) historical figures to which the authors refer, and where applicable, to provide references to sources where the reader may pursue further information (for these additional sources, only abbreviated citations are provided in the footnotes; for full bibliographical information, see the bibliography).

Accordingly, we have sought to shed light on the issues under discussion. Although most commentary on the texts has been reserved for the General Introduction and the Editor's Introductions to each article, further brief commentary on specific points of importance has occasionally been provided in footnotes to facilitate understanding of the significance of the arguments.

We hope that our practice throughout will help bring these remarkable texts to life again for a new century, while also allowing the authors to be heard in their own authentic voices.

Acknowledgments

Volume Editor

As volume editor, I thank Bradford Littlejohn, the founding editor of this series, for the opportunity to edit this volume and, thereby, make a small contribution to the Mercersburg Theology Study Series. I thank David Layman for his excellent work as the general editor of this volume. I thank Charles Hambrick-Stowe for his contribution to this volume (in *Tome* 1). I also take this opportunity to thank Charles for his positive contribution to my life. While serving as Academic Dean of Northern Seminary in Lombard, IL, Charles hired me to join his teaching team. I thank Patrick Carey of Marquette University. When I informed Patrick that I wanted to focus my doctoral studies on American Protestant ecclesiology, he introduced me to John Nevin; he, then, wisely directed my dissertation—"John Williamson Nevin: The Christian Ministry" (1990). I thank Linden DeBie, editor of the first two volumes in The Mercersburg Theology Study Series, for paving the way for the editors who follow in his impressive wake. I frequently referred to Linden's first two volumes for editorial guidance and quickly gave up on trying to keep up with the depth and breadth of his editorial comments. I thank Wipf & Stock for its commitment to Mercersburg Theology; this volume marks our third project together on that subject. I thank the Mercersburg Society for its support; I have been a member nearly since its inception and have benefited immensely from *The New Mercersburg Review* and the society's annual conferences. Finally, I thank by wife Debbie for her support throughout the project.

General Editor

David Layman thanks Brad Littlejohn for the energy and passion that initiated this project, and for his continued counsel and assistance. He is grateful to Lee Barrett for sharing the task of continuing this invaluable work as fellow general editor. Sam Hamstra Jr. took on an enormous task; the general editor primarily limited his contributions to providing cross-references to the growing body of texts and commentary within the Mercersburg Theology Study Series, along with tracking down especially obscure references. The latter task was made immensely easier by Google Books, a searchable repository of digital texts. This volume now fills out the first six volumes in the projected series, which is identified throughout by the abbreviation "MTSS".

The general editor also continued to rely on the resources of the Philip Schaff Library of Lancaster (Pennsylvania) Theological Seminary and the Archives of the Evangelical and Reformed Historical Society. Finally, he thanks his daughter, Karen Louise Layman, for assistance in the final copy editing.

General Editor's Introduction to *Tome 2*

For readers who come to this tome first, this brief introduction will summarize the themes that emerge from Nevin's work on ecclesiology between 1844 and 1849, and prepare the reader for the texts in this tome. The interested reader can find several exceptional biographical summaries in earlier volumes of the Mercersburg Theology Study Series.[1] There are two basic theories in modern scholarship for the origins of Nevin's ecclesiology. The traditional one locates Nevin in German Romanticism and "idealism and speculative theology."[2] A partial corrective to this position thinks that Nevin was, at least in theological and spiritual origins, a "high-church Calvinist".[3] In the latter view, Nevin began his work at Mercersburg as a conservative "old-school" (i.e., non-revivalist) Presbyterian, simply transplanted into a German Reformed context.[4]

The first monograph in *Tome 1*, *Anxious Bench*, lends support to the latter view. As Sam Hamstra Jr. explains in his general introduction, the most dynamic religious expression in American Christianity at the beginning of the national period was revivalism, or as it was reified by later evangelicals, the Second Great Awakening. Preachers used innovative methods, such as protracted meetings and camp meetings, to draw people and stimulate emotional intensity among the listeners. A particular technique

---

1. Littlejohn, series introduction to *Mystical Presence*; DeBie, biographical essay in *Coena Mystica*. Born in 1803, Nevin grew up in a Presbyterian community in central Pennsylvania. After theological education at Princeton and a decade at Western (now Pittsburgh) Theological Seminary, in 1840 he accepted a call from the Mercersburg (Pennsylvania) Seminary of the German Reformed Church. Four years later, he was joined by Philip Schaff, a church historian fresh from the best universities in Germany. Together they created "Mercersburg Theology," a "high-church" movement that called for a renewed appreciation of the resources of pre-Reformation Christianity, restoration of a "high" Calvinistic doctrine of the presence of Christ in the Eucharist, and liturgical renewal. Nevin finished his career as a teacher and administrator at Franklin and Marshall College in Lancaster, Pennsylvania.

2. Nichols, *Romanticism in American Theology*; DeBie, editor's introduction to Nevin, *The Mystical Presence*, MTSS ed., esp. xxxv. See also DeBie's biographical essay in *Coena Mystica*, MTSS, vol. 2, and *Speculative Theology and Common-Sense Religion*.

3. Hart, *John Williamson Nevin: High Church Calvinist*; Layman, general introduction to *Born of Water and the Spirit*, MTSS, vol. 6, 12–19.

4. Nevin himself seemed to have some of this attitude: *One, Holy, Catholic, Apostolic, Tome 1*, 176n35.

was the "anxious bench," located at the front of the congregation, where those who were "anxious" for their conversion would gather to receive the prayers of the community—and the hectoring of the preacher and his assistants. As Hamstra describes in his introduction to *Anxious Bench*, Nevin had a visceral reaction to a ministerial candidate's introduction of the device at the Mercersburg, Pennsylvania congregation in 1842, and he wrote the work to explain his response. He thought it a manifestation of religious "quackery," psychological manipulation that generated the appearance of spiritual transformation rather than its reality. The bad pushed out the good: emotional display and theatrical appeals to sentiment replaced real moral change. The real issue—would the listener of the gospel experience God's converting grace—was replaced by a false issue: would the listener come forward to the anxious bench?[5]

In the first edition of *Anxious Bench* (1843), Nevin had pointed to "the system of the catechism" as the proper method of conversion and nurture, which required faithful, consistent attention of the pastor to the spiritual needs of the congregation, not the spasmodic enthusiasm of itinerant preachers and mass gatherings. In the second edition (presented in *Tome* 1), he developed his claim by describing the ministry of seventeenth century English Puritan Richard Baxter as a model of the earnest and arduous spiritual endeavor required of a pastor who wanted to bring genuine renewal to his parish. Extraordinary revivals were authentic phenomena, so long as they occurred *in* the ordinary patterns of pastoral ministration.[6] This sociological pattern corresponded to Nevin's emergent theological organicism:

> The sinner is saved then by an inward living union with Christ as real as the bond by which he has been joined in the first instance to Adam. This union is reached and maintained, through the medium of the Church, by the power of the Holy Ghost. It constitutes a new life, the ground of which is not in the particular subject of it at all, but in Christ, the organic root of the Church.[7]

This fundamental thesis would undergo a number of changes; but its core vision can be traced through all the monographs and essays in *One, Holy, Catholic, and Apostolic*. A subtle shift can already be detected in a sermon delivered six months later. Nevin was arguing that the organic grounding of every Christian in Christ required the "Catholic Unity" of the church. The church is a *whole* in Christ, and not merely an *all*, a collection of individuals. The individual life of the believer flows out of this common source, which must be *one*. With this sermon, Nevin began to manifest Hegelian readings of ideality and actuality as applied to the church.[8] He recognized that this unity was

---

5. See Nevin, *One, Holy, Catholic, and Apostolic*, Tome 1, 23–24; *Anxious Bench* in ibid., 52–55, 61–70.

6. Ibid., 98–100.

7. Ibid., 91–92. For an extended restatement and development, see "Hodge on the Ephesians" below, 98–101.

8. See Payne, "Schaff and Nevin, Colleagues at Mercersburg," 170.

not yet "actual," yet it was the "ideal," and in the nature of life must be externalized.⁹ Recent reading suggests that Nevin's immediate source for this Hegelian view, Frederick Rauch,¹⁰ had in fact left Nevin an idiosyncratic fusion of theological Hegelianism and Aristotelianism. Aristotelianism posits a distinction of matter and form, also known in the philosophical tradition as "potentiality" and "actuality." Rauch thought "potentiality" was equivalent to "genus" (e.g., "tree"), itself invisible but becoming manifested in the "species and individual" (e.g., "white oak tree," "*this* tree"). To close the circle, Rauch then claimed that genus/potentiality was approximately equivalent to the Hegelian "idea."¹¹ This formulation enabled Nevin to synthesize his underlying biological metaphor of a plant that grows and manifests its "germ" with the idealism that was becoming increasingly attractive to him. In other words, it is precisely at this time—sometime between February and August of 1844—that the theory of the influence of idealism can accurately explain Nevin's position.

Two years later, Nevin presented another sermon on "The Church." He immediately leapt into a more detailed explanation of the distinction between the "Ideal Church" and the "Actual Church." He had obviously thought more deeply about this formulation, and was prepared to express it more rigorously. Three further conceptual developments also manifest themselves: Nevin began to explore how Christians could perceive the ideal church within its flawed actuality. His answer was that one needed to have *faith* in the church. The ideal was not a matter of empirical observation but of supernatural conviction. Most of the evangelicals around Nevin were attempting to *produce* the church through revivalistic enthusiasm and sectarian primitivism. They thought they were recapitulating an allegedly pure apostolic Christianity, although in fact their actual religious expression was a thoroughly modern notion of personal, democratized religious experience.¹² Nevin rather thought that the church was already present, but had to be seen through the transformed perception of faith. Secondly, he was coming to believe that the "essence" of this church, apprehended through faith, was expressed in the Apostles' Creed: "*Credo* in God . . . in Jesus Christ his only Son, . . . [and in] the holy catholic church." It must be believed to be seen at all. More technically, Nevin had assimilated the theory of Philip Schaff (his new colleague at Mercersburg after the death of Rauch) that the "development of the church" was *evolution*, "regular development."¹³ For the next five or six years, this understanding of

---

9. "Catholic Unity," in Nevin, *One, Holy, Catholic, and Apostolic*, Tome 1, 120.

10. Rauch was a German émigré, and Nevin's first colleague at Mercersburg. Linden DeBie provides more background on the relationship of Rauch and Nevin in the editor's introduction to *Mystical Presence*, MTSS ed., xxvi.

11. This interpretation is based on Rauch, "Ecclesiastical Historiography in Germany," 314–15n. Rauch stated the "idea of the Church" according to "Hegel's school" in the body of the text. The editor first discovered this text through a citation by DeBie in *Speculative Theology*, 61n9; DeBie was using a reprint in *Reformed Church Review* (1905).

12. Hatch, *Democratization of American Christianity*.

13. Nevin, *One, Holy, Catholic, and Apostolic*, Tome 1, 145n10. In October 1844, Schaff had

development would overlay Nevin's native biological metaphor of the organism.[14] But the first two themes would remain with Nevin for the rest of his life, and are ever more energetically stated and explored in the present tome.

Now that Nevin had established his central vision of Christian catholicity grounded in the supernaturally revealed presence of Jesus Christ, he turned his attention to the realities of American church life, which saw a plethora of antagonistic Christian communities, each competing for its share of the "religious market." In this he was doubtless inspired by Schaff. Schaff had labeled sectarianism as "one-sided practical subjectivism," in contrast to "Rationalism," which was "one-sided theoretic subjectivism."[15] That is, Schaff thought that sectarianism was religious individualism and privatized spirituality as manifested in the concrete organization of religious communities. Nevin's first major foray against sectarianism was a theological analysis of sectarianism as the contemporaneous American expression of the "antichrist." No longer identifying it with the pope—as most Protestants since the Reformation had done—Nevin rather tied it to the denial that the Church was an ongoing manifestation of Christ's incarnation in the world, the historical extension of the Incarnate Christ.[16] He began with a biblical-theological account of what "antichrist" meant in 1 John 4: a denial that Jesus Christ "is come in the flesh." He proceeded to interpret this root error as he thought it was manifested in the later heresies of the early church. Here he resorted to convenient dichotomies: Docetism and Ebionism, Pelagianism and Manichaeanism, Nestorianism and Eutychianism. He attempted to show that the errors manifested on each side were also characteristic of contemporaneous sectarianism. The total of twelve "marks" can be distilled to the following claim: the sects of his day denied that Jesus Christ in his person united divinity and humanity, and was a supernatural presence who continued to reveal himself, continually and historically embodied in the Church. This denial either left God remaining in heaven, or humanity left on earth, with no union in "actuality".

Some of the arguments of *Antichrist* will likely appear forced to the contemporary reader. In contrast, "The Sect System" (in two essays) is energetic, Nevin at his acerbic best. He had reluctantly bought John Winebrenner's *History of all the Denominations in the United States* at "the request of a persistent itinerant book salesman."[17] Wine-

---

presented his lectures on "The Principle of Protestantism" in German, which Nevin translated: Schaff, *Principle of Protestantism*, MTSS, vol. 3. Schaff's full theory is stated in *What is Church History?*, MTSS, vol. 3, 287–307.

14. The present writer argues Nevin eventually abandoned it: Layman, general introduction to Nevin, Schaff, and Gerhart, *Born of Water and the Spirit*, 23–4, 31.

15. Schaff, *Principle of Protestantism*, MTSS, vol. 3, 128–41. See 120 for "Rationalism."

16. For the shift in Nevin's identification of the antichrist, see Nevin, *One, Holy, Catholic, and Apostolic, Tome* 1, 161. For the latter phrase, see Borneman, *Christ, Sacrament, and American Democracy*, 89.

17. Nevin, *One, Holy, Catholic, and Apostolic, Tome* 1, 235. Winebrenner was an ex-German Reformed pastor who had formed his own evangelical denomination.

brenner's production consisted of essays on as many of the different sects and religious communities as he could locate. Most of the essays were written by adherents of the sect described. In response, Nevin perceptively skewered the pretensions of each sect to represent the whole truth of Christianity. Most of them professed to simply and directly obey the Bible, but that supposed common foundation brought no relief from ecclesiastical enmity. Sects endeavored to interpret that common Bible through a hermeneutics of "private judgment," but each only held to intellectual independence so long as it led a person into its own communion. They were simultaneously rationalistic and superstitious, claiming to use reason to interpret the Bible and exposit the truths of Christian belief, yet bound to a narrow range of notions invented by their founder. Sectarianism was therefore incapable of bearing the universality and supernatural life of the church, a life that was necessarily recognized in and through faith.

After "Sect System," Nevin turned his attention to the history and thought of the early church. He was motivated in part by the claim of most of the sects to be the repristination of primitive Christianity. This was of course self-contradictory, since they contradicted each other. They could not *all* be faithful reenactments of apostolic faith and practice. His intellectual interests were also moved in this direction by the influence of Schaff, whose concept of historical development said that in historical and theological change, in the annulment of earlier periods, one should be able to discern new and higher expressions of the same spiritual and moral life.[18] So Nevin wanted to determine the content of patristic spirituality and thought, and thereby evaluate the authority claims of contemporaneous evangelicalism. His study produced three essays on "Early Christianity," and four on "Cyprian" (the third-century bishop of Carthage).[19]

The first essay in the present Tome was written around the beginning of 1851, some six or eight months *prior* to his immersion into the life and thought of the early church. Nevin seemed full of hope that Christian catholicity could provide a unifying vision for a future Christendom. This vision would be sorely tested over the next two years ("Cyprian" was completed in November, 1852). Nevin's conclusion about contemporaneous Christianity's claims to ground itself in the apostolic era (or, for Anglicans, in the Nicene era) was clear: evangelicalism was *not* a repristination of primitive Christianity.[20] Less certain is Nevin's attitude to Schaff's theory of historical development, but he was beginning to intellectually distance himself from it.[21] What

---

18. Schaff, *What is Church History*, MTSS, vol. 3, 288–91. Schaff applied the specifically Hegelian word *aufheben* on p. 289. (Literally *aufheben* can be translated both "cancel" and "lift up," but as a technical philosophical term is usually rendered "sublate".)

19. At present, the most recent edition of "Early Christianity" is in Yrigoyen and Bricker, ed., *Catholic and Reformed*. "Cyprian" has no modern edition; but both sets of essays are scheduled for publication in a further volume of MTSS.

20. Nevin, "Early Christianity," in *Catholic and Reformed*, 204–5, 254, 309; "Cyprian," 418–19 ("Third Article").

21. See the summary in Layman, general introduction to *Born of Water and the Spirit*, 31.

is *least* certain is how he finally incorporated the apparent authority claims of the patristic era generally, and Cyprian's claims particularly. Nevin asserted in "Cyprian" and later that he was simply attempting to present the facts for detached consideration, but some scholars find this claim disingenuous.[22] In any case, there can be no doubt that the spiritual and ecclesiastical claims of the early church left their mark in the essays that follow.

---

22. Nevin's claim can be found in "Cyprian," 560, 562–63 and "Wilberforce on the Eucharist," 150–51. Later critical readings are in Nichols, *Romanticism in American Theology*, 203–6 and Littlejohn, "Sectarianism and the Search for Visible Catholicity," 410n20. For this entire episode in Nevin's career, see Payne, "Schaff and Nevin, Colleagues at Mercersburg." The present writer is more inclined to take Nevin at his word: Layman, "Revelation in the Praxis of the Liturgical Community," 114–38.

DOCUMENT 1

"Catholicism" (1851)

Editor's Introduction

As noted in the general introduction to *Tome* 1, the "Church Question" boils down to this query: is the Church, as represented by appropriately constituted local congregations and served by properly instituted and ordained pastors, essential in the Triune God's strategy to seek and save the lost?[1] If the answer is "Yes," as Nevin asserted, then the ministry of the local church is the normal divine instrument by which children within the church are nurtured in the faith and adults outside of the church are brought to faith. That answer to the "Church Question" naturally leads to another series of questions: How do I find this church among the religious options in my community? How do I know if a congregation is the true church and not an imposter? What are the marks of the true church?

Throughout history, Christians have answered those questions by corporately creating succinct lists of the marks of the true church. During the Reformation era, the Protestants insisted that the list include the proper preaching of the Word of God and administration of their abbreviated list of sacraments: the Lord's Supper and baptism. More recently, John Howard Yoder and William Visser 't Hooft identified three essential functions of the true church: witness, service, and communion.[2] Back in the fourth century, Christians included four marks of the church in the Nicene-Constantinople Creed: one, holy, catholic, and apostolic. By so doing, the church followed the example of those who had come before them. In the time period immediately following that of the apostles, the church developed baptismal creeds that included marks of the true church, such as holy and catholic. The Apostles' Creed, the complete text of which doesn't appear until the eighth century, grew out of these creeds. For this reason and more, Philip Schaff calls it the "Creed of creeds" and described it "as an admirable popular summary of the apostolic teaching, and in full harmony with the spirit and even the letter of the New Testament."[3]

---

1. Hamstra, general introduction to *One, Holy, Catholic, and Apostolic*, Tome 1, 17.

2. See Nikolajsen's discussion on marks of the church in *The Distinctive Identity of the Church*, 117–18.

3. Schaff, *History of the Creeds of Christendom* I.2.7. The Mercersburgian writings on the Apostles' Creed are slated to appear in volume 8 of MTSS.

Document 1: "Catholicism" (1851)

Of all the lists of the true marks of the church created throughout the history of the Christian church, John Nevin gravitated towards those of the ante-Nicene and Nicene era—in particular, one, holy, catholic, and apostolic. Throughout his extensive career, Nevin commented upon and defended each of those as they provided a positive vision for an American Protestant church ruptured by sectarianism and individualism. Of those four marks, Nevin dedicated a significant amount of energy to catholicity. In the process, he distinguished the ecclesiology of Mercersburg Theology from that of both the Roman Church and the Anglican Church, as well as from most of Protestantism, thereby earning his reputation as "Catholic and Reformed"[4] or "High-Church Calvinist."[5]

In his revealing and remarkable article entitled "Catholicism," Nevin systematically and carefully unpacks the catholicity of the true church. While most Christians "generally understood" catholicity as universal, Nevin suggested an alternative, one rooted in the incarnation. Brad Littlejohn has noted, "For the Church to be 'catholic' means that it constitutes the proper wholeness of mankind and creation; it is no mere universal convocation of men from all over the world, but the renewal of the human race as a whole."[6] Richard Wentz adds,

> Nevin here suggests that Christianity, perhaps more accurately Christ as the Incarnation, represents the introduction of wholeness into the life of the world. The world can never again escape the fact that claims to truth are particular and partial realizations of a truth that is greater than the sum of its parts. Any claim to exclusiveness is inevitably challenged by the inclusive wholeness already present in "the earth in its natural form". . . . For Nevin Christianity was catholic in the sense that it represents the universal *in our midst*, already present, but judging and beckoning us to a more radical realization than is present among individuals, whether they are aware of it or not.[7]

For Nevin, then, catholicity is "no vague dedication to universality, even in some morally ideal sense." Instead, "it is the discovery of wholeness amid the penultimate claims of the world, as expressed in human history."[8]

---

4. See Yrigoyen and Bricker, *Catholic and Reformed*.

5. See Hart, *Nevin: High-Church Calvinist* and Layman, general introduction to *Born of Water and the Spirit*, 12–19.

6. Littlejohn, *Mercersburg Theology*, 149.

7. Wentz, *Nevin: American Theologian*, 66–67.

8. Ibid., 69.

Catholicism[1]

Among the attributes which Christianity has claimed to itself from the beginning, there is none perhaps more interesting and significant than that which is expressed by the title *Catholic*.[2] It is not the product in any way of mere accident or caprice; just as little as the idea of the Church itself may be taken to have any origin of this sort. It has its necessity in the very conception of Christianity and the Church. Hence it is that we find it entering into the earliest christian confession the Apostles' Creed, as an essential element of the faith that springs from Christ. As the mystery of the Church itself is no object of mere speculation, and rests not in any outward sense or testimony only, but must be received as an article of faith which proceeds with inward necessity from the higher mystery of the Incarnation, so also the grand distinguishing attributes of the Church, as we have them in the Creed, carry with them the same kind of inward necessary force for the mind in which this Creed truly prevails. They are not brought from abroad, but spring directly from the constitution of the fact itself with which faith is here placed in communication. The idea of the Church as a real object for faith, and not a fantastic notion only for the imagination, involves the character of catholicity, as well as that of truth and holiness, something which belongs inseparably to its very nature. To have true faith in the Church at all, we must receive it as one, holy, apostolical, and catholic. To let go any of these attributes in our thought, is necessarily to give up at the same time the being of the Church itself as an article of faith, and to substitute for it a mere chimera of our own brain under its sacred name. Hence the tenacity with which the Church has ever held fast to this title of *catholic*, as her inalienable distinction over against all mere parties or sects bearing the christian name. Had the title been only of accidental or artificial origin, no such stress would have been laid on it, and no such force would have been felt always to go along with its application. It has had its reason and authority all along, not so much in what it may have been made to mean exactly for the understanding in the way of formal definition

---

1. [J. W. N[evin], *The Mercersburg Review* 3 (January 1851) 1–26.]

2. [The term "Catholic" as applied to the church occurs first in the second century writings the *Epistles of Ignatius* and the *Martyrdom of Polycarp*. See Schaff, *History of the Creeds of Christendom* I.2.7.]

and reflection, as in the living sense rather of christianity itself, the consciousness of faith here as that which goes before all reflection and furnishes the contents with which it is to be exercised.

The term catholic, it is generally understood, is of the same sense immediately with *universal*; and so we find some who are jealous of the first, as carrying to their ears a popish sound, affecting to use this last rather in the Creed. They feel it easier to say: "I believe in a holy universal or general church," than to adopt out and out the old form: "I believe in *the* holy catholic, or in *one* holy catholic, church." In this case however it needs to be borne in mind that there are two kinds of generality or universality, and that only one of them answers to the true force of the term catholic; so that there is some danger of bringing in by such change of terms an actual change of sense also, that shall go in the end to overthrow the proper import of the attribute altogether.

The two kinds of universality to which we refer are presented to us in the words *all* and *whole*. These are often taken to be substantially of one and the same meaning. In truth however their sense is very different. The first is an abstraction, derived from the contemplation or thought of a certain number of separate individual existences, which are brought together in the mind and classified collectively by the notion of their common properties. In such view, the general is of course something secondary to the individual existences from which it is abstracted, and it can never be more broad or comprehensive than these are in their numerical and empirical aggregation. It is ever accordingly a limited and finite generality. Thus we speak of *all* the trees in a forest, *all* the stars, *all* men, &c., meaning properly in each case the actual number of trees, stars, or men, individually embraced at the time in our general view, neither more nor less, a totality which exists only by the mind and is strictly dependent on the objects considered in their individual character. We reach the conception by a process of induction, starting with single things, and by comparison and abstraction rising to what is general; while yet in the very nature of the case the generality can never transcend the true bounds of the empirical process out of which it grows and on which it rests. But widely different now from all this is the conception legitimately expressed by the word *whole*. The generality it denotes is not abstract, a mere notion added to things outwardly by the mind, but concrete; it is wrought into the very nature of the things themselves, and they grow forth from it as the necessary and perpetual ground of their own being and life. In this way, it does not depend on individual and single existences as their product or consequence; although indeed it can have no place in the living world without them; but in the order of actual being they must be taken rather to depend on it, and to subsist in it and from it as their proper original. Such a generality is not finite, but infinite, that is without empirical limits and bounds; it is not the creature of mere experience, and so is not held to its particular measure however large, but in the form of idea is always more than the simple aggregate of things by which it is revealed at any given time in the world of sense.

The *all* expresses a mechanical unity, which is made up of the parts that belong to it, by their being brought together in a purely outward way; the *whole* signifies on the contrary an organic unity where the parts as such have no separate and independent existence, but draw their being from the universal unity itself in which they are comprehended, while they serve at the same time to bring it into view.[3] The whole man for instance is not simply all the elements and powers that enter empirically into his constitution, but this living constitution itself rather as something more general than all such elements and powers, in virtue of which only they come to be thus what they are in fact. In the same way the whole of nature is by no means of one sense simply with the numerical aggregate, the actual all, of the objects and things that go to make up what we call the system of nature at any given time; and humanity or the human race as a whole may never be taken as identical with all men, whether this be understood of all the men of the present generation only or be so extended as to include all generations in the like outward view. Even where the thing in view may appear by its nature to exclude the general distinction here made, it will be found on close consideration that where the terms before us are used at all appropriately they never have just the same sense, but that the whole of a thing implies always of right something more than is expressed merely by its all. The whole house is not of one signification with all the house, the whole watch with all its parts, or the whole library with all the certain books that are found upon its shelves. Two different ways of looking at the object, whatever it may be, are indicated by the two terms, and also two materially different conceptions, the force of which it is not difficult to feel even where there may be no power to make it clear for thought.

And now if it be asked: which of these two orders of universality is intended by the title *catholic,* as applied to the Christian Church, the answer is at once sufficiently plain. It is that which is expressed by the word *whole* (a term that comes indeed etymologically from the same root[4]), and not that whose meaning lies more fitly in the word *all*. A man may say "I believe in a holy universal Church," when his meaning comes merely to this at last, that he puts all Christians together in his own mind, and is willing then to acknowledge them under this collective title. The universality thus reached, however, is only an abstraction and, as such, falls short altogether of the living concrete mystery which is set before us as an object, not of reflection simply, but of divine supernatural faith, in the old ecumenical symbols. The true universality of Christ's kingdom is organic and concrete. It has a real historical existence in the world in and through the parts of which it is composed; while yet it is not in any way the sum simply or result of these, as though they could have a separate existence beyond

---

3. [Nevin's distinction of *all* and *whole* may be derived from his first colleague at Mercersburg Seminary, Frederick Rauch; see Rauch's *Psychology*, 281. For background to their relationship, see Hart, *John Williamson Nevin*, 76–7; DeBie, *Speculative Theology*, 48–9, 62–4.]

4. ["Catholic" is derived from the Greek phrase καθ' ὅλου, "on the whole" ("catholic, adj. and n.". *OED Online*. June 2016. Oxford University Press. http://www.oed.com/view/Entry/28967).]

and before such general fact; but rather it must be regarded as going before *them* in the order of actual being, as underlying them at every point and as comprehending them always in its more ample range. It is the *whole*, in virtue of which only the parts entering into its constitution can have any real subsistence as parts, whether taken collectively or single. Such, undoubtedly, is the sense of the ancient formula, "I believe in the holy *catholic* church," as it meets us in the faith of the early christian world.

But the idea of wholeness is variously determined of course by the nature of the object to which it may be applied. We can speak of a whole forest, a whole continent, or a whole planet; of a whole species, or of animated nature as a whole; of a whole man, a whole nation, a whole generation, or a whole human world. What now is the whole, in reference to which attribute of the Church here under consideration is affirmed, as a necessary article of christian faith?

The only proper answer to this question is that the attribute refers to the idea of universal humanity, or of this world as a whole. When christianity is declared to be *catholic*, the declaration must be taken in its full sense to affirm, that the last idea of this world as brought to its completion in man is made perfectly possible in the form of christianity, and in this form alone, and that this power therefore can never cease to work until it shall have actually taken possession of the world as a whole, and shall thus stand openly and clearly revealed as the true consummation of its nature and history in every other view.

The universalness here affirmed must be taken to extend in the end, of course, over the limits of man's nature abstractly considered, to the physical constitution of the surrounding world (according to Rom. viii, 19–23; 2 Peter iii, 13, and many other passages in the Bible); for the physical and moral are so bound together as a single whole in the organization of man's life, that the true and full redemption of this last would seem to require a real παλιγγενεσία or renovation[5] also of the earth in its natural form. The proper wholeness even of nature itself, ideally considered, lies ultimately in the power of christianity, and can be brought to pass or made actual only by its means. But it is more immediately and directly with the world of humanity as such that this power is concerned, and such reference is to be acknowledged too, no doubt, as mainly predominant in the ecclesiastical use of the title which we have now in hand. Christianity is catholic, and claims to be so received by an act of faith, inasmuch as it forms the true and proper wholeness of mankind, the round and full symmetrical *cosmos* of humanity, within which only its individual manifestations can ever become complete, and on the outside of which there is no room to think of man's life except as a failure.

There are two ways of looking at the human world, under the conception its totality. The view may regard simply the area of the world's life outwardly considered, humanity in its numerical extent, as made up of a certain number of nations, tribes and individual men; or it may be directed more particularly to the world's life

---

5. [This is the word used in Matt 19:28: " . . . at the renewal of all things (NRSV)."]

inwardly considered, humanity in its intensive character, the being of man as a living fact or constitution made up of certain elements, laws, forces and relations, which enter necessarily into its conception aside from the particular millions of living men as such by which it may be represented at any given time. These two conceptions are plainly different; while it is equally plain, at the same time, that neither of them may be allowed with any propriety to exclude the other, but that the true and real wholeness of humanity is to be found only in the union of both. Christianity or the Kingdom of God is catholic, as it carries in itself the power to take possession of the world both extensively and intensively, and can never rest short of this end. It is formed for such two-fold victory over the reign of sin, and has a mission from heaven accordingly to conquer the universe of man's life in this whole and entire way.

Here precisely lies the *missionary* nature and character of the Church. It has a call to possess the world, and it is urged continually by its own constitution to fulfil this call. The spirit of missions, wherever it prevails, bears testimony to the catholicity of christianity, and rests on the assumption that it is the only absolutely true and normal form of man's life, and so of right should, and of necessity also at last must, come to be universally acknowledged and obeyed.

As regards the numerical view of the world, or its evangelization *in extenso*, this is generally admitted. All christians are ready to allow, that the world in this view belongs of right to Christ, and that it is his purpose and plan to take possession of it universally in the end as his own. The commission, "Go ye into all the world and preach the gospel to every creature,"[6] at once makes it a duty to seek the extension of the gospel among all men, and authorizes the confident expectation that this extension will finally be reached. The world needs christianity, and it can never rest satisfied to be anything less than a full complement for this need. It has regard by its very nature, not to any section of humanity only, not to any particular nation or age or race, but to humanity as such, to the universal idea of man, as this includes all kindreds, tribes, and tongues under the whole heaven. "The field is the world."[7] Christianity can tolerate no Heathenism, Mohammedanism, or Judaism at its side. It may not forego its right to the poorest or most outcast and degraded tribe upon the earth, in favor of any other religion. Wherever human life reaches, it claims the right of following it and embracing it in the way of redemption. The heathen are given to the Son for his inheritance, and the uttermost parts of the earth for his possession. It is a sound and right feeling thus which enters into the cause of missions in its ordinary form, and leads the church to pray and put forth action in various ways for the conversion of the nations.

But it is not always so clearly seen, that the intensive mastery of the world's life belongs just as truly as this extensive work to the idea of the kingdom of God, and that it ought to be therefore just as much also an object of missionary interest and

6. [Mark 16:15.]
7. [Matt 13:38.]

zeal. The two interests indeed can never be entirely separated; since it belongs to the very nature of christianity to take possession in some way of the interior life of men, and the idea of salvation by its means unavoidably involves something more than a simply outward relation to it under any form. Hence a mere outward profession of it is felt on all hands to be not enough; although even this, as far as it goes, forms a part also of that universal homage which is its due; but along with this is required to go also some transformation of character, as a necessary passport to the heavenly world towards which it looks.

So in nominally christian lands, and within the bounds of the outward visible church itself, there is recognized generally the presence of a more inward living evangelization, a narrower missionary work which consists in the form of what is sometimes called experimental religion, and has for its object the interior form of the life it pretends to take possession of, its actual substance, rather than the mere matter of it outwardly taken. In this country particularly no distinction is more familiar, than that between the mere outward acknowledgment of christianity and the power of religion in the souls of its true subjects; although the line of this distinction is more or less vaguely and variously drawn to suit the fancy of different sects. But still it is for the most part a very inadequate apprehension after all, that seems to be taken in this way of the inner mission of christianity. Even under its experimental and spiritual aspect, the work of the gospel is too generally thought of as something comparatively outward to the proper life of man, and so a power exerted on it mechanically from abroad for its salvation, rather than a real redemption brought to pass in it from the inmost depths of its own nature. According to this view, the great purpose of the gospel is to save men from hell and bring them to heaven; this is accomplished by the machinery of the atonement and justification by faith, carrying along with it a sort of magical supernatural change of state and character by the power of the Holy Ghost, in conformity with the use of certain means for the purpose on the part of men; and so now it is taken to be the great work of the Church to carry forward the process of deliverance almost exclusively under such mechanical aspect, by urging and helping as many souls as possible in their separate individual character to flee from the wrath to come and to secure for themselves, through the grace of conversion, a good hope against the day of judgment. With many of our sects, the idea of religion (evangelical or experimental religion as they are pleased to call it), would seem to run out almost entirely into a sort of purely outward spiritualism in the form now noticed, with almost no regard whatever to the actual contents of our life as a concrete whole. Their zeal looks to the conversion of men in detail, after their own pattern and scheme of experience, as a life boat looks to the preservation of as many as possible from a drowning wreck; but beyond this seems to be in a great measure without purpose or aim. Once converted and made safe in this magical way, the mission of the Church in regard to them (unless it should be found necessary to convert them over again), is felt to be virtually at an end; and if only the whole world could be thus saved, there would be an end of the same mission for mankind altogether; we should have the millenium, and to preserve it for a thousand years[8] would only need afterwards to look well to the whole conversion of each new generation subsequently, as it might come of age for such purpose.

But, alas, how far short every such view falls of the true glorious idea of the kingdom of God among men, as it meets us in the Bible and in the necessary sense of the grand mystery of the Incarnation, on which the whole truth of the Bible rests.

Even in case of the individual man, singly and separately considered, the idea of redemption can never be answered by the imagination of a merely extensive salvation, a deliverance in the form of outward power, under any view. All admit that his translation bodily as he now is in his natural state into heaven, would be for him no entrance really into a heavenly life. It is not in the power of locality or place of itself to set him in glory. Precisely the like contradiction is involved (although it may not be at once so generally plain) in the supposition of a wholly *ab extra* transformation of the redeemed subject into the heavenly form of existence. This at best would be the creation of a new subject altogether, as much as if a stone were raised by Divine fiat to the dignity of a living angel, and in no real sense whatever the redemption of the same subject into a higher order of life. No redemption in the case of man can be real, that is not from within as well as from without; that is not brought to penetrate the inmost ground of his being, and that has not power to work itself forth from this, outwards and upwards, till it shall take possession finally of the whole periphery of his nature, body as well as soul. This in the very nature of the case is a process, answerable to the universal character of our present life. To conceive of it as something which is brought to pass suddenly and at once, without mediation and growth, is to sunder it from the actual constitution of humanity, to place it on the outside of this, and so to reduce it, in spite of all spiritualistic pretensions the other way, to the character of a simply mechanical salvation that is at last no better than a dream. And it is of course much the same thing, to make the beginning here stand for the whole; and so to swell the starting point of the new life out of all right proportion, that instead of being, like the beginning of the natural life itself, in a great measure out of sight and knowledge (or at most as a grain of mustard the least of all seeds), it is made to stand forth to view empirically as the proper whole of salvation in this world, throwing the idea of the process which should follow completely into the shade, or turning it into dull unmeaning monotony and cant. Every such restriction of the idea of christianity to a single point of the christian life, even though it be the point where all individual salvation begins, is chargeable with deep and sore wrong to the idea as a whole, and cannot fail to be followed with disastrous consequences, wherever it may prevail, in

---

8. [Until approximately the Civil War, most Protestantism was "postmillennial": the church would bring about Christ's millennial reign on earth through its own activity, and Christ would return at its end (thus "post-"). For this concept's relation to Nevin's own thought, see Layman, general introduction to *Born of Water and the Spirit*, 29.]

some form of practical one-sided divergency, more or less morbidly fanatical, from the true and proper course of the new creation in Christ. The full salvation of the man turns ultimately on his full sanctification; the kingdom of heaven must be in him as a reign of righteousness, in order that it may be revealed around him as a reign of glory. It must take up his nature into itself intensively, as leaven works itself into the whole measure of meal in which it is hid, in order that it may be truly commensurate with the full volume of his being outwardly considered. The new birth is the beginning of a progressive maturation, which has its full end only in the resurrection; and this last, bringing with it the glorification of the entire man, can be rationally anticipated only as it is felt to have its real possibility in the power of such a whole renovation ripening before to this blessed result.

But to understand fully the inner mission of christianity now under consideration, we must look beyond the merely individual life as such to the moral organization of society, in which alone it can ever be found real and complete. Pure naked individuality in the case of man is an abstraction, for which there is no place whatever in the concrete human world. The single man is what he is always, only in virtue of the social life in which he is comprehended and of which he is a part. His separate existence is conditioned universally by a general human substance beyond it, from which it takes root, and derives both quality and strength. The idea of redemption then, in his case, implies of necessity far more than any deliverance that can have place for his life separately regarded. As it must lay hold of this as such in an inward way, in order to become outwardly actual, so also to do this effectually it must have power to reach and change the general substance of humanity out of which the individual life is found to spring. In other words, no redemption can be real for man singly taken, or for any particular man, which is not at the same time real for humanity in its collective view, for the fallen race as a whole. Hence it is that christianity, which challenges the homage of the world as such a system of real redemption, can never possibly be satisfied with the object of a simply numerical salvation, to be accomplished in favor of a certain number of individual men, an abstract election of single souls,[9] whether this be taken as large or small, a few only or very many or even all of the human family. The idea of the true necessary wholeness of humanity is not helped at all by the numerical extent of any such abstraction. It stands in the general nature of man, the human life collectively considered, as this underlies all such distribution, and goes before it in the order of existence, filling it with its proper organic force and sense in the constitution of society. Here especially comes into view the full form and scope of the work, which must take place intensively in the life of the world before the victory of the gospel can be regarded as complete. Humanity includes in its general organization certain orders and spheres of moral existence that can never be sundered from its idea without

---

9. [Nevin here begins a critique of "election" as an absolute decree selecting a specific, limited number of individuals for salvation. See "Hodge on Ephesians" below for his detailed critique of scholastic predestinarianism.]

overthrowing it altogether; they enter with essential necessity into its constitution, and are full as much part and parcel of it all the world over as the bones and sinews that go to make up the body of the outward man. The family, for instance, and the state with the various domestic and civil relations that grow out of them, are not to be considered factitious or accidental institutions in any way, continued for the use of man's life from abroad and brought near to it only in an outward manner. They belong inherently to it; it can have no right or normal character without them; and any want of perfection in them, must even be to the same extent a want of perfection in the life itself as human, in which they are comprehended. So again, the moral nature of man includes in its very conception the idea of art, the idea of science, the idea of business and trade. It carries in itself certain powers and demands that lead to these forms of existence, as the necessary evolution of its own inward sense. Humanity stands in the activity of reason and will, under their proper general character. Take away from it any interest or sphere which legitimately belongs to such activity, and in the same measure it must cease to be a true and sound humanity altogether. No interest or sphere of this sort then can be allowed to remain on the outside of a system of redemption, which has for its object man as such in his fallen state. If christianity be indeed such a system, it must be commensurate in full with the constitution of humanity naturally considered; it must have power to take up into itself not a part of this only but the whole of it, and by no possibility can it ever be satisfied with any less universal result.

All this we say falls to the inner mission of christianity, its destination to raise humanity inwardly considered to a higher power, a new quality and tone, as well as to take possession of it by territorial conquest from sea to sea and from pole to pole. And it needs to be well understood and kept in mind, that the first object here is full as needful as the second, and belongs quite as really to the cause of the world's evangelization. "The field is the world,"[10] we may say with quite as much solemnity and emphasis in this view, as when we speak of it under the other. As the kingdom of God is not restricted in its conception to any geographical limits or national distinctions, but has regard to mankind universally; so neither is it to be thought of as penetrating the organization of man's nature only to a certain extent, taking up one part of it into its constitution and leaving another hopelessly on the outside; on the contrary it must show itself sufficient to engross the whole. Nothing really human can be counted legitimately beyond its scope; for the grand test of its truth is its absolute adequacy to cover the field of human existence at all points, its *catholicity* in the sense of measuring the entire length and breadth of man's nature. Either it is no redemption for humanity at all, or no constituent interest of humanity may be taken as extrinsical ever to its rightful domain. It will not do to talk of any such interest as profane, in the sense of an inward and abiding contrariety between it and the sacredness of religion; as though religion might be regarded as one simply among other coordinate forms of life, with a certain territory assigned to it and all beyond foreign from its control. What is really

10. [Matt 13:38.]

human, a constitutive part of the original nature of man, may be indeed profaned, by being turned aside from its right use and end, but can never be in itself profane. On the contrary, if religion be the perfection of this nature, all that belongs to it must not only admit but require an inward union with religion, in order to its own completion; and as christianity is the end and consummation of all religion besides, it follows that such completion in the case of every human interest can be fully gained at last only in the bosom of its all comprehensive life. The mission of christianity is not to denounce and reject any order of life belonging to primitive humanity as intrinsically hostile to God (that would be a species of Manichean[11] fanaticism); nor yet to acknowledge it simply as a different and foreign jurisdiction; but plainly to appropriate every order to itself, by so mastering its inmost sense as to set it in full harmony with the deeper and broader law of its own presence. Art, science, commerce, politics, for instance, as they enter essentially into the idea of man, must all come within the range of this mission; and so far as it falls short of their full occupation at any given time with the power of its own divine principle, it must be regarded as a work still in process only towards its proper end; just as really as the work of outward missions is thus in process also, and short of its end, so long as any part of the world remains shrouded in pagan darkness. It is full as needful for the complete and final triumph of the gospel among men, that it should subdue the arts, music, painting, sculpture, poetry, &c., to its sceptre, and fill them with its spirit as that it should conquer in similar style the tribes of Africa or the islands of the South Sea. Every region of science, as it belongs to man's nature, belongs also to the empire of Christ; and this can never be complete, as long as any such region may remain unoccupied by its power. Philosophy too, whose province and need it is to bring all the sciences to unity and thus to fathom their deepest and last sense, falls of right under the same view. Some indeed pretend, that christianity and philosophy have properly nothing to do with each other; that the first puts contempt on the second; that the second in truth is a mere *ignis fatuus*[12] at most, which all good christians are bound to abhor and avoid. But if so, it must be considered against humanity to speculate at all in this way; whereas the whole history of the world proves the contrary; and it lies also in the very idea of science, that knowledge in this form should be sought as the necessary completion of it under other forms. To pronounce philosophy against humanity, is virtually to place science universally under the like condemnation. And so to treat it as profane or impertinent for the kingdom of God, is in truth to set all science in similar relation; the very result to which fanaticism has often shown itself prone to run. But what can be well more monstrous than that or more certainly fatal in the end to the cause of christianity? Philosophy, like science and art in other forms; is of one birth with man's nature itself; and if christianity be the

11. [Manicheanism held that that human soul had been contaminated and darkened by matter, and must be freed through an esoteric knowledge of divine illumination.]

12. [Lit., "foolish fire," e.g., flitting phosphorescent lights, and thus something that misleads; an illusion.]

last true and full sense of this nature, it is not possible that it should be either willing or able to shut it out from its realm. We might as soon dream of a like exclusion towards the empire of China; for it is hard to see surely how the idea of humanity would suffer a more serious truncation by this, than by being doomed to fall short of its own proper actualization the other way. The world without China would be quite as near perfection, we think, as the world without philosophy. Its full redemption and salvation, the grand object of the gospel and so the necessary work and mission of christianity among men, includes it is plain both interests, and we have no right to magnify the one ever at the cost of the other.[13]

Such being the general nature of this missionary work intensively taken, we may see at once how far it is still from its own proper end even in the case of the nominally christian world itself. It is melancholy to think, that after nearly two thousand years which have passed since Christ came, so large a part of the human race should still be found beyond the line of christianity outwardly considered. But it is not always properly laid to heart, that the shortcoming in the other view, the distance between idea and fact within this line is, to say the least, no less serious and great. If when we think of the millions of Africa, India, and China, we must feel that the gospel thus far has been only in progress towards its full triumphant manifestation in the world; this feeling must prevail no less, when we direct our attention to the moral, scientific, and political fields, which all around us appear in like barbarous estrangement from its inward law. In this view, even more emphatically than in the other, may we not adopt the language (Heb. ii: 8): "We see not yet *all things* put in subjection under him"—though nothing less than such universal subjection be needed to carry out the first sense of man's life (Gen i: 26; Ps viii: 6–8), and so nothing less can satisfy the enterprise of his redemption? Alas, how quite the reverse of this are we made to behold in every direction. Not alone do the wild powers of nature refuse to obey at once the will of the saints, but it is only a most partial dominion at best also that the christian principle has yet won for itself even in the moral world. Whole territories and spheres of human life here, have never yet been brought to any true inward reconciliation and union with the life of the Church. Romanism has pretended indeed to bring them into subjection; but so far as the pretension has yet been made good, it has been ever in a more or less outward and violent way only; whereas the problem from its very nature requires that the relation should be one of free loving harmony and not one of force. Protestantism seeing this, has in large measure openly surrendered the whole point; falling over thus to the opposite extreme; carrying the doctrine of freedom so far that it is made not only to allow but even to justify, in many cases, a full dissociation of certain spheres of humanity from the rightful sovereignty of religion. In our own time especially there is a fearful tendency at work under this form, which rests throughout on the rationalistic assumption that christianity has no right to the universal lordship

---

13. [Nevin would become less confident of the place of science in the redemption of humanity over the next decade. See "Jesus and the Resurrection," 151, and "Nature and Grace," 504–5.]

of man's life, and which aims at nothing less accordingly than the emancipation of all secular interests from its jurisdiction. It has become a widely settled maxim, we may say, that whole vast regions of humanity lie naturally and of right on the outside of the kingdom of God, strictly taken, and that it must ever be wrong to think of stretching its authority over them in any real form. Hence we find the arts and sciences to a great extent sundered from the idea of the Church as such; and more particularly politics and religion are taken to be totally separate spheres. It is coming to seem indeed a sort of moral truism, too plain for even children or fools to call in question, that the total disruption of Church and State, involving the full independence of all political interests over against the authority of the new constitution of things brought to pass in Christ, is the only order that can at all deserve to be respected as rational, or that may be taken as at all answerable to man's nature and God's will. And yet what a conception is that of christianity, which excludes from its organic jurisdiction the broad vast conception of the Commonwealth or State?[14] We may say, if we please, that such dissociation is wise and necessary for the time being, and as an interimistic transitional stadium in a process that looks towards a far different ulterior end; but surely we are bound to pronounce it always in its own nature wrong, and false to the true idea of the gospel; something therefore which marks not the perfection, but the serious imperfection rather, of the actual state of the world. The imagination that the last answer to the great question of the right relation of the Church to the State, is to be found in any theory by which the one is set completely on the outside of the other must be counted essentially antichristian. Christianity owns the proper freedom of man's nature under its common secular aspects, and can never be satisfied with the violent subjugation of it in a merely outward way; but it requires, at the same time, that this shall be brought to bow to its authority without force; and it can never acknowledge any freedom as legitimate and true that may affect to hold under a different form. So far short then as its actual reign in the world is found to fall of this universal supremacy over all the interests of life, it must be regarded as not having yet reached its proper end, as being still in the midst of an unfulfilled mission.

Of the two parables setting forth the progressive character of the kingdom of God, Matt xiii: 31–33, it is not unnatural to understand the first, that of the mustard seed namely, as referring mainly to its extensive growth, while the other, that of the leaven hid in three measures of meal, is taken to have respect rather to this intensive growth, by which the new divine nature of christianity is required to penetrate and pervade always more and more the substance of our general human life itself, with a necessity that can never stop till the whole mass be wrought into the same complexion. It is certain at all events, that the parables together refer to both forms of increase; for the mere taking of volume outwardly is just as little sufficient of itself to

---

14. [See DeBie, *Speculative Theology*, 72 for the problem of the state raised by Hegelianism; for Nevin's position see Borneman, *Church, Sacrament, and American Democracy*, 121–24. Borneman quotes the important text in Nevin, "Early Christianity" in *Catholic and Reformed*, 299.]

complete the conception of organic growth in the world of grace, as it is notoriously to complete the same conception in the world of nature. The taking of volume must be joined in either case with a parallel progressive taking of answerable inward form. The growth of the mustard seed itself involves this two-fold process; for it consists not simply in the accumulation of size, but in the assumption at the same time of a certain type of vegetable life throughout the entire compass of its leaves and branches. It is, however, more particularly the image of leaven that serves to bring out this last side of the subject in all its force, and that might seem accordingly to be specially designed for this purpose, in distinction from all regard to the other more outward view. The parallel, as in the case of all the N. T. parables, is no mere fancy or conceit, but rests on a real analogy, by which a lower truth or fact in the sphere of nature is found to foreshadow and as it were anticipate a higher one in the sphere of the spirit. Leaven is a new force introduced into the mass of meal, different from it, and yet having with it such inward affinity that it cannot fail to become one with it, and in doing so to raise it at the same time into its own higher nature. This however comes to pass, not abruptly nor violently, but silently and gradually, and in such a way that the action of the meal itself is made to assist and carry forward the work of the leaven towards its proper end. The work thus is a process, the growing of the new principle continually more and more into the nature of the meal, till the whole is leavened. And so it is with the new order of life revealed through the gospel. Involving as it does from the start a higher form of existence for humanity as a whole (new and yet of kindred relation to the old), it is still not at once the transformation of it, in a whole and sudden way, into such higher state. It must grow itself progressively into our nature, taking this up by degrees into its own sphere and bringing out thus at the same time its own full significance and power, in order to take possession of our nature at all in any real way. In the case of the single believer accordingly it is like leaven, a power commensurate from the first with the entire mass of his being, but needing always time and development for its full actual occupation; and so also in the case of our human life as a social or moral whole. Christianity is from the very outset potentially the reconstruction or new creation of man's universal nature (including all spheres and tracts of existence which of right belong to this idea), just as really as a deposit of leaven carries in it from the first the power of transformation for the whole mass of meal in which it has been hid; but it is like leaven again also in this respect, that the force which it has potentially needs a continuous process of inward action to gain in a real way finally its own end. There is an inner mission in its way here, which grows with as much necessity out of its relation to the world, as the mission it has to overshadow the whole earth with its branches, and which it is urged too with just as much necessity, we may add, to carry forward and fulfil. The prayer, *Thy kingdom come*, has regard to the one object quite as much as to the other. This comes by the depth of its entrance into the substance of humanity, as well as by the length and breadth of it, as a process of intensification no less than a process of diffusion.

Document 1: "Catholicism" (1851)

And it deserves to be well considered, that these two processes are not just two different necessities, set one by the side of the other in an external way; that they are to be viewed rather as different sides only of one and the same necessity; since each enters as a condition into the fulfilment of the other, and neither can be rightly regarded without a due regard to both. The power of christianity in particular to take possession of the world extensively, depends at last on the entrance it has gained into the life of the world intensively, so far as it may have already come to prevail. And it may well be doubted, whether it can ever complete its outward mission, in the reduction of all nations to the obedience of the gospel, without at least a somewhat parallel accomplishment of its inward mission, in the actual christianization of the organic substance of humanity, to an extent far beyond all that is now presented within the bounds of the outward Church. The leaven masters the volume of the meal in which it is set, only by working itself fully into its inmost nature. The conversion of the world in the same way is to be expected, not just from the multiplication of individual converts to the christian faith, till it shall become thus of one measure with the earth, but as the result rather of an actual taking up at the same time of the living economy of the world more and more into the christian sphere. The imagination that the outward mission here may be carried through first, and the inner mission left behind as a work for future leisure, is completely preposterous. The problems then which fall to this last have a direct and most important bearing always, on the successful prosecution also of the object proposed to the first. To make the reign of Christ more deep and inward for the life of the world, is at the same time to prepare the way correspondingly for its becoming more broad and wide. The proper solution of a great theoretic question, lying at the foundation of the christian life, and drawing after it consequences that reach over nations and centuries, may be of more account for the ultimate issues of history, than the present evangelization of a whole continent like Africa. At this very time it is of more account far, that the power of christianity should be wrought intensively into the whole civilization of this country (the weight of which prospectively no one can fully estimate); that it should have in it not merely an outward and nominal sovereignty, but be brought also fully to actuate and inform its interior collective life, filling its institutions as their very soul, and leavening them throughout into its own divine complexion; that it should solve the problem of Church and State in a really christian way, so as to bind them into one with free inward reconciliation, instead of throwing them hopelessly apart; that it should take possession truly of the art and literature of the country, its commerce and science and philosophy as well as its politics, passing by no tract of humanity as profane and yet acknowledging no tract as legitimate on the outside of its own sphere and sway: all this, we say, is an object far more near to the final redemption of the world, and of far more need at this time (if it might be accomplished), for the bringing in of the millenium, than the conversion of all India or China. The life of the Church is the salvation of the world.

From the whole subject we draw in conclusion the following reflections:

1. From the view now taken of the proper catholicism or wholeness of christianity, we may see at once that it by no means implies the necessary salvation of all men. This false conclusion is drawn by Universalists, only by confounding the idea of the whole with the notion of all; whereas in truth they are of altogether different force and sense. As hundreds of blossoms may fall and perish from a tree, without impairing the true idea of its whole life as this is reached finally in the fruit towards which all tends from the beginning, so may we conceive also of multitudes of men born into the world, the natural posterity of Adam, and coming short of the proper sense of their own nature as this is completed in Christ, without any diminution whatever of its true universalness under such form. Even in the case of our natural humanity, the whole in which it consists is by no means of one measure merely with the number of persons included in it; it is potentially far more than this, being determined to its actual extent by manifold limitations that have no necessity in itself; for there might be thousands besides born into the world, which are never born into it in fact. Why then should it be thought that the higher form of this same humanity which is reached by Christ, and without which the other must always fall short of its own destination, in order to be full and universal in its own character must take up into itself literally all men? Why may not thousands fail to be born permanently into this higher power of our universal nature, just as thousands fail of a full birth also into its first natural power, without any excluding limitation in the character of the power itself? Those who thus fail in the case of the second creation fail at the same time of course of the true end of their own being, and so may be said to perish more really than those who fall short of an actual human life in the first form; yet it by no means follows from this again that such failure must involve annihilation or a return to non-existence. It may be a continuation of existence; but of existence under a curse, morally crippled and crushed, and hopelessly debarred from the sphere in which it was required to become complete. To be thus out of Christ is for the subjects of such failure indeed an exclusion from the true and full idea of humanity, the glorious orb of man's life in its last and only absolute and eternally perfect form; but for this life itself it involves no limitation or defect. The orb is at all points round and full.

2. As the wholeness in question is not one with the numerical all of the natural posterity of Adam, so neither may it be taken again as answerable simply to any less given number, selected out of the other all for the purpose of salvation. This idea of an abstract election, underlying the whole plan of redemption, and circumscribing consequently the real virtue of all its provisions by such mechanical limitation, is in all material respects the exact counterpart of that scheme of universal salvation which has just been noticed. It amounts to nothing, so far as the nature of the redemption is concerned that it is made to be for all men in one case and only for a certain part of them in the other. In both cases a mere notional all, a fixed finite abstraction, is substituted for the idea of an infinite concrete whole, and the result is a mechanical *ab*

extra[15] salvation, instead of a true organic redemption unfolding itself as the power of a new life from within. The proper wholeness of christianity is more a great deal than any arithmetical sum, previously made up under another form, for its comprehension and use. It implies parts of course, and in this way at last definite number and measure, and so in the case of its subjects also a veritable "election of grace;"[16] but it makes all the difference in the world, whether the parts are taken to be the factoral making up the whole, or come into view as its product and growth, whether their number and measure be settled by an outward election or determined by an election that springs from within. A tree has a definite number of branches and leaves—so many, and not more nor less; but who would think of looking for the ground of this beyond the nature of the tree itself, and the conditions that rule the actual development of its life? The law of determination here is something very different, from the law that determines the imitation of a tree in wax or the composition of a watch. So the election of grace in the case of the new creation holds *in Christ*, and not in any view taken of humanity aside from his person.

3. The catholic or universal character of the Church thus, we may easily see farther, does not depend at any time upon its merely numerical extent, whether this be large or small. An organic whole continues the same (the mustard seed for instance) through all stages of its development, though for a long time its actual volume and form may fall far short of what they are destined to be in the end, and must be too in order to fulfill completely its inward sense. So the *whole* fact of christianity gathers itself up fundamentally into the single person of Christ, and is found to grow forth from this literally as its root. The mystery of the incarnation involves in itself potentially a new order of existence for the world, which is as universal in its own nature as the idea of humanity, and by which only it is possible for this to be advanced finally to its own full and perfect realization. Those who affect to find this unintelligibly mystical and transcendental, would do well to consider that every higher order of existence, even in the sphere of nature itself, carries in it a precisely similar relation to the mass of matter, surrounding it under a lower form, which it is appointed to take up and transform by assimilation into its own superior type. The Second Adam is the root of the full tree of humanity in a far profounder sense than the First; and it is only as the material of it naturally considered comes to be incorporated into this, that it can be said to be raised into the same sphere at all; its relation to it previously being at best but that of the unleavened meal to the power at work in its bosom, or that of the unassimilated element to the buried grain which is destined by means of it to wax into the proportions of a great plant or tree. So too from the root upwards, from the fountain onwards, the new order of life which we call the Church or the Kingdom of God remains throughout one and catholic. It owns no coordination with the idea of man's life under any different form. It is the ultimate universal sense of man's nature,

15. [Literally "from outside".]
16. [Rom 11:5.]

the entire sphere of its perfection, the whole and only law of its final consummation. With this character however, the Church can never be content to rest in a merely partial revelation of its power among men, but is urged continually by its very nature to take actual possession of all the world, as we have already seen, both extensively and intensively. Here we have of course the idea of a process, as something involved in the very conception itself which we have in hand. As an article of faith, the catholicity of the Church expresses a present attribute in all ages; it is not drawn simply from future, as a proleptical declaration of what is to be true hereafter, though it be not true now; the *whole* presence of the new creation is lodged in its constitution from the start and through all centuries. But who will pretend that this has ever yet had its proper actualization in the living world? The catholic quality and force of christianity go always along with it; but innumerable hindrances are at hand to obstruct and oppose its action; and its full victory in this view accordingly, as well as in the view of its other attributes, is to be expected only hereafter. To believe in the Church as universal or catholic, it is not necessary that we should see it in full actual possession of the whole world; for when has that been the case yet, and what less would it be than the presence of the millenium in the most absolute sense? It is to believe however that the whole power by which this is to be reached is already at work in its constitution, and that its action looks and strives always towards such end, as the only result that can fairly express its necessary inward meaning and truth.

4. The catholicity of the Church, as now described, involves of course the idea also of its unity and exclusiveness. As being the true whole of humanity, it can admit no rival or co-ordinate form of life (much less any more deep and so more comprehensive than itself), and it must necessarily exclude thus as false and contrary to humanity itself all that may affect to represent this beyond its own range and sphere.

5. No other order of human life can have the same character. It is not of the nature of the civil state or commonwealth, to be thus catholic; and still less does it belong to any single constituent sphere of such political organization, separately taken. Even religion, which claims to be the last sense of man's life from the start, and which is therefore in consistency bound and urged under all forms to assert some sort of whole or universal title in its own favor, is found to be in truth unequal always to this high pretension, till it comes to its own proper and only sufficient completion in Christ. No system of Paganism of course could ever be catholic. So a catholic Mohammedanism is a contradiction in terms. More than this, it never lay in the nature of Judaism itself, with all its truth, to take up into itself the whole life of the world. To do so, it must pass into a higher form, and so lose its own distinctive character, in Christianity. No faith could say truly, "I believe in a holy catholic Judaism"—even if all nations were brought to submit to circumcision before its eyes; for it is not in the power of Judaism as such to possess and represent in full harmony the *whole* idea of humanity; and what is thus not in itself possible, and so not true, can never be the object really of faith in its true form. Judaism is not the deepest power of man's life in the form of religion, and

for this reason alone it must be found in the end a comparatively partial and relative power; leaving room for a different consciousness over against itself, with a certain amount of legitimacy and right too in the face of its narrow claims, under the general form of Gentilism. This contradiction is brought to an end in Christ (the true Peace of the world as we have it Eph. ii: 14–18), in and by whom religion, the inmost fact of man's nature, is carried at once to its last and most perfect significance, and so to the lowest profound of this nature at the same time; with power thus to take up the entire truth of it into its own universally comprehensive law; healing its disorders, restoring its harmony, and raising it finally to immortality and glory. Only what is in this way deeper than all besides, can be at the same time truly catholic, of one measure with the whole compass and contents of our universal life.

6. As no other form of religion *can* be catholic, so it lies in the very nature of Christianity as here shown to have this character. It *must* be catholic. Conceive of it, or try to exhibit it, as in its constitution less comprehensive than the whole nature of man, or as not sufficient to take this up universally into its sphere of redemption, and you wrong it in its inmost idea. It must be commensurate with the need and misery of the world as a whole, or come under its own reproach of having begun to build where it has no power to finish. Say, that it is for all mankind, except the Malay race or the many millions of China; and our whole sense at once revolts against the declaration as monstrous. Substitute for such geographical limitation the notion of an invisible line, in the form of an outward unconditional decree, setting a part of the race on one side in a state of real salvability, and another part of it on the other side in a state of necessary reprobation, the atonement being in its own nature available or of actual force in one direction only and not in the other; and the spirit of the whole New Testament again rises into solemn protest. Under the same general view again it is monstrous, as we have already seen, to conceive of a line being interposed in the way of Christianity, in the interior organism of man's general nature itself; leaving one tract of it free to the occupancy of this new power, but requiring it to stop on the frontier limits of another (politics, trade, science, art, philosophy); as though it were deep enough and broad enough to take in a part of the great fact of humanity only, but not the whole. Or take now finally another form of limitation, not unfrequently forced on the idea of what is called the Church in these last days. Suppose a line cutting the universal process of humanity, as a fact never at rest but in motion always from infancy to old age, into two great sections; for the one of which only there is room or place in the restorational system here under consideration while the other including all infants is hopelessly out of its reach—unless death so intervene as to make that possible in another world by God's power, which is not possible here by his grace.[17] Is the thought

17. [The argument of this paragraph is that catholicity transcends all apparent divisions in humanity: so far he has mentioned geographical separation, an "unconditional decree" that separates the elect from the non-elect, and a dichotomy between religion and culture or politics. In this obscure sentence, the hypothetical division appears to be between infancy and adulthood. Nevin's point would in that case be that infants are just as much in the "reach" of Christianity as adults. One can find a

less monstrous, we ask, than any of the suppositions which have gone before? The redemption of the gospel, as it is the absolute end of all religion besides and the full destiny of man, cannot be less broad in its own nature than the whole life it proposes to renovate and redeem. Shall there be imagined any room or place in this for the dark reign of sin—any island of the sea, any remote nation or tribe, any reprobate caste, any outside moral tract, any stadium of infancy or unripe childhood—where the reign of grace (formed to overwhelm it, Rom. v: 15–21) has no power to follow and make itself triumphantly felt? That were indeed to wrong this kingdom in its primary conception. It must be catholic, the true whole of God's image in man, the recovery of it potentially from the centre of his nature out to its farthest periphery, in order to be itself the truth and no lie.

7. As the attribute of catholicity is distinctively characteristic of the Church as such, it follows that no mere sect or fragment of this can effectively appropriate the title. The idea of a sect is, that a part of the christian world has been brought to cut itself off from the rest of it, on the ground of some particular doctrinal or practical interest, and now affects to have within itself under such isolated view all church powers and resources, though admitting at the same time the existence of such powers & resources in other bodies also with which it owns no real church union. This is a vast contradiction from the very start, which is found to work itself out afterwards into all sorts of anomaly and falsehood. The sect virtually puts itself always into the place of the Church, and in spite of its own principle of division is then forced to arrogate to itself the proper rights and prerogatives of this divine organization, as though it were identical with its own narrow limits. In other words, it is forced to act as the whole, when it is in truth by its own confession again only a segment or part. So far as any remnant of church feeling remains (such as is needed for instance to distinguish a sect in its own mind from a voluntary confederation for religious ends), it must necessarily include in it the idea of catholicity or wholeness, as an indestructible quality of such thought; for as it lies in the very conception of a sphere to be round, so precisely does it lie in the very conception of the Church to be catholic, that is to be as universal in its constitution as humanity itself, with no tract or sphere beyond. Hence every sect, in pretending to be sufficient within itself for all church ends, practically at least if not theoretically asserts in its own favor powers and prerogatives that are strictly universal, as broad as the idea of religion itself under its most perfect and absolute form; an assumption that goes virtually to deny and set aside all similar church character in the case of other sects; for the case forbids the notion of two or more systems, separately clothed with the same universal force. Nothing short of such claim to exclusive wholeness is involved in the right each sect asserts for itself, to settle doctrines, make laws, and ply the keys, in a way that is held to be for the bounds of its own communion absolutely whole and final. Such ecclesiastical acts either mean nothing, sink into the character of idle sham, or else they are set forth as the utterances of a real church

fuller argument for this claim in "Noel on Baptism," 98–101.]

authority which is taken to be as wide as the idea of the Church itself. Every sect in this way, so far as it secretly owns the power of this idea, puts on in mock proportion at least all the airs of Rome. But now, on the other hand, the inward posture of every sect again, as such, is at war with catholicity, and urges it also to glory in the fact. The sect mind roots itself in some subjective interest, made to take the place of the true objective whole of christianity, and around this it affects to revolve pedantically as an independent world or sphere. Then it is content to allow other spheres beyond itself, under the like independent form. So its universal rights and powers as we had them just before (rights and powers that mean nothing ecclesiastically save as they *are* thus catholic and not partial) shrink into given bounds; often ridiculously narrow; much like the power of those old heathen deities, whose universal sway was held to stop short with the limits of the nation that worshipped at their shrines. It is a power dogmatical, diatactical, and diacritical,[18] as they call it, which is of full conclusive force (the "keys of the kingdom of heaven") for one man but not for another his next neighbor; for James but not for John; for such as have agreed to own it but not for those who have been pleased to own a different church; universal as the boundaries of the particular denomination from which it springs, the numerical all of a given sect, but of no force whatever beyond this for the mighty whole of which the sect is confessedly only a fraction and part. Here comes out of course the inward lie of the sect system, forcing it to falsify on one side what it affirms of itself on another. Sects are constitutionally uncatholic. Commonly they dislike even the word, and are apt to be shy of it, as though it smacked of Romanism, and as having a secret consciousness that it expresses a quality of the Church which their position disowns. By this however they in truth condemn themselves. It is the very curse of sect, to bear testimony here to the true idea of the Church, while it must still cry out, "What have I to do with thee thou perfection of beauty!"[19] No sect as such has power to be catholic; just as little at least as Judaism has ever had any such power.

No one can say truly, "I believe in a holy catholic Lutheranism, Presbyterianism, Methodism, or any like partial form of the christian profession," as he may say, "I believe in the holy catholic Church." For every such interest owns itself to be a part only of what the full fact of christianity includes, and is so plainly in its own nature. How then should it ever be for faith the whole? What sect of those now existing, Lutheran, German Reformed, Methodist, &c., can seriously expect ever to take up the universal world of man's life into its bosom—unless by undergoing at last such a change in its own constitution, as shall cause the notion of sect to lose itself altogether in another far higher and far more glorious conception? No such has faith, or can have faith, in

18. [This three-fold power of the church is a commonplace in Reformed dogmatics: see T. E. Peck, *Notes on Ecclesiology*, 120 citing Turretin, *Institutio Theologiae Elencticae*, Locus 18, Q. 29, ¶ 5 (vol. 3 [Geneva: Samuelem de Tournes, 1686], 308). The three powers are interpreting scripture, creating "rules of order," and church discipline: Forbes, "Christ the Head of the Church," in *Lectures on the Headship of Christ*, 24–5.]

19. [Possibly an allusion to Lam 2:15–16; see also Ps 50:2.]

any universality of this sort as appertaining to itself; for to have it, would be to feel in the same measure a corresponding right and necessity to extend its authority over the whole world; which we know is not the case. It belongs to that which is in its own nature universal, to lay its hand imperatively on what it is found to embrace. Catholicity asks willing subjects indeed, but not optional. It says not, you may be mine, but you must. The true whole is at the same time inwardly and forever necessary. But what sect thinks of being catholic in this style? Is it not counted catholic rather in the sect vocabulary, to waive altogether the idea of any such universal and necessary right, and to say virtually: "We shall be happy to take charge of you if you see fit to be ours—but if not, may God speed you under some different conduct and care!" Not only the sect itself, but the sect consciousness also, the sect mind, is constitutionally fractional, an arbitrary part which can by no possibility feel or act as a necessary whole.

8. In this way we are brought finally to see the difference, between the true catholicism of christianity, and the mock liberalism which the world is so fond of parading on all sides in its name. This last appears in very different forms, though it ends always in the same general sense. Sometimes it openly substitutes the idea of mere humanism for that of christianity, and so prates of the universal brotherhood of man, as though this were identical with the kingdom of God, and sentimental philanthropy the same thing with religion. In another shape, it is found preaching toleration among opposing sects, exhorting them to lay aside their asperities and endeavoring it may be to bring them to some sort of free and independent confederation (such as the Peace Society[20] aims at among nations), that shall prove the Church one in spite of its divisions. Then again it comes before us in the character of an open war against all sects, calling upon men to forsake them as in their very nature uncatholic; and to range themselves under the standard of general christianity, with no creed but the Bible and no rule for the use of it but private judgment. And here it is that the spirit in question often comes to look like an angel of light, by contrast with the demon of sectarianism which it pretends to cast out; so that to many it seems impossible to distinguish it from the true genius of catholicity itself, as we are taught to acknowledge this in the old church Creed. But there is just this world-wide difference between the two, that the one is positive and concrete, while the other in all its shapes is purely negative and so without real substance altogether. This is at once apparent, where mere philanthropism is made to stand for religion; the liberality it affects has indeed no limits, but it is just because the religion it represents has no contents; it is of one measure with the natural life of man, because it adds nothing to this and has no power whatever to lift it into any higher

---

20. [On May 8, 1828, William Ladd (1778–1841) brought together existing peace groups into The American Peace Society. Its stated purpose was to "promote permanent international peace through justice; and to advance in every proper way the general use of conciliation, arbitration, judicial methods, and other peaceful means of avoiding and adjusting differences among nations, to the end that right shall rule might in a law-governed world ("American Peace Society Records," http://www.swarthmore.edu/library/peace/DG001–025/DG003APS.htm)."]

sphere.[21] The same vast defect however goes along with the pseudo-catholic theory also in its other more plausible forms. The universality it proposes is not made to rest in the idea of the Church itself, as the presence of a real concrete power in the world, with capacity and mission to raise the natural life of man to a higher order (the *Body of Christ*) which in such view implies historical substance, carrying within itself the laws and conditions of its own being; which men may believe, but have no ability to make, more than they may pretend to make the natural world: not in this is it made to rest, we say, the indubitable sense of the old Creed, but in the conception rather of the mere outward all of a certain number of men, or parties of men in world convention represented, who consent to be of one mind in the main on the great subject of the gospel, and only need to extend such voluntary association far enough to take in finally the entire human family. All ends in an abstraction, which resolves itself at last simply into the notion of humanity in its natural character, as bringing into it no new whole whatever for its organic elevation to a higher sphere. There is no mystery accordingly ever in this pseudo-catholicism; it needs no faith for its apprehension; but on the contrary falls in readily with every sort of rationalistic tendency and habit. Sects too, that hate catholicism in the true sense, find it very easy to be on good terms with it under such mock form; the most unchurchly and uncatholic among them, taking the lead ordinarily in all sorts of buttery twaddle and sham in the name of christian union. The purely negative character of the spirit is farther shown, in its open disregard for all past history. It acknowledges no authority in this form, no confession, no creed; but will have it, that christianity is something to be produced by all men, in every age, as a new fact fresh from the Bible *and themselves.* But how then can it be taken to have any substance of its own in the actual world, any wholeness that is truly concrete, and not simply notional and abstract? Catholic and historical (which at last means also apostolical) go necessarily hand in hand.

J. W. N.

---

21. [For later denunciations of "natural philanthrophism" and "merely humanitarian praxis," see "The Internal Sense of Holy Scripture," 9, 37–8 and "Once for All," 124.]

DOCUMENT 2

"The Christian Ministry" (1854)

Editor's Introduction

The issues of pastoral function, pastoral authority, and private judgment have been debated since the Protestant Reformation. The debate became especially intense in American during the years following the American Revolution. At stake was the necessity of the pastoral office. The egalitarian principles of republicanism and the success of itinerant preachers encouraged the populace to reject the age-old distinction that set clergy apart as a separate order. Most rejected the notion that the office of the pastoral ministry was a necessary medium in the order of salvation. They denied that the properly installed pastor possessed unique authority as an officeholder to study, interpret, and proclaim the truths of the Bible. They believed, instead, that this authority was common to all Christians; each had the right of private judgment, a right which minimized the need for pastors.

Nevin, in prophetic fashion, called the denomination back to its theological roots, especially those of the Reformation and Patristic periods.[1] He proposed a pastoral office that is an indispensable extension of the life-bearing quality of the church and a necessary link in the process of salvation. He also asserted that the properly installed pastor dispenses objective and spiritual realities that cannot be obtained anywhere else. In other words, in Nevin's theory, salvation is impossible outside of the pastoral office in the church, the divinely ordained medium of saving grace. Furthermore, the pastoral office is clothed with apostolic authority to administer the means of grace, interpret and proclaim the scriptures, and discipline the wayward.

Nevin's articulated his doctrine of the pastoral ministry in six documents. The first document is "Personal Holiness," a lecture delivered in June of 1837, at the opening of the summer term at the Western Theological Seminary.[2] The second document is an "Inaugural Address," offered May 20, 1840, during his installation as Professor of Theology at Mercersburg Seminary. It affirms the "grandeur and solemnity of the work in which the Church has embarked" through the support of a theological semi-

---

1. For more see Hamstra, "Nevin on the Pastoral Office."

2. Nevin, *Personal Holiness*. This lecture was published at the request of the Western Seminary student body. It is identical to "Lecture Three" in his Mercersburg Seminary course on pastoral theology, as published in Hamstra, ed., *The Reformed Pastor: Lectures on Pastoral Theology by John Williamson Nevin*, 15–35.

Document 2: "The Christian Ministry" (1854)

nary.³ Nevin returned to the theme of personal fitness for the ministry in a sermon delivered on July 10, 1842, entitled "The Ambassador of God: or the True Spirit of the Christian Ministry as Represented in Jesus Christ".⁴ The fourth document is the present sermon. This systematic portrait of the pastoral office was delivered toward the end of November 1854 in Zion's Church of Chambersburg during the installation of Bernard C. Wolff (1794–1870), Nevin's successor as Professor of Theology. The fifth work is a liturgical form. As a member of the committee of the German Reformed Church that produced the "Provisional Liturgy" of 1857, Nevin developed the services for ordination and installation of ministers. The ordination service was approved with minimal changes for inclusion in the *Order of Worship* of 1866, an official publication of the German Reformed Church.⁵ Finally, we now have the recently resurrected lectures on pastoral theology, transcribed and published by the present editor.⁶

While from different periods in his career—and thus developing contrasting emphases—these six sources advance a consistent view-point. The earlier writings emphasize the personal qualities of the pastor as the "Ambassador of God," reflecting the influence of Pietism. In "Personal Holiness," for example, Nevin offers this exhortation to his students:

> Resolve, then, now, in the strength of God's grace, to save your own souls from the shipwreck of the second death. It should terrify you certainly to think of being damned, with the title of *Reverend* upon your head. It were better to descend to hell from any other height, than that you should go down thither from the sacred desk. Let your resolution be taken, then, now, within the walls of this Seminary, to make your calling and election sure. Consider it part of your necessary preparation for that perilous office to which you are looking, to have your souls so strengthened in the principles of piety, that when you shall hereafter be thrown forth upon the world, there may be no danger of your falling away from your own steadfastness.⁷

The later writings deal with pastoral office and function, particularly the importance of properly installed pastors providing Christian nurture through the sacraments and catechism. The following text, "The Christian Ministry," may be his most significant statement on the subject. In this three-point sermon on Ephesians 4:8–16, Nevin proposed that the pastoral office is of divine origin, is of supernatural force, and functions as a conduit of the life-transforming power of God.

---

3. Nevin, "Inaugural Address of Professor Nevin," in *Addresses Delivered at the Inauguration of Rev. J. W. Nevin, D.D. . . .* , 27.

4. Nevin, *The Ambassador of God*.

5. Maxwell, *Worship and Reformed Theology*, 237, 295–96. Maxwell only considers the liturgy for the ordination of ministers, which he presents on pp. 457–66, with an analysis of its sources. Nichols gives excerpts from the 1866 edition of this liturgy in Nichols, ed., *Mercersburg Theology*, 346–48.

6. Hamstra, ed., *The Reformed Pastor*.

7. Ibid., 32.

This text marks an important development in Nevin's understanding of the church and the pastoral office. He links the pastoral ministry to the church in such a way that they cannot be separated. He asserts that since the so-called "Great Commission" of Matthew 28 to the apostles precedes the church and the pastoral ministry originates with the apostles, we may conclude that the pastoral ministry precedes, even constitutes the church. Hence, while the church is a wider concept than the pastoral ministry, they are inseparable; where you find one, you will find the other. In "The Christian Ministry," then, Nevin takes a "decisive step providing visible definition for the church catholic" through the mandatory presence of the pastoral ministry; he furthermore took a "decisive step away from the Protestant doctrine of the priesthood of all believers" by rooting the pastoral ministry, not in the communion of saints, but in the apostles.[8] This development, as James Nichols suggests, may reflect the influence on the Mercersburg theologians of the German Lutheran theologian Andreas Osiander (1498–1552). Nichols tracks the thought of Osiander to "that whole group of high-church theologians noted in Schaff's background," including Johann Löhe (1808–72),[9] and then quotes Emanuel Hirsch:

> The really characteristic doctrinal mark of this group of theologians emerges as the Osiander-Löhe teaching on the ministerial office. The powers of the clergy are not those common to all Christians and assigned to the ministry for exercise, but those peculiar to Christ, conferred by him on the Apostolate and transmitted in the church through ordination up to the contemporary holders of the office. The dichotomy of church and ministry is thus fundamental, and the ministry possesses the power basic to all church government.[10]

---

8. Littlejohn, "Sectarianism and the Search for Visible Catholicity," 411. The paragraphs that are the primary basis of Littlejohn's critique are below, 42, 46.

9. Nichols, *Romanticism in American Theology*, 259. Nichols remains the best study on the topic. See further Nichols, ed., *Mercersburg Theology*, 345–46; Maxwell, *Worship and Reformed Theology*, 36–39, and 237–43 on whether ordination was a sacrament for Nevin.

10. Emanuel Hirsch, *Geschichte der Neuern Evangelischen Theologie*, V: 194, trans. and quoted in Nichols, *Romanticism in American Theology*, 259.

The Christian Ministry[1]

[Introduction]

> Ephesians 4:8–16 Wherefore he saith, When he ascended up on high, he led captivity captive, and gave gifts unto men. (Now that he ascended, what is it but that he also descended first into the lower parts of the earth? He that descended is the same also that ascended up far above all heavens, that he might fill all things.) And he gave some, apostles; and some, prophets; and some, evangelists; and some, pastors and teachers; For the perfecting of the saints, for the work of the ministry, for the edifying of the body of Christ: Till we all come in the unity of the faith, and of the knowledge of the Son of God, unto a perfect man, unto the measure of the stature of the fullness of Christ: That we henceforth be no more children, tossed to and fro, and carried about with every wind of doctrine, by the sleight of men, and cunning craftiness, whereby they lie in wait to deceive; But speaking the truth in love, may grow up into him in all things, which is the head, even Christ: From whom the whole body fitly joined together and compacted by that which every joint supplieth, according to the effectual working in the measure of every part, maketh increase of the body unto the edifying of itself in love.

We propose to consider from this passage, without farther introduction, the Origin, Nature, and Design of the Christian Ministry.

[The Origin of the Christian Ministry]

In the first place, its ORIGIN. This is here referred by St. Paul explicitly to what may be denominated the *Ascension Gift* of our Lord Jesus Christ. When he ascended up on high, we are told, leading captivity captive, far above all heavens, that he might fill all things, he gave gifts unto men; and he gave some apostles, and some prophets, and some evangelists, and some pastors and teachers. The ministry was the result and fruit

---

1. [John W. Nevin, *The Mercersburg Review* 7 (January 1855) 68–115.]

of his glorification at the right hand of God, when he became "head over all things to the Church, which is his body, the fulness of him that filleth all in all."[2] All lay in the Gift of the Holy Ghost, as his presence began to reveal itself in the world on the day of Pentecost.

This gift forms in a certain sense the end or completion of the Gospel. In it the "Mystery of Godliness," the economy of redemption, came first to its full perfection as the power of God, not in purpose merely, but in actual reality, for the salvation of the world. What was begun when the Word became Flesh in the Virgin's womb, was brought here to its proper consummation. The Incarnation of Christ and the Mission of the Holy Ghost stand related to each other, not simply as cause and effect, but as commencement and conclusion of one and the same grand fact. The first was in order to the last, and looked forward to it continually as its own necessary issue and scope. Short of this, the design of Christ's coming into the world could not be reached. He took upon him our nature, that he might die for our sins and rise again for our justification, that is, that having by his death exhausted the curse which lay upon the world through the fall, and having broken thus the power of death and hell, be might be constituted by his resurrection and glorification the head of a new creation, the principle and fountain of a new order of life among men, in the bosom of which it should be possible for the believing and obedient, through all time, to be saved from their iniquities and made meet for the inheritance of the saints in light. All this took place by the mission of the Holy Ghost, for which it was necessary that room should in this way be first made by the whole previous manifestation and work of the Redeemer.

The New Testament is full of this thought; so that it is truly wonderful there should ever be any doubt in regard to it, with those who pretend to take the Scriptures as their guide. The Gospel goes throughout upon the assumption that the power which Christ carried in himself for the salvation of the world could not make itself felt with free, full, constant action among men, till it had gone through a certain course of qualification previously in his own person. The Spirit dwelt in him, we know, without measure; but so long as he continued in our present mortal state, it was necessarily confined to his own individual life. Between it and the surrounding world of humanity, comprehended as this was in the order of mere nature, rose as a high wall of separation, the law of sin and death which reigns throughout this constitution, making it impossible for the law of spiritual life in Christ Jesus to reach it under its own form. Death and sin must first be conquered on their own territory by the Son of God himself; which however implied, of course, that he should with real victory transcend, at the same time, their domain, and so take possession of the world under the form of a new, higher existence, no longer natural, but supernatural, from the plain of which it might be possible for him to extend to men generally the power of his redemption in a corresponding real and truly supernatural way. The order of nature could never be the platform of any such work; and therefore it must be left behind for the sake of

2. [Eph 1:23]

the work itself; and room must be found for the mystery of righteousness in another system altogether, in the order of grace, as this was to be constituted and made permanent in the world by the resurrection of Jesus Christ from the dead.

This great idea underlies all our Saviour's instructions, as it may be said also to be the actuating sense of his own entire life. "Except a corn of wheat fall into the ground and die," we hear him saying (John 12:24), "it abideth alone; but if it die, it bringeth forth much fruit." This refers to himself; but then he adds immediately, as the standing law and general conception of the Christian salvation: "He that loveth his life shall lose it; and he that hateth his life *in this world,* shall keep it unto life eternal."[3] So after his resurrection (Luke 24:25–26), "O fools, and slow of heart to believe all that the prophets have spoken! *Ought* not Christ to have suffered these things, and to *enter into his glory?*" Everywhere we may see, that in the mind of our Saviour, the whole purpose and force of his life were felt to be conditioned by his dying, and so entering upon a new mode of existence, in which he should no longer be subject to the limitations of his mortal state, but have his humanity itself exalted above nature, and clothed with dominion over it for the benefit of his Church. His removal from the world of sense in this way was to be no loss to his disciples, but on the contrary great gain. He would be put to death in the flesh, as St. Paul expresses it, only that he might be quickened *in the Spirit.*[4] His presence with his people, under this form, would be not less real than it had been before, but in some sense, we might say, even more real, as being at the same time far more unrestrained, and intimately near, and powerfully efficacious for the ends of the Gospel, than it was ever possible for it to be previously to his glorification. For it is by the Spirit that he enters into living communication with the members of his mystical body; and the Spirit or Holy Ghost, we are told (John 7:39), could not be given, or was not, as the original text has it—that is, was not as the actual revelation of the Saviour's higher presence in the world—till Jesus was glorified. "I will not leave you orphans," he says (John 14:18–19), "I will come to you. Yet a little while, and the world seeth me no more; but ye see me because I live, ye shall live also." So again (John 16:7), "*It is expedient for you* that I go away; for if I go not away, the Comforter will not come unto you, but if I depart, I will send him unto you." The presence in the flesh must be withdrawn, to make room for a higher, better, and far more glorious presence in the Spirit.

The great burden indeed of our Saviour's valedictory discourse may be said to turn upon this thought; and after his resurrection, accordingly, all is made to depend with him on what was to be now brought to pass by his formal ascension into heaven. "Behold I send the promise of my Father upon you," it was said (Luke 14:49. Acts 1:4–5), "but tarry ye in the city of Jerusalem, until ye be endued with power from on high. For John truly baptized with water; but ye shall be baptized with the Holy Ghost not many days hence." The mission of the Spirit is made thus to be the great object

---

3. [John 12:25.]
4. [Nevin might have conflated 1 Pt 3:18 with either Eph 2:5 or Col 2:13.]

of his whole previous life. It formed the travail of his soul, from the commencement of his sufferings to their close. For this he wrestled with the powers of hell. This was emphatically the purchase of his death, the boon of salvation which he came into the world to obtain for our fallen race. He became the author and finisher of our faith (Heb 12:2), by enduring the cross, with all its shame, and so being set down at the right hand of the throne of God; ascending up far above all heavens, that he might fill all things; leading captivity captive, and taking possession of the world as its supernatural king and head, that he might bestow gifts upon men. And all these gifts were comprehended primarily in the Holy Ghost, as the form under which it was now made possible for the power of his glorified life to reveal itself with free effect in the world. The Holy Ghost, in this view, is not one among other gifts for which the world is indebted to Christ, but the sum and absolute unity at once of the whole; the Gift of gifts; that without which there could be no room to conceive of any other, and through which only all others have their significance and force. It is that which men need as the very complement of their life, that they may be redeemed from the power of the fall, and raised to a participation of the divine nature (2 Peter 1:4), having escaped the corruption that is in the world through lust. For "except a man be born of water and of the Spirit, he cannot enter into the kingdom of God;" and only what is thus born of God, as distinguished from all that is the birth of mere flesh (1 John 5:4), can ever have power to overcome the world. So wide and vast is the grace procured for man by the death and resurrection of the Son of God, and bestowed upon them after his ascension through the gift of the Holy Ghost.

This Gift now forms the origin and ground of the Christian Church; which by its very nature, therefore, is a supernatural constitution, a truly real and abiding fact in the world, and yet, at the same time, a fact not of the world in its natural view, but flowing from the resurrection of Christ and belonging to that new order of things which has been brought to pass by his glorification at the right hand of God; a fact not dependent, accordingly, on the laws and conditions that reign in "this present evil world,"[5] and not at the mercy of its changes in any way—"against which the gates of hell shall not prevail,"[6] and that is destined to outlast and conquer in the end all other institutions, interests and powers of the earth. As a supernatural presence among men in any such constant and really historical way as the Gift and Promise of Christ seem necessarily to imply, the Spirit must have his own supernatural sphere, in distinction from the order of nature, within which to carry forward his operations as the power of a new creation over against the vanity and misery of the old. This constitution or order of grace is what our faith is taught to receive in the article of the Holy Catholic Church; that great mystery which is denominated Christ's Body, and within which is comprised, according to the Creed, the whole supernatural process of man's salvation, from baptism for the remission of sins, onward to the resurrection of the flesh and

5. [Gal 1:4.]
6. [Matt 16:18.]

the life everlasting. It is not of the first creation, like the art and science, and political institutions of mankind in every other view. It holds directly from Christ in his capacity of glorified superiority to the universal order of nature. He is "head *over all things* to the Church."[7] It is in virtue of his having conquered, and ascended up on high, leading captivity captive, far above all heavens—far above all principality (Eph 1:21), "and power, and might, and dominion, and every name that is named, not only in this world, but also in that which is to come"—that he has by his Spirit created for himself this glorious constitution, and continues to reign over it through all ages as "the beginning (Col 1:18) and firstborn from the dead." So when he commissioned his Apostles for their great work, all was made to depend on what had thus been accomplished in his own person. "All power," he said (Matt 28:18–20), "is given unto me in heaven and in earth: Go ye *therefore*"—because it is so and I am able, as the conqueror of sin and death and hell, having all power in my hands, to become the author, the principle and ground of a new creation, against which the gates of hell shall not prevail; because it is so, go ye therefore—"and teach all nations, baptizing them in the name of the Father, and of the Son, and of the Holy Ghost; teaching them to observe all things whatsoever I have commanded you: And, lo, I am with you always, even unto the end of the world."

And here we are brought directly to the point which we have now before us for particular consideration, namely, the origin of the Christian Ministry. It is, by the terms of this commission, identified with the institution of the Church itself. The two things are not just the same. The Church is a much wider conception than the Ministry. But still they are so joined together, that the one cannot be severed from the other. The idea of the Church is made to involve the idea of the Ministry. The first is in truth constituted by the commission that creates the second; for it has its whole existence conditioned by an act of faith in the reality of this commission, and this tested again by an act of real outward homage to its authority, the sacrament of baptism being interposed as the sign and seal of every true entrance into the system of grace thus mysteriously consigned to its charge. "He that *believeth*, and is *baptized*," it is said (Mark 16:16), "shall be saved; but he that believeth not, shall be damned."

The appointment of the Ministry in the form now mentioned, took place just before our Saviour's ascension; but it was not until the day of Pentecost that the appointment was fairly armed with its own proper supernatural force, as an institution springing from the glorious sovereignty with which Christ was invested, when he took his seat at the right hand of God as head over all things to the Church. The Apostles were directed to wait at Jerusalem, accordingly, till they should be endued with power from on high. Then, when the right time was fully come, the Spirit descended in symbols of wind and flame. The great promise of the gospel was fulfilled. The Ministry received its baptism of fire. The Church came to its solemn inauguration; all as an order of things proceeding really and truly from the Saviour's glorification. "Being

---

7. [Eph 1:22.]

by the right hand of God exalted," the people were told at the time (Acts 2:33), "and having received of the Father the promise of the Holy Ghost, he hath shed forth this which ye now see and hear."

[The Nature of the Christian Ministry]

We are to consider, in the next place, the NATURE of the Christian Ministry, the peculiar quality and constitution of the office, as related to its origin in one direction and to its general purpose or design in another.

And what we need first and chiefly to fix in our minds here, is its *supernatural* character. This lies in what we have now seen to be the source from which it springs. It refers itself at once to the ascended and glorified Christ. When he went up, leading captivity captive, far above all heavens, and was constituted head over all things at God's right hand, then it was, and in this capacity and posture, that he gave gifts unto men, and foremost among these the institution of the Ministry, endued with power from on high for its own heavenly ends.

Let us endeavor to apprehend well the full force of this thought. We may speak of a divine agency in the order of nature. "The heavens declare the glory of God, and the firmament sheweth his handiwork."[8] And still more room is there to refer the life of man, in its higher forms, to his ordination and care. "The inspiration of the Almighty giveth him wisdom."[9] In this way, we are prompted to ascribe remarkable providences to his hand, and are accustomed to talk of nations and men as having been raised up by him for the accomplishment of particular ends. There may be a vocation thus, and along with it a corresponding commission, for purposes embraced in the economy of our present life, which are as truly referable to the divine will as this economy itself is in all its parts. Cyrus had his mission from God; so had Alexander the Great; and so also our own more illustrious Washington. Great statesmen, great artists, and great scholars, may be regarded as men sent of God for their own special work. We ascribe to them at times an actual inspiration from on high, a sort of truly divine afflatus, answerable to the idea of such a mission. And so the Bible itself teaches us to look upon the domestic constitution and upon civil government, as existing by the authority and will of heaven. Parents have a divine right to the respect and obedience of their children; and magistrates, according to St. Paul, are to be obeyed for conscience' sake. "The powers that be," he tells us (Rom 13:1–2), "are ordained of God: Whosoever, therefore, resisteth the power, resisteth the ordinance of God; and they that resist shall receive to themselves damnation." Thus it is, we may see, that the order of nature admits, not only the idea, but the actual reality also of heaven-appointed functions and functionaries, in its own sphere, on all sides.

---

8. [Ps 19:1.]
9. [Job 32:8 (KJV says "understanding").]

DOCUMENT 2: "THE CHRISTIAN MINISTRY" (1854)

But is the Christian Ministry now a divine institution, only in the same general view? Such seems to be the opinion of many. They attach much the same force to the commission claimed by Calvin or John Wesley, that they are ready to allow also to that of Oliver Cromwell. Both the authority of the office, and the vocation to it, are supposed to be lodged in some way in the moral constitution of the world under its ordinary form, and to be divine only in virtue of those general relations to God, which this must be allowed on all hands to carry in its bosom. But this is in truth to mistake and deny the supernatural character of the Ministry altogether, and to turn it into an institution of mere nature, the very thing which our faith is required to contradict. The peculiarity of the office is, that it does not originate in any way out of the order of this world naturally, but proceeds directly and altogether from a new and higher order of things brought to pass by the Spirit of Christ in consequence of his resurrection and ascension. It belongs to that constitution which we call the Church; which starts from him who is the resurrection and the life, and who has passed into the heavens as its glorified head; which is by its very conception therefore, a supernatural fact; and whose whole existence in the world, accordingly—its actual relations, capabilities, and powers—is a mystery that can be apprehended only by faith. To conceive properly of the divine character of the sacred office, we must make full earnest with the relation it bears to the glorification of Christ, as the cause and source of an order of things higher than nature in the world, which was not and could not be in it before. It holds from him immediately as head over all things to the Church.

And as regards this point, it is plain that no account is to be made of the distinction that is justly enough drawn between the ordinary and extraordinary forms of the office. "He gave some, apostles," it is said, "and some, prophets; and some, evangelists, and some, pastors and teachers;"[10] various classes and orders, some special and for a time only, others for the ordinary use of the Church through all ages; but so far as their origin is concerned, all of precisely the same character and nature; since all alike are referred to the same ascension gift. The source of the apostleship, is the source also of the common pastoral episcopate. As the Church is a supernatural constitution, and so an object rightly of faith, in its ordinary history, no less than in the midst of Pentecostal miracles, so does the Ministry also derive its force really and truly from Christ, in his capacity of head over all things to the Church, whether exercised by inspired or by uninspired men. This deserves to be well considered and laid to heart. Either the office in its ordinary form is a mere sham, an idle mockery without reality or power, or else it must be allowed to represent and embody in itself actually the force of a supernatural commission.

It becomes easy, in this view, to determine its relation to the world, as it exists in the order of nature. The office is no product, in any sense, of the life of humanity in this form. It holds, as we have seen, from another economy or system, founded in a power which has actually surmounted the order of nature, and reigns above it in its

10. [Eph 4:11.]

own higher sphere. On this ground it is, that we declare the Church to be higher and greater than the State. Patriotism after all is not the first virtue of man, if we are to understand by it devotion to the will of the State, regarded as an absolute end. To make this will the absolute measure of truth and duty, to find in it the last idea of right and wrong, to denounce the conception of a real jurisdiction on the part of the Church that shall be taken as owing no subordination whatever to the jurisdiction of the State (in the style of some who carry on the war blindly with the Church of Rome), is in fact to betray Christ into the hands of Caesar, and to treat the whole mystery of his ascension and glorification as a cunningly devised fable. Governments have no right to place themselves at the head of the Church, or over it, in its own sphere; converting it into a department of State, as in Prussia;[11] or making the civil power the source and fountain of ecclesiastical authority, as since the days of Henry the Eighth and Cranmer in England.[12] What can be more monstrous than the conception of such a pretended headship of the Church, resting as it does at this moment in the person of Queen Victoria, because she happens to be the political sovereign of the British nation![13] But if it be monstrous for any civil power to usurp this sort of lordship over God's heritage, affecting to play the part of sovereign in the sphere of powers that belong not to this world, can it be at all less monstrous to think of making these powers dependent on the constitution of the simply natural world in another view? The people have just as little right here as parliaments and kings, to shape the Church to their own ends, or to take the creation of its Ministry into their own hands. The fond notion which some have of a republican or democratic order in Christianity, by which the popular vote, or the will of any mass or majority of men, shall be regarded as sufficient to originate or bring to an end the sacred office wherever it may be thought proper, and even to create if need seem a new *Church*, as they dare to prostitute that glorious name, for its service and use—is just as far removed from the proper truth of the Gospel as any other that could well be applied to the subject. It is completely at war with the Creed. It makes no account of the strictly supernatural character of Christ's kingdom, as a real polity not of this world, and yet from its own higher sphere entering into it and taking hold upon its history in the most real way. It drags the whole mystery down continually to the level of the simply natural understanding, and forces it thus to lose itself at last altogether in the world of mere flesh and sense.

11. [In 1817, the Evangelical Church of the Prussian Union, by order of King Frederick William III (1797–1840) of Prussia, united the Lutheran and Reformed Churches of his kingdom. In addition to that initiative, the King of Prussia established the framework for a state church (*Landeskirche*). See Bigler, *The Politics of German Protestantism*.]

12. [During the reign of Henry VIII (1491–1547), the 1534 Act of Supremacy established the English monarch as the official head of the Church of England, supplanting the power of the Catholic pope in Rome. The King then appointed Thomas Cranmer (1489–1556) as Archbishop of Canterbury. Contemporaneous with the previous chapter, Nevin had criticized English Erastianism in "The Anglican Crisis."]

13. [Alexandrina Victoria (1819–1901) reigned as Queen of the United Kingdom of Great Britain and Ireland from 1837–76.]

Document 2: "The Christian Ministry" (1854)

The relation of the Ministry to the world on the outside of the Church, however, as now described, does not determine at once its relation to the mass or body of men who belong to the Church itself; and there is room here, accordingly, for the democratic notion just dismissed, to return upon us again under another and much more plausible form. The office may be viewed as something which proceeds from Christ, not indeed through the constitution of nature as is the case with that of the civil magistrate, but yet through the constitution of grace itself as this is comprehended in the general Christian community. We are thus confronted with the question concerning the order which the Ministry and the Church hold to each other, in the system of Christianity. Both spring from the same source, and date from the same time. Still there is room to distinguish between them, as regards inward priority and dependence, and to ask, whether the Church is to be regarded as going before the Ministry, or the Ministry before the Church. To this question, however, an answer has been in fact already returned, in speaking of the commission originally given to the Apostles. The terms of that commission are such as of themselves plainly to show, that the Church was to be considered as starting in the Apostles, and extending itself out from them in the way of implicit submission to their embassy and proclamation. They were to stand between Christ and the world; to be his witnesses, his legates, the representatives of his authority, the mediators of his grace among men. They were to preach in his name, not merely a doctrine for the nations to hear, but a constitution to which they were required to surrender themselves, in order that they might be saved. The new organization was to be formed, and held together, by those who were thus authorized and empowered to carry into effect officially its conditions and terms. Hence the Church is said to be builded upon Peter, as the central representative of the college of the Apostles (Matth. 16:18), and in another place, again (Eph. 2:20), "upon the foundation of the apostles and prophets, Jesus Christ himself being the chief corner stone." So in the passage we have taken for our text, the Ministry both in its extraordinary and ordinary character, is exhibited as the great agency which Christ is pleased to employ for the edification of his mystical body. There is no room then for the theory, by which the Church at large, or any particular part of it, is taken to be the depository in the first instance, of all the grace and force which belong to the ministerial office, just as in a political organization the body of the people may be supposed to contain in themselves primarily the powers with which they choose to invest their own officers and magistrates. The order of dependence here is not ascending but descending. The law of derivation is downwards and not upwards, from the few to the many, and not from the many to the few. The basis of Christianity, as it meets us in the New Testament, is not the popular mind and popular will as such in any form or shape. It starts from Christ. It reaches the world through the mediation of his ministers. Their mission is from him only. "As my Father hath sent me," he says (John 20:21), "even so send I you." They are overseers set over the house of God by the Holy Ghost. By whatever names they may be distinguished, apostles, prophets, presbyters, rulers, or pastors, their office is in its essential constitution episcopal. They are shepherds under Him who is the Chief Shepherd, clothed by delegation with his authority, and appointed to have charge of the flock in his name (1 Peter 5:2–4), with a power so real in its own sphere, and so absolutely irresponsible, at the same time, in any democratic or republican sense, that they are warned before Christ not to use it as lords over God's heritage. However well then the famous watchword may sounds for the popular ear: "A Church without a bishop, and a State without a king,"[14] it must be held to be, so far at least as the first part of it is concerned, absolutely treasonable to the true conception of Christianity. The question is not of the episcopal office in some special given form; but of the office in its broad New Testament sense, as involving the idea of a real pastoral jurisdiction over the Church, representing in it immediately the authority of Jesus Christ, and deriving its force from the sovereignty of heaven and earth to which he has been advanced by his resurrection from the dead.

To say that there may be a Church without a bishop, in such view, a purely republican assembly of Christians in simply lay capacity, able to generate and produce from itself a full, valid ministration of the mystery of grace contained in the Gospel, without the intervention, in any way, of the ministry constituted and commissioned for the purpose by the ascended Saviour himself; to say, in other words, that the Church is before the Ministry, in the order of existence, and in no way dependent upon it, but complete without it (the very thing the maxim *does* mean to say if it has any meaning whatever), is a heresy which at once strikes at the root of all faith in the supernatural constitution of the Church, and turns both the apostolical commission and the gift of Pentecost into a solemn farce.

Both from its origin, as already considered, and from its design, which yet remains to be considered, it may be inferred with necessary consequence that the office in question must be a single institution, in harmony with itself in all its parts. The commission given to the Apostles implied that they were to act in concert. It was not an authority which each one of them was left to himself to exercise, in his own way and for his own pleasure. It belonged to them only in their collective capacity. They were bound by it to the real and fixed constitution of grace with which it was concerned, in the capacity of a college or corporation. And so as the Ministry assumed other forms, whether ordinary or extraordinary, it remained necessarily subject still to the power of the same law. Just as among the Jews, the Priesthood was one, though the Priests were many and of different orders; so in the Christian Church, however the Ministers might be multiplied, and the forms of their office varied, the office itself could be of force only as it retained always the character of a single body bound together, and in union with itself. As there can be by the very conception of Christianity, but one faith,

---

14. [Nevin's quote is the refrain from the poem "The Pilgrim's Legacy" by the Rev. Charles Hall. The poem appears to have been very popular in nineteenth-century America, as it appears in several journals and magazines, including the pamphlet *An Oration Delivered at Plymouth December 22, 1824*, 38–39.]

one baptism, and one Church, so can there be also but one Ministry; and this unity must be taken to extend to all times and ages, as well as to all lands.

And thus we have, in the next place, the idea of apostolical succession; and along with that the conception also of ordination, as the veritable channel through which is transmitted mystically, from age to age, the supernatural authority in which this succession consists. It is easy, of course, to deride everything of this sort, and to make sport with the notion of a tactual communication, as it is sneeringly styled, of heavenly powers, and of grace that is supposed to trickle from consecrated fingers in the imposition of hands; but it comes certainly with a very bad grace from those who pretend to make a merit of their respect for the Bible. The Old Testament is full of this way of ordering spiritual things; and in the New Testament also exemplifications of it occur on all sides. The derision in question only serves to reveal and expose the unbelieving habit of mind from which it proceeds. What is in truth the subject of skeptical scorn in the case, is the existence in the world of any such supernatural constitution, any such mystery of faith, as the Church claims to be in virtue of her derivation from him who has "ascended up far above all heavens, that he might fill all things."[15] The mockery regards the whole reality of the order of grace, as an abiding economy among men, different from the order of nature and above it. Let this first conception be admitted, with some felt sense of its being a fact, and not merely a speculation or notion; and then it will be easy comparatively to allow also all other points belonging in any way to the same grand article of faith. Sacramental grace will follow as a matter of course. And so will the idea of the Ministry, as an institution proceeding from Christ's commission, and armed with power by his Spirit, and having all its force accordingly in the unity and perpetuity of its first appointment. This involves succession; and the succession, to be valid, must be kept up in some way within the bosom of the institution itself. For, as we have seen, this holds not from the natural life of the world, nor even from the higher life of the Church collectively taken, but directly and wholly from the commission and ordination of Christ; and so can be maintained with its original character from age to age, only as it may have power to transmit the actual virtue of this first supernatural appointment from one generation still onward to another.

It remains to notice, finally, under our present head, the force and power of the office. It is not properly of this world; for the sphere of existence to which it belongs is that higher economy of the Spirit, which has been introduced by the triumph of Christ over the whole constitution of nature. The virtue which it carries in itself for its own ends, therefore, is not to be measured by any merely natural or worldly standard. The preaching of the cross is foolishness to the Greek and a stumbling block to the Jew, we are told, and yet the wisdom and power of God for salvation to them that believe.[16] "The weapons of our warfare," St. Paul says (2 Cor. 10:4), "are not carnal, but mighty through God to the pulling down of strong holds." The power of the Ministry stands

15. [Eph 4:10.]
16. [A paraphrase of 1 Cor 1:23–24.]

not in the wisdom, or eloquence, or art and policy of men in any form. It is a quality derived from the kingdom of Christ, and answerable to its heavenly constitution. In its own form and sphere, however, it has to do with relations that are most real, and takes hold of interests which are lasting and solemn as eternity itself. It involves the stewardship of the mysteries of God (1 Cor. 4:2), the administration of the keys of the kingdom of heaven (Matth. 16:19; 18:18; John 20:28), the negotiation of the terms of eternal life (Mark 16:16; 2 Cor. 2:15–16; 5:18–20). All this supernatural force, in the case of those by whom it is thus exercised, is of course official and not personal. It belongs to the institution of the Ministry, and not to the men privately considered who may be charged at any given time with the sacred trust. Their personal character may come in to enforce or to prejudice its claims to respect; but the claims themselves are independent of this, and rest upon other ground altogether. They go with the office; and the whole case supposes, that so long as it may be held to its legitimate form this will be found true and equal to the purposes of its original institution. Even a simply human organization, where the mind and action of the individual functionary are necessarily ruled by the spirit of the body as a whole, is found to have a wonderful power of self-consistency and self-conservation in this way; as we may see, for instance, in the case of our civil courts, where the decisions of a judge, circumscribed and controlled by the fixed relations of his office in the general system of which it is a part, are something very different from his merely personal will, and carry with them rightly and safely an authority to which out of such position he could lay no good claim whatever. And why should it be thought strange then, if the same law of organized corporate life, raised from the sphere of nature to the sphere of grace, and having to do with the "powers of the world to come," be represented as carrying with it in the Church, by virtue of Christ's Spirit, not only a general moral security, but an absolutely infallible guaranty, for the truth and trustworthiness of its results? What less than this can the commission mean, that clothes the Ministry with Christ's own authority, and requires the nations to bow to it under penalty of damnation? Whatever may be said of single ministers in their private character, or in particular acts of their office, the institution as a whole, and taken in its corporate unity, must be held to be equal in full to the terms of this appointment. It cannot prove false and recreant to its supernatural trust. "On this rock," Christ says, "I build my Church: He that heareth you, heareth me; and he that despiseth you, despiseth me: Lo I am with you always even to the end of the world."[17]

[The Design of the Christian Ministry]

We come now, in the third place, to the design of the Christian Ministry. The whole office is, as St. Paul expresses it,

---

17. [Matt 16:18; Luke 10:16; Matt 28:20.]

for the perfecting of the saints, for the work of the ministry, for the edifying of the body of Christ: till we all come in the unity of the faith, and of the knowledge of the Son of God, unto a perfect man, unto the measure of the stature of the fulness of Christ. That we henceforth be no more children, tossed to and fro, and carried about with every wind of doctrine, by the sleight of men, and cunning craftiness, whereby they lie in wait to deceive; but speaking the truth in love, may grow up into him in all things, which is the head, even Christ: from whom the whole body fitly joined together, and compacted by that which every joint supplieth, according to the effectual working in the measure of every part, maketh increase of the body unto itself in love.[18]

Here we have the great thought, which may be said to form the key note of this whole Epistle to the Ephesians, Christ "head over all things to the Church, which is his body, the fulness of him that filleth all in all."[19] The Church is no congregation merely of persons professing Christianity, brought together in an outward way, the result in such view of private and separate piety supposed to be brought to pass under such form on the outside of its communion. It is a living constitution which starts from Christ himself, in virtue of his resurrection from the dead, forms the home of the Spirit in the world, and includes in itself powers altogether above nature for the accomplishment of its own heavenly ends; within the bosom of which only is comprehended all the grace that men need for their salvation, as truly as deliverance from the Flood was to be found only within the Ark in the days of Noah. Here is the forgiveness of sins, the illumination of the Holy Ghost, the manna of heaven, the communion of saints, the victory of faith, the resurrection of the dead, and the life everlasting. And these benefits are conditioned by the vitality of the whole system or constitution to which they belong. Thus the Church is viewed as being to Christ in the world of grace, what the body is to the head in the natural world. It is the form in which he reveals his presence among men through the Spirit, and the organ by which he carries into effect the purposes of his grace. His people in this view are members of himself, and at the same time "members one of another," by their common relationship to the Church. "For as the body is one," the Apostle writes (1 Cor. 12:12–13; Comp. Rom. 12:5), "and hath many members, and all the members of that one body, being many, are one body; so also is Christ. For by one Spirit are we all baptized into one body, whether we be Jews or Gentiles, whether we be bond or free, and have been all made to drink into one Spirit." It is as comprehended in the general organization of the Church that its members grow up more and more into him who is the head, and this process of growth on their part is, at the same time, the edification of the Church as a whole.

The mystery of the general Christian life goes forward thus by the activity of its several parts, working unitedly together for a common end, in obedience to the law of its own supernatural constitution. The whole is an organic process. The growth of

---

18. [Eph 4:12–16.]
19. [Eph 1:22b–23.]

the Church is carried forward by the growth of its members; while at the same time the plastic power[20] from which this last comes resides only in the Church itself. There it flows from Christ, through the Spirit, fashioning and building up the new nature according to its own divine type. Its operation is primarily by the faith and knowledge of the Son of God, that living apprehension of the truth as it is in Christ, which faith only has power to produce, when brought into communication with the realities of the Gospel in their own sphere. Such knowledge is, as far as it goes, an actual entrance into the truth itself, and so a real participation in the life of him who is the absolute light of the world. What serves thus to redeem the understanding from darkness, brings into the will also the law of charity or love; which becomes then a perpetual fountain of grace, and the source of all Christian sanctification.

Such wealth of salvation, according to the Apostle, is comprehended in the knowledge of Jesus Christ as it is made possible to men in the Church! His prayer for Christians was accordingly, that God might give unto them the Spirit of wisdom and revelation in this form, the eyes of their understanding being enlightened, to know the hope of his calling, and the riches of the glory of his inheritance in the saints, and the exceeding greatness of his power towards them who believe (Eph. 1:17–19). His soul struggles seemingly with the greatness of the theme, and no language is found strong enough in its service. "For this cause," he says (Eph. 3:14–19),

> I bow my knees unto the Father of our Lord Jesus Christ, of whom the whole family in heaven and earth is named, that he would grant you, according to the riches of his glory, to be strengthened with might by his Spirit in the inner man; that Christ may dwell in your hearts by faith; that ye, being rooted and grounded in love, may be able to comprehend with all saints, what is the breadth, and length, and depth, and height; and to know the love of Christ, which passeth knowledge, that ye might be filled with all the fulness of God.

So in our text, the edification of the body of Christ is represented as going forward by the perfecting of the saints in this very process of faith and knowledge; whose scope is "the measure of the stature of the fulness of Christ;" and through which, "speaking the truth in love," or rather as the original word means, *being one with the truth* in love, it is their privilege to "grow up into him in all things, which is the head," from whom the power of growth and spiritual completion is conveyed to the whole Church.

And here it is precisely, we say, that the Christian Ministry has its grand purpose and use. It is the agency, through whose intervention in the Church, Christ is pleased by his Spirit to provide for the building up of his people in the faith and hope of the gospel unto everlasting life. The representation of the Apostle implies that the faith

---

20. [Here Nevin reverts to language he learned from Frederick Rauch: the "germ" of vegetable life "is the product of a *plastic power*, which is the principle of individual life and its preservation, which . . . will confine the form of each individual to its species" (*Psychology*, 28–9, emphasis original).]

and knowledge of the Son of God, by which the saints are carried forward towards their proper perfection, are conditioned by this arrangement as its necessary medium. And how much again this involves may be understood, by considering what results are supposed to be reached after and gained by its means. The case has to do with the mysteries of the kingdom of God, with the treasures of wisdom which are hid in Jesus Christ, with the deep things of the Spirit which surpass all natural thought and comprehension. It has to do with a knowledge that begins altogether in faith, and supposes, therefore, an actual order of supernatural life and truth answerable to such faith, brought home to the soul in the form of revelation, and challenging its implicit submission. The obedience of faith, as it is called, is made to be in this way, over against all speculation and opinion, the ground of the whole Christian salvation. Men are required to surrender themselves to the economy of the gospel, in order that they may be formed by it to its own purposes and ends; and it is assumed, that in doing so they will come really and truly under the action of the truth as it is in Christ, so as to "be no longer children, tossed to and fro, and carried about with every wind of doctrine, by the sleight of men, and cunning craftiness, whereby they lie in wait to deceive;" but having their very being in the element of truth and charity, "may grow up in all things into him" who "is the head, even Christ." When we are told then, that the Ministry is the agency by which all this is brought to pass, we are not only enabled to form some right conception of its design, but from this come to see again what must necessarily be its constitution, agreeably to what we have already found to be true of the same, in looking at it from the side simply of its supernatural origin. The nature of the office is determined and explained by the object it is formed to serve, no less than by the source from which it springs; and from this view full as much as from the other, may be easily found to require all the qualifications which we have before shown it to possess. In no other form could it mediate safely between Christ and his Church, and promote the perfecting of the saints, "till we all come in the unity of the faith and of the knowledge of the Son of God," as distinguished from the winds and waves of all merely human doctrine, "unto a perfect man, unto the measure of the stature of the fulness of Christ."[21]

[Conclusion]

IN CONCLUSION, it becomes us to consider seriously from the whole subject what are the general tests and conditions of a true Ministry, and to ponder well the misery and danger of a false one, both for those who exercise it and for those who trust themselves to its care.

The Ministry under its true form supposes, as we have seen, a divine commission, a strictly supernatural appointment and source. And as there has been in fact

---

21. [Quotes from the Eph 4 text previously quoted.]

but one such commission, that which was given by Christ when he passed into the heavens as head over all things to the Church, it must be able, all the world over and through all time, to refer itself to this as the actual charter of its authority, in clear exclusion of every other title pretending to take its place.

From this it follows necessarily in the next place that the Ministry under its true form, wherever it exists, must be comprehended in the unity of the office as a whole, and so also at the same time in the unity of that one true Church which we all own and acknowledge, as an object of faith, in the Apostles' Creed. One Lord, one faith, one baptism. All starts from Christ; all subsists by his Spirit; all rests on the same foundation of the apostles and prophets. The very thought of a loose and divided Ministry, in such a constitution, destroys itself, by overthrowing the conception on which alone the whole authority of the office must rest. To see and feel the reality of the commission from which it flows, is at once to see and feel also that it must be in union and harmony with itself through all its parts, that it must have the character of a single organization, and that the whole force of it must fall to the ground whenever it is pretended to sever it from such connection, and to exercise its functions in an independent and isolated way. In any government, the powers by which it exists and carries on its affairs, must form one single constitution. However they may be distributed, they must remain still bound together as one orb, whose parts all meet in the unity of a common centre. Laws, titles, offices, functions, all have force only by virtue of their comprehension in the order which originates and sustains the whole. To think of powers being validly exercised, or rights validly claimed, in the name of the government without regard to this order would be a monstrous contradiction. And can it be any less monstrous to suppose the possibility of any similar disruption of authority and office in the kingdom of Christ, and under the great seal which imparts to the Christian Ministry its supernatural warrant and force? "Is Christ divided?"[22] May the same seal be attached here to different ministries, in no connection with one another, held by no common law, and moving in no common sphere? Is the connection something which a man may carry away with him wherever he pleases, to use in his private capacity as to himself shall seem right and good? The imagination is preposterously absurd. The force of the commission holds only in the office considered as a whole. To rend it from this unity, is to reduce it to nothing.

And so from this we have by necessary consequence again the third condition of a true Ministry, namely, submission to a living rule or order in which this unity of office may be actually exhibited in a real way as a fact coming down from the time of the Apostles. To act officially in any polity, the single functionary must not only join himself with its general organization, but in doing so must bow also to the authority which already belongs to it as an actually existing constitution in its own sphere. How much more is it meet and fit that this should be the case also, where the administration regards the supernatural constitution of the Church, and the mysteries of the

---

22. [1 Cor 1:13.]

kingdom of God! Christianity, in its very nature, involves the idea of authority, under a form not dependent on human thought or will; so that here above all, the conception of office must be taken to imply, at the same time, submission to the actual polity or order from which it springs, regarded as a living permanent constitution. And if this polity be represented by the unity of the Ministry, as we have seen it to be, there must be a line of historical continuance by which both together shall be found falling back to the great commission, in which the Church originally took its start. The unity of the Ministry in this way is not the consent merely of any number of men, whether many or few, who may agree to take the office upon them and exercise it in the same way. It exists always as a historical fact already at hand, and dating from the day of Pentecost, to the authority of which in such view, accordingly, all must bow, who are brought from time to time to have part truly in its commission.

Such seem to be necessarily, from the nature of the subject, the great tests of the Christian Ministry in its legitimate and true form. Where these are wanting, we may have the show and sham, but not, it is to be feared, the reality of the sacred office. It is hardly necessary to say, however, how widely different from all this is the reigning popular view of the subject, especially in our own country at the present time. Few appear to make serious account either of the supernatural commission of the Ministry, or of its necessary unity, or of its dependence upon an actual succession in this form, handed down from the time of the Apostles. Indeed nothing is more common, than to hear ministers themselves, those at least who call themselves such, openly deriding every requirement of this nature, as a sort of exploded superstition, fit only for Catholics and Old Testament *Jews*. Any evangelical sect, they take it, has power to originate the office for its own use; or at all events may be satisfied if it has been able to carry off with it some small fragment or particle of an older succession, in breaking away violently from some other Church; as Micah felt that all was right, when he obtained a wandering Levite for his priest (Judges 17:13), or as the children of Dan considered it an object afterwards to steal away the same unprincipled priest, and to make him the source of a new, separate priesthood for their own false worship (Judges 18:18–31). The flaw of schism, in such a case, is not felt to be of any consequence; for the persons in question have no sense whatever of the necessary oneness or corporate solidarity of the sacred office. They laugh at the idea of its legitimacy and force being conditioned, in their own case or in the case of others, by any such relation. They are bound by no such consciousness. Their commission is felt to be a sort of private property, which holds good to themselves directly and separately, from the great head of the Church. Enough, it may be, that it is acknowledged by a single congregation. Or, at most, that it is comprehended in the organized ministry of some particular sect. They care for no wider comprehension. And with such unbelieving indifference to the idea of the Church as a present whole, how should they be expected to have any such faith in its historical character, as to feel the least real concern about the derivation of their title through its living succession in past ages. The only authority they think it necessary to bow to, in such view, is the constitution and tradition again of their own sect. What though this be only of yesterday, and its creed confessedly a mere opinion or "persuasion?"[23] They are willing to trust themselves blindly to its guidance, and then make a merit of what they call their Christian liberty and independence by throwing off all respect for Church authority under every broader and older view.

Need we say that such a habit of thought always involves in its last analysis, an entire want of faith in the supernatural constitution of the Church, and in the divine order of the Ministry as we have had it under consideration at this time. We have a right to say of it, indeed, that it is absolutely at war with the mystery of Christianity from first to last. It substitutes for it another Gospel.

By comprehending what the Ministry involves in its true form, we are prepared to understand how great must be the calamity of a false Ministry for all who are concerned with it in any way. It is by its very nature an imposture and usurpation, where it is most dreadful to think of any such outrageous wrong. By pretending to be the truth, at the same time, under such false character, it contradicts and opposes the truth itself in its own proper form. It belongs in this way necessarily to the realm of Antichrist. For this precisely is the true conception of the power we call Antichrist, that it exalts itself against Christ by wickedly thrusting itself into his place, and seeking to pass itself off under his name. The grand criterion of the spirit, according to St. John (1 John 4:3), is just this, that it "confesseth not that Jesus Christ is come in the flesh," is not willing to know and own the actual of a new and higher order of life in him as the Word made Flesh for us men and our salvation; but pertinaciously insists on resolving the whole "mystery of godliness" (1 Tim 3:16), either directly or indirectly, into the form of a mere abstract spiritualism belonging to nature in its own sphere. Thus a spurious Christ, existing only in the thought and fancy of men, and having no power to effect a real union, and so a real reconciliation between the natural and supernatural worlds, is set up in mockery and rivalry of the true Christ, and made to challenge the faith of the world under the usurpation of his glorious name. And what else is it but the same spirit at work, when the true supernatural constitution of the Church, proceeding as this does from the mystery of the incarnation "justified in the Spirit"[24]—the Son of Man received up into glory—is ignored, or virtually denied, and made to be practically of no account, by the substitution for it of another conception altogether, reducing it in fact to a simply rationalistic and natural form! Or when, in full conformity with this, the supernatural origin of the Ministry is sublimated into a sort of Gnostic idealism merely, its commission converted into a religious myth, the idea of its necessary unity and apostolical succession derided as a silly dream of the

---

23. [Nevin's use of quotation marks may point the reader to Winebrenner's *History of all Religious Denominations*, the lengthy sub-title of which includes *containing authentic accounts . . . of the different persuasions:. . . .* Nevin's response to Winebrenner's *History* is presented in *One, Holy, Catholic, and Apostolic, Tome* 1, "The Sect System."]

24. [1 Tim 3:16.]

middle ages, and an institution of wholly different form and nature, excluding these characteristics in their true sense altogether, is brought forward and exhibited as fully equal to all the purposes and ends of the sacred office? Could any presumption more certainly refer itself, by St. John's criterion, to the domain of Antichrist?[25] Whatever any such false Ministry may affect or pretend, it is a Ministry in truth, not of faith, but of unbelief, not of righteousness, but of sin. It practically proclaims God a liar (1 John 5:10), by "not believing the record that he has given of his Son," not owning the mystery of the Gospel in its own form, but daring to put it into another form agreeably to its own taste. Christ, having risen from the dead, establishes his Church as a constitution above nature, and in virtue of the power that belongs to him as the fountain and head of this new creation solemnly commissions the Ministry in his own form, clothing it in a real way with powers answerable to the economy to which it belongs, and promising to surround it with the guaranty of his own presence in the Spirit through all time; bids it go teach all nations, baptizing them into his name; makes salvation to depend on believing and obeying the order which he has been pleased thus, in his sovereign goodness, to appoint. And now, in the face of all this, the false ministry of which we are speaking stands forward, and preaches to men that salvation depends on no such special constitution whatever, and that if they will but trust themselves to its guidance all may be expected to come out right in the end. Is not this, we ask again, the very spirit of Antichrist? And what shall we say of those, who commit themselves to the care of such an episcopate, in the prosecution of eternal life? The very thought is dismal in the extreme, and the case, if Christianity be more than a dream, one of the most deplorable that can well be presented to the contemplation of a believing mind.

Of such vast significance is the question concerning a true Ministry and the true Church. It has to do, not merely with the accidental form of Christianity, but with its inmost constitution and life.[26] All are bound, as they value their salvation, to look well to the nature of the commission and charter under which they propose to secure this all important object. Indifference with regard to the matter, is itself a just occasion for apprehension and alarm; for it implies at once serious infidelity towards the whole subject—infidelity at the very point too, where Christ makes all to depend on faith, when he says; "He that *believeth*, and is baptized, shall be saved, but he that believeth not shall be damned."[27] As every minister is bound to be well assured, that he is a minister, not merely of this or that sect, but of the true Church Catholic, and has part thus in that one great commission from which hangs the unity of the whole office; so also are all other persons under obligation to satisfy themselves, on good and sufficient grounds, that they are in the bosom of the Church in its true form, and under the guidance and care of a legitimate and true Ministry.

25. [*Antichrist* in Nevin, *One, Holy, Catholic, and Apostolic*, Tome 1.]
26. [See below, "Thoughts on the Church," 146n13.]
27. [Mark 16:16.]

DOCUMENT 3

"Hodge on the Ephesians" (1857)

Editor's Introduction

From 1851 to 1852, an exhausted Nevin believed his death near. In 1851 he resigned from Mercersburg Seminary. Two years later he resigned as president of Marshall College. During his premature retirement, Nevin devoted himself to the study of the ancient church and considered defecting to Roman Catholicism. James Hasting Nichols writes of Nevin:

> Almost all his theological writing for a year and a half was devoted to the study of the ancient church, toward which he adopted much of the Roman view. His friends and associated watched anxiously as his articles showed increasingly a despair of Protestantism and a loss of confidence in the Mercersburg offices in the German Reformed Church.[1]

Nevin did not defect. "As far as Nevin was concerned," notes Linden DeBie, "his articles on St. Cyprian concluded his case for evangelical Catholicism," which would be rooted in "the historic, Catholic faith," recognizing "Roman Catholic weaknesses" in regards to the authority of Scripture, while "anticipating a new synthesis in the union of Protestants and Roman Catholics in a future age."[2]

Nevin ended his premature retirement in 1861, returning to the classroom as instructor of history at Franklin and Marshall College in Lancaster, where the college had moved in 1853. In the years preceding, he was occupied with the development of the official liturgy of the German Reformed Church, but also took time to re-engage with Charles Hodge, his former mentor with whom he sparred throughout most of his career. The two theological heavy-weights engaged in one of the more interesting theological debates of their generation. Hodge favored common sense realism, Nevin preferred German Idealism. One was a product of the Enlightenment, the other perhaps of Romanticism.[3] One approached the biblical text like a scientist seeking certainty, the other like a historian comfortable with mystery. One may be described as low-church, and the other as high-church. One viewed himself as the one holding

---

1. Nichols, *Romanticism in American Theology*, 192.
2. DeBie, "Biographical Essay" in *Coena Mystica*, xxxvi.
3. See Nichols, *Romanticism in American Theology*.

the moderate center,[4] and the other viewed himself as a confessional reformer within the Reformed tradition.

As a result of those differences, while Hodge and Nevin "came from the same broader Reformed tradition and shared the same doctrinal beliefs on the surface ... their understandings of these doctrines often proved to be light-years apart."[5] Such is surely the case in their understandings of election as reflected in Hodge's *Commentary on the Epistle to the Ephesians* and Nevin's review of that commentary. Hodge, the Old School Presbyterian, staunchly defended the Westminster Confession wherein we read: "By the decree of God, for the manifestation of His glory, some men and angels are predestinated unto everlasting life; and others foreordained to everlasting death" (III.3). The same confession also specifies that the elect are "effectually called unto faith in Christ by His Spirit" (III.6) and that "the catholic or universal Church, which is invisible, consists of the whole number of the elect" (XXV.1). In his *Commentary*, Hodge not only affirmed the Calvinistic doctrine of predestination defined by the Westminster Confession, he also viewed the same doctrine as the golden thread of the entire letter. On that foundation, Hodge could only conclude that the church is not a visible organization, but just a hyperspiritual entity known only to God. There follows, then, in Hodge's scheme, no necessary connection between the ministry of the local church and the process by which the elect are effectually called to faith in Christ. "Salvation history," then "is simply a mechanism designed to bring God's eternal decrees to fruition—an epiphenomenon at best."[6]

Nevin, in contrast, charted an understanding of predestination flowing from his view of the one, holy, catholic church as a visible "historical economy of redemption in which believers actually participate in the powers of the world to come." Instead of confirming the "Calvinistic decretal system," Nevin opened "the Scriptures in the light of Christ, the Sun of Righteousness, by holding up Christ as the alpha and omega of the Christian salvation." He chose that option, notes one biased biographer, A.B. Kremer, in place of "an abstract deity exercising an arbitrary will in blessing and cursing, saving and damning, 'for His own glory.'"[7] Theodore Appel (granted another biased biographer) still offers a clear window through which we may better understand Nevin's thoughts on the divine decrees and appreciate his review of Hodge's *Commentary on the Ephesians*:

> Nevin was born and educated in a Calvinist Church, and in his younger days it is not probable that he ever presumed to question the doctrine of predestination as taught in the Westminster Confession of Faith.[8] When he became

---

4. See Wallace, "History and Sacrament"; Wallace, "The Defense of the Forgotten Center;" and Stewart, "Mediating the Center."

5. Wallace, "History and Sacrament," 177.

6. See DiPuccio on this subject in *The Interior Sense of Scripture*, 180–86.

7. Kremer, *Biographical Sketch of John Williamson Nevin*, 199.

8. Appel may not have been aware of Nevin's sermon on "Election Not Contrary to a Free Gospel,"

professor of theology at Mercersburg he still held it in a moderate sense, but seldom, if ever, preached on the subject. After stating the doctrine cautiously in its different phases to his classes, he was accustomed to close his remarks by saying that the whole subject was "a deep, unfathomable mystery." In the progress of his theological thinking he came to feel that it could not in all respects be made to harmonize with Calvin's doctrine of the Lord's Supper, and he allowed his view of the decrees to be considerably modified. He was also led to believe that it could not be reconciled with Scriptural views of the Church.[9]

---

offered in 1833 while Nevin was at Western Theological Seminary in Allegheny, Pennsylvania. In this sermon, Nevin questions but affirms both the doctrine of election and the freedom of all who are willing to accept the blessings of the Gospel.

9. Appel, *Life and Work of John Williamson Nevin*, 566. Nevin's belief that Calvin's doctrines of election and the sacraments were incompatible was probably wrong. Thompson and Bricker claim that he was persuaded of this belief by Hodge: editors' preface to *Mystical Presence* (1966), 13. Cf. Gerrish, *Tradition in the Modern World*, 70.

Hodge on the Ephesians [First Article][1]

A COMMENTARY ON THE EPISTLE TO THE EPHESIANS. *By Charles Hodge, D. D., Professor in the Theological Seminary, Princeton, N. J. New York: Robert Carter & Brothers. 1856.*

The distinguished character and high position of the author of this work, taken in connection with the wide significance of its subject, must be allowed on all hands to clothe it with more than ordinary claims to attention. The Epistle to the Ephesians is of cardinal authority, in particular for the doctrine of the Church; and it forms in such view the key, we may say, for the right understanding of all St. Paul's Epistles generally, which must serve of course also at the same time, to open the true sense of all the other Epistles of the New Testament. Knowing this, we could not be indifferent to the view that might be taken of it by such a man as Dr. Hodge. His theory of the Church, as it has been presented to the world in various ways, is commonly understood to be very low; so low indeed, that it has given serious dissatisfaction to many in his own communion. It has been a matter of interest with us to see, how such a theory would be applied in his hands to the interpretation of the Epistle to the Ephesians. We have, accordingly, examined the new commentary with respectful consideration and care; and having done so, we propose now to make it the occasion for some earnest criticism and discussion, in our present article. Our object is not to go into exegetical details; to speak of particular excellencies belonging to the work, or of what we may suppose to be its particular errors and defects. Our concern rather is with the work, viewed as a whole; with its general theological standpoint; with its reigning idea of the Gospel; with the scheme of Christianity which underlies all its thinking, and so gives form and determination to its particular expositions from beginning to end. We feel that there is an advantage in this. It leaves free room for all proper acknowledgment of the merits of the commentary, in its own order and system of thought. Indeed if we did not honor it in such view as the fruit of real learning and piety, we should hardly

---

1. [J. W. N[evin], *Mercersburg Review* 9 (January 1857) 46–83.]

feel it necessary to notice it in the way of controversy at all. As it is, we contend with it because we hold it in respect. It represents ably the system of theological opinion in whose bosom it stands; and by doing so, challenges attention to its peculiar pretensions and claims, while it furnishes a fair opportunity also for bringing them into trial. For our readers generally also, we take it for granted, the general criticism we propose is likely to be of more interest than any discussion of single and separate points of exegesis. Such points it may indeed fall in our way occasionally to take in band; but when that is the case, it will not be so much on their own particular account, as for the sake of their bearing on what is more comprehensive and broad. Our consideration of single passages and texts, will be steadily subordinated to the wider purpose of explaining, exemplifying, exposing and overthrowing, so far as with God's help we may be able, the general theological theory which we find employed with so much learning and ability in the commentary before us, to darken, as it seems to us, the true sense of this most interesting and important portion of God's Word.

In any case, the theological scheme with which an interpreter comes to the exposition of the Bible, is more deserving of consideration than any isolated results of his exegetical learning aside from this. Our theology, or want of theology, must always rule our exegesis. The notion of a purely grammatical exegesis, as urged by the school of Ernesti,[2] is simply absurd. No amount of philological or historical learning can of itself lead to a trustworthy exposition of what the Scriptures actually say and teach. The case requires, in addition to this, an inward correspondence and sympathy of mind on the part of the expositor, with the world of truth which he is called to expound. It needs the living spirit of any science or art, to read aright the true sense of its utterances and speak forth the hidden power of its creations. And just so, it requires the inward standpoint of a positively right and sound theology, to understand and explain to full purpose the theological teachings of the Bible. It may sound well, to talk of coming to the Scriptures without any theory or scheme; but there is not in fact, and cannot be, any such freedom from all prepossession. The Bible supposes the existence of Christianity as a fact already at hand, and utters all its oracles from the bosom of this new creation alone. We must come to it then with the prepossession of faith, or else with the prepossession of unbelief, the worst possible preparation for understanding it, on the supposition of its being more than an empty fable. Of what account here can the greatest knowledge of words be, without any actual sense of the things with which the words are concerned? An infidel pretending to explain the Bible, is like a man born blind discoursing of colors. All mere rationalism or naturalism must necessarily travesty its sense. But for the very same reason that faith in general, or power to acknowledge the supernatural character of Christianity, as distinguished from full un-

---

2. [Johann August Ernesti (1707–1781) developed the definitive statement of what was to be known as the "grammatical–historical method" of biblical interpretation. See Sailhamer, "John August Ernesti: The Role of History in Biblical Interpretation." Nevin regularly expressed dissatisfaction with Ernesti's hermeneutics: e.g., *Mystical Presence*, MTSS ed., 130, 131n.]

belief, forms thus the necessary habit of a good interpreter of the sacred text, it is plain that it must be of vast account also for such an interpreter to possess this habit of faith in a form approaching as nearly as possible to the very nature of the things themselves with which it is employed. And therefore it is always of the first consequence, as we have already remarked, to look to the theological scheme which an interpreter brings with him to the exposition of the Bible and from which as a stand-point he takes his observations upon its sense.

It is hardly necessary to say, that this *Commentary* of Dr. Hodge is constructed upon a general theory of the nature of Christianity, thus previously established and fixed in his own mind. If it were not so, the work would be entitled to but small regard. We find no fault with it merely on this ground. Only let the fact be fairly understood and kept in sight; that we may make due account of it, in examining the work itself. It is not an attempt to explain the Epistle to the Ephesians purely and exclusively from its own text, and without any sort of theological preconception or bias. It can hardly be said, indeed, to pretend to such independence. However it may suit the view of some to make light of all authority in this form, and to look upon tradition of every kind as an embarrassment to the right use of the Scriptures more than a help, we meet with no such pedantry in Dr. Hodge. He has his theological system, his ecclesiastical tradition, that serves him continually as a medium through which to study the features and proportions of the inspired text. Neither is it difficult at all to determine the character of this system. It is well defined, openly acknowledged, and for the most part, though not always, consistently maintained. We may see at once, in such circumstances, how necessary it is that we should try the merits of the system, in order to estimate aright the merits of the *Commentary*.

No one can have read the Epistles of the New Testament with any sort of attention, without being made sensible in his own mind of a certain difficulty in them, standing not so much in particular passages as in the whole hypothesis which is made to underlie their construction. Two seemingly opposite views are embraced in this, which it is found exceedingly hard to reconcile or hold in steady union. Let us endeavor to exemplify and explain.

Nothing can be more clear, in the first place, than that these Epistles are not addressed to the world at large in its natural character and state. For the world in such view, the Gospel universally has but one form of address. It calls on all men everywhere to "repent and believe," to submit themselves to Christ, to be "converted," to be "baptized in the name of Jesus Christ for the remission of sins," as the absolutely indispensable condition of holiness and salvation.[3] "He that believeth and is baptized," the proclamation runs, "shall be saved; but he that believeth not shall be damned."[4] All depends on this obedience of faith. All begins here. Without this preliminary act of submission to Christ's authority, the opportunities and possibilities

---

3. [Mark 1:15, 4:12; Acts 2:38.]
4. [Mark 16:16.]

of grace in any farther view are not regarded as being at hand for the use of men at all. The Gospel never offers its grace for the purposes of sanctification, to those who refuse to place themselves by such preliminary obedience within the range and scope of its supernatural provisions; and it never allows itself, therefore, to waste upon such its lessons of piety or its motives to a holy life. So with these New Testament Epistles. They are full of doctrine, instruction in righteousness, warnings, admonitions, promises, encouragements to Christian duty; but all this for a certain class of persons only, and not for the race of mankind indiscriminately. This is at once evident from their inscriptions and salutations. They are addressed not to countries or towns as such, but to particular bodies of people in them separated and distinguished in some way from the·world in general. St. Jude writes "to them that are sanctified by God the Father, and preserved in Jesus Christ, and called."[5] St. Peter, in one place, "to them that have obtained like precious faith with us, through the righteousness of God and our Saviour Jesus Christ;"[6] in another, to dispersed strangers of Pontus, Galatia, &c., who are regarded, at the same time, as gathered together and elect "according to the foreknowledge of God the Father, through sanctification of the Spirit, unto obedience and sprinkling of the blood of Jesus Christ."[7] So in every Epistle of St. Paul. One is: "To all that be in Rome, beloved of God, called to be saints;" another: "Unto the Church of God which is at Corinth, to them that are sanctified in Christ Jesus, called to be saints;" a third: "Unto the church of God which is at Corinth, with all the saints which are in all Achaia;" a fourth: "Unto the churches of Galatia;" a fifth: "To the saints which are at Ephesus, and to the faithful in Christ Jesus;" and in similar style throughout.[8] And the restriction thus made in the first address, is always carefully observed in every Epistle on to the end. The writers do not allow themselves to fall away from the conception with which they start, by gliding into any more loose and general view. They have before their mind always, not men at large, but the particular class or description of persons to whom they address themselves in the beginning. Their instructions and exhortations are everywhere for the "church," for the "called," for those who are known as the "faithful in Christ Jesus."

Nothing, moreover, can be more plain, than that the distinction thus kept in view always by these sacred writers was considered by them to be far more than one of name only and mere outward profession. Nominal and outward indeed it is assumed to be, as implying an external separation of some sort from the rest of the world, which might be known and spoken of in such view as a really existing society, bearing its own name and having its own terms of fellowship and communion. The society of the "faithful in Christ Jesus" is referred to, not as a fellowship of opinion only, not as the presence merely of a common sentiment in a number of minds, but as being in

5. [Jude 1.]
6. [2 Pt 1:1.]
7. [1 Pt 1:2.]
8. [In order: Rom 1:7; 1 Cor 1:2; 2 Cor 1:1; Gal 1:2; Eph 1:1.]

some way actually at hand, and open to observation, in the form of an externalized historical fact. But in this character again, as we now say, it is never represented as a simply factitious distinction, turning upon the fancy and pleasure of those who had come to set themselves apart in such style from the surrounding world. It is continually carried along with it benefits and privileges, opportunities and powers, of the very highest order. So much is suggested at once by the titles and terms of address, which are employed, as we have just seen, to characterize those to whom the Epistles are directed. These are quite too bold and strong, to be resolved into the notion of rhetorical declamation simply or gracious compliment. "Beloved of God" (Rom. 1:7), "called to be saints" (Rom. 1:7; 1 Cor. 1:2), " the called of Jesus Christ" (Rom. 1:6), "those that are sanctified in Christ Jesus" (1 Cor. 1:2), "saints in Christ" (Eph. 1:1, Phil. 1:1, &c.); how unreasonable to imagine for a moment that terms of this description might be used, under the guidance of inspiration, without any meaning answerable to their high sound. We are not left here, however, to such inferences only, as it might seem natural to draw from any titles of this sort taken by themselves. The Epistles in question proceed throughout on the supposition, that the persons whom they address are really and truly in a state or condition corresponding with these titles; and references are made in them continually to what are conceived to be the actual privileges of this state, in such a way as to show that there is not considered to be any exaggeration whatever in the terms thus used for its description.

Take, for example, the First Epistle of St. Peter. No sooner has the Apostle saluted those whom he addresses, than he is led to break out in the language of adoring worship and praise, on account of what appears to him the unspeakable mercy of God bestowed upon them through the Gospel.

> Blessed be the God and Father of our Lord Jesus Christ, which according to his mercy hath begotten us again unto a lively hope by the resurrection of Jesus Christ from the dead; to an inheritance incorruptible, and undefiled, and that fadeth not away; reserved in heaven for you, who are kept by the power of God through faith unto salvation, ready to be revealed in the last time.[9]

It is not the salvation of the Gospel as a general boon to the world, not the mere fact at large that Christ has risen from the dead and made salvation possible, that is here made the subject of such joyful praise. It is plainly the special relation rather, in which those addressed are regarded as standing to this grace by virtue of their Christian profession and position. We may congratulate all men that life and immortality have been brought to light, that redemption is placed within the reach of our guilty and lost race; but in the case before us, the congratulation extends a great deal farther than this. The persons to whom it is offered, are considered to be already, in a most material sense, the recipients and subjects of God's redeeming mercy. They have come actually within the range of its action. They have a present interest in it, and a right

---

9. [1 Pt 1:3–5.]

to its opportunities and privileges, going vastly beyond any form it may be supposed to carry along with it for the world at large. This very fact, accordingly, is made the ground of all that follows in the way of exhortation to Christian duty. "Wherefore gird up the loins of your mind," it is said,

> be sober, and hope to the end for the grace that is to be brought unto you at the revelation of Jesus Christ: as obedient children, not fashioning yourselves according to the former lusts in your ignorance; but as he which hath called you is holy, so be ye holy in all manner of conversation.[10]

No such exhortation is dreamed of as suitable for men in other circumstances, however desirable it might be that they too should practice the virtues of Christianity; it proceeds throughout on the supposition, that a certain position in the way of grace has been already secured, that an actual foothold in the kingdom of God has been already gained, by which a life of true holiness is rendered practicable, and without which it must ever be vain to bestow either precept or exhortation on the subject. So again:

> Ye are a chosen generation, a royal priesthood, an holy nation, a peculiar people; that ye should show forth the praises of him who hath called you out of darkness into his marvellous light. Which in time past were not a people, but are now the people of God; which had not obtained mercy, but now have obtained mercy. Dearly beloved, I beseech you as strangers and pilgrims, abstain from fleshly lusts, which war against the soul; &c.[11]

The order of thought still is: Ye are the subjects of a glorious distinction in the way of grace; ye have passed out of darkness into God's marvellous light; ye have purified your souls in obeying the truth; ye have come out of the world into the Church: therefore follow diligently after holiness, without which no man shall see the Lord.[12] Your privilege involves, not merely the duty, but also the power of overcoming the world and entering into everlasting life. See then that it be used with earnestness, and perseverance to the end, for this purpose. The same idea pervades the entire Epistle; as any one may readily see who will take pains to read it with proper attention, bearing in mind the restriction which characterizes its address in the beginning, and observing how all along in conformity with this it is written, not for men at large, but only for those who have come into the bosom of the Church.

St. Paul's Epistles all, in like manner, only if possible in a still more striking way, take for granted everywhere the existence of a most real distinction between those whom they address as saints and the world in its general and natural character. Let any one consider in this view particularly the Epistle to the Ephesians. No terms seem to

---

10. [1 Pt 1:13–15.]
11. [1 Pt 2:9–11.]
12. [Last phrase from Heb 12:14.]

be too strong for the Apostle, no conceptions too high, in setting forth the condition of grace and privilege to which he considers those advanced, whom he addresses as "the saints which are at Ephesus and the faithful in Christ Jesus."[13] They are already, by their position and calling, "blessed with all spiritual blessings in heavenly places in Christ;" the subjects, along with other saints, of a heavenly election and adoption; made accepted in the Beloved, in whom they had "redemption through his blood, the forgiveness of sins, according to the riches of his grace."[14] In virtue of their faith, they are said to have been "sealed with that Holy Spirit of promise," which is the earnest of the inheritance that awaits the Christian in the world to come.[15] They needed a special illumination, only to be able themselves to form any proper conception of the high and glorious significance of their own position; and the most earnest prayer of the Apostle in their behalf accordingly, was that God might give unto them the spirit of wisdom and revelation in the knowledge of Christ; the eyes of their understanding being enlightened, that they might know what was "the hope of his calling, and what the riches of the glory of his inheritance in the saints, and what the exceeding greatness of his power"[16] towards them that believe. Their relation to Christ is represented as being nothing less than a present actual comprehension in the new order of life, which was exhibited in his resurrection from the dead, and in his glorification at the right hand of God. They were quickened and raised up together with him, and made to sit with him in heavenly places. They were "no more strangers and foreigners, but fellow-citizens with the saints, and of the household of God."[17] They were, "built upon the foundation of the Apostles and prophets, Jesus Christ himself being the chief cornerstone."[18] Such is the strain in which the Apostle speaks throughout of the high condition and state of those to whom he writes; and all his instructions and practical exhortations, addressed to them as Christians, are so formed as to involve continually the same view. Their spiritual exaltation as the elect of God, the called of Christ, the sealed of the Spirit, the heirs of the heavenly inheritance, is assumed everywhere as an admitted postulate, on the ground of which they are urged upon to cultivate piety and avoid sin. In view of this precisely, they are besought to "walk worthy of the vocation wherewith they are called."[19] Their privileges made the great reason for their "putting off concerning the former conversation the old man, which is corrupt according to the deceitful lusts," so as to be "renewed in the spirit of their mind," and to "put on the new man, which after God is created in righteousness and true holiness."[20] What is

13. [Eph 1:1.]
14. [Eph 1:3.]
15. [Eph 1:13–14.]
16. [Eph 1:18.]
17. [Eph 2:18.]
18. [Eph 2:20.]
19. [Eph 4:1.]
20. [Eph 4:22–24.]

particularly worthy of observation, moreover, is that the consideration thus pressed is brought forward, not simply as a motive to recommend and enforce Christian virtue, but as being itself the whole ground of its possibility. The order of thought is in part certainly: Ye are exalted in Christ, and it is, therefore, fit and right for you to cultivate corresponding dispositions and habits. But mainly it goes far beyond this, and means: Ye are highly exalted in Christ, and it is, therefore, practicable for you to cultivate successfully a corresponding character. It is not so much the idea of what ought to be, as the idea of what may be and can be, in virtue of the Christian position that is urged as the grand argument for a Christian life. "Ye were sometime darkness," it is said, "but now are ye light in the Lord; walk as children of light: for the fruit of the Spirit is in all goodness, and righteousness, and truth."[21]

All this, we say, forms one general aspect, under which the conception of Christianity is continually presented to us in the New Testament Epistles. Along with this, however, in the second place, there runs throughout another view, which seems at first to look in quite a different direction, and to place the whole subject in a new and different light. It may be denominated, with propriety perhaps, the human side of the case, as distinguished from its divine side.

We are confronted with it at once in all those representations, which require us to descend from the idea of the lofty privileges of believers, to the thought of the manifold infirmities with which they are still compassed about in their present state. Who has not experienced at times some sense of incongruity, in passing directly from the wonderful terms in which these privileges are described by St. Peter or St. Paul, to the topics of ordinary morality they are made to enforce? It sounds strangely, to hear those who are spoken of as sitting in heavenly places in Christ Jesus, exhorted, at the same time, to avoid the most common sins, such as lying and stealing, and warned against "fellowship with the unfruitful works of darkness" among the heathen, including things done by them in secret, of which it was a "shame even to speak."[22] It sounds strangely, when the power of the Spirit and the power of the flesh, the life of grace and the life of nature, are brought before us in such close proximity as we find ascribed to them in the fifth chapter of the Epistle to the Galatians. "Walk in the Spirit," it is there said,

> and ye shall not fulfil the lust of the flesh. For the flesh lusteth against the Spirit, and the Spirit against the flesh: and these are contrary the one to the other; so that ye cannot do the things that ye would. But if ye be led by the Spirit, ye are not under the law. Now the works of the flesh are manifest, which are these: adultery, fornication, uncleanness, lasciviousness, idolatry, witchcraft, &c.[23]

---

21. [Eph 5:8.]
22. [Eph 5:11–12.]
23. [Gal 5:16–20.]

Document 3: "Hodge on the Ephesians" (1857)

The occasion for admiration here is, not that such sins are condemned as contrary to Christianity, but that those who are addressed should be supposed to be at all liable to the power of them in the immediate and near way that seems to be implied by such a style of exhortation. But the case becomes, in this view, still worse, when we find that the bad possibilities of the Christian state, as thus described, are represented as frequently passing into actual effect. We need not go beyond the New Testament, to get clear of the idea that the early churches were, in a great measure, free from corruption and sin. We have abundant evidence of the contrary in the New Testament itself. The sacred writers use no sort of reserve on the subject. They not only warn Christians against the danger of sin, but bewail and denounce it at times as really present under very gross forms in their communion. We hear of some in the church who denied the Lord that bought them, privily introducing damnable heresies, and bringing upon themselves swift destruction; of certain men, who "turned the grace of God into lasciviousness,"[24] walking after their own ungodly lusts; and strange indeed are the terms in which they are spoken of by St. Peter, bringing into immediate juxtaposition; as they do, the exaltation of their Christian state on the one hand, and their enormous abuse of it, to the purposes of sin, on the other.

> Spots they are and blemishes, sporting themselves with their own deceivings while they feast with you. Having eyes full of adultery, and that cannot cease from sin; beguiling unstable souls; an heart they have exercised with covetous practices; cursed children. Which have forsaken the right way, and are gone astray, following the way of Balaam the son of Bosor, who loved the ways of unrighteousness. [. . .] When they speak great swelling words of vanity, they allure through the lusts of the flesh, through much wantonness, *those that were clean escaped from them who live in error.* While they promise them liberty, they themselves are the servants of corruption: for of whom a man is overcome, of the same is he brought in bondage. For it *after they have escaped the pollutions of the world through the knowledge of the Lord and Saviour Jesus Christ,* they are again entangled therein, and overcome, the latter end is worse with them than the beginning.[25]

Compare with this Heb. 6:4–6 and 10:26–29, where we have the same startling picture of extremes thrown together, in a way which many have found it exceedingly difficult to understand. The difficulty, however, is not confined to passages of this sort, in which the bright and dark sides of the Christian profession are opposed to each other in such direct and vivid contrast. It meets us with full force, likewise, in all those numerous cases, in which reference is made to ruinous errors or gross corruptions in the Church, without any particular stress being laid at the time on the idea of its abused grace. References of this sort abound on all sides. We meet with them in every Epistle.

---

24. [2 Pt 2:1; Jude 1:4.]
25. [2 Pt 2:13–15, 18–20, emphases Nevin's.]

Lofty as the terms are in which St. Paul addresses the several churches to which he wrote, while his eye is fixed on the thought of their high and glorious privileges, he finds it quite as easy again apparently to admit the existence among them of offences and scandals, which seem to turn the other conception into a mere flourish of empty words. We need not cite examples. They will come up readily of themselves to the mind of every one, who is at all familiar with his writings.

Here then is a peculiar and difficult problem to be solved in the interpretation of these Epistles. How are we to bring together the two sides that enter thus into their general hypothesis of Christianity, seemingly incongruous as they are, in such a way that we shall have a result doing full justice to both, and uniting them in real logical harmony for our thoughts? It is plain, that no scheme of exegesis which fails to do this, however much it may have to recommend it on other grounds, can be entitled to confidence; since it must be constructed on a view of the Gospel different from that which pervades the Epistles themselves, and can never serve, therefore, as a sufficient key to unlock their sense.

Now there are two general ways in which a theory of interpretation may wrong the New Testament conception of Christianity, as we have just had it under consideration. It may not do justice to the first side of the hypothesis, or it may not do justice to the second. In the one case, we shall have the idea of nature overwhelmed in a certain sense by a false sublimation of the idea of grace; in the other case, the order will be reversed, and we shall have the idea of grace merged and lost in the idea of nature. For the sake of distinction, we may call one the Calvinistic and the other the Arminian tendency.

The Arminian view proceeds on the supposition, that there is no essential difference between the order of nature and the order of grace. It acknowledges, of course, the existence of grace, regarded as a supernatural power exerted upon the minds of men; but this is not felt to depend on any other order or constitution than that of the world under a simply natural view, considered in the general relation which it sustains to God. Man in his natural character is possessed of intellectual and spiritual faculties, which carry his thoughts above and beyond the present world, and qualify him for entering into communication with the realities of a higher life in the way of religion; and the idea here is, that in order to do so, he needs no other help than what is comprehended in the notion of a common divine influence exercised upon his powers for this purpose. The whole conception of grace thus resolves itself into this, that God by his Spirit, is supposed to act on the minds of men, just as they are, directly and indirectly, without any intervention whatever; and it is supposed also to depend upon themselves, in the use of their natural ability, whether such gracious influence shall be of avail or not for the purposes of salvation. Such a view, of course, leaves no room for the idea of the Church, as a real economy or constitution different from the world. It is easy to see, accordingly, how it must work, when brought to bear exegetically on the New Testament problem which we have at present under consideration. This

Document 3: "Hodge on the Ephesians" (1857)

Arminian tendency has no power to make any earnest account of the lofty terms, in which St. Peter and St. Paul allow themselves to speak of the privileges of the Christian state, regarded as anything more than the inward condition in general of the truly pious. It is admitted, indeed, that these terms are applied immediately to outward and visible bodies of people; but this is considered sufficient of itself to show, that they are not to be construed strictly, but with great latitude rather and accommodation. The titles "elect," "beloved of God," "called to be saints," "sanctified in Christ Jesus," &c., are taken to refer only to the profession of Christians and the avowed object of their being gathered into ecclesiastical associations. They are for the most part borrowed too from the old Jewish economy, being a simple transfer to the Christian Church, outwardly considered, of forms of thought and modes of speech, with which the Jewish mind had long been familiar as applied to the Old Testament theocracy, under a like outward view. Christianity, however, it is assumed, is of altogether too spiritual a nature to be adequately measured by any such simply outward conceptions; and it is held to be clear enough, that there was very much in the actual condition of those to whom they are thus collectively applied, which forbids the thought of their being employed in any other light. In this way, these conceptions, great as they may seem to be in sound, are virtually shorn of significance and force. The heavenly or divine side of Christianity, as represented by them, falls away before its merely human or earthly side. The Church comes to be nothing more than a particular form of the general life of the world, in its relation to religion and piety. It offers facilities and opportunities for spiritual culture; but these are by no means confined to its bosom. All resolves itself at last into the sincere belief of certain doctrines, and the earnest practice of certain virtues, which have no *necessary* dependence on the Church.

How completely this system of thought fails to do justice to the Epistles of the New Testament, we need not spend time now in endeavoring to show. Our business at present is more immediately with the opposite form of onesided thinking presented to us by the Calvinistic tendency; for this it is that governs throughout the New Testament exegesis of Dr. Hodge, as it comes before us in his *Commentary on the Epistles to the Ephesians*.

Here we have a false sublimation of the idea of grace, by which in the end serious wrong is done to the proper human side of the Christian salvation. All is made to resolve itself into divine agency, under such a form as fairly lifts the process of redemption out of the sphere of man's proper life, and causes it to go forward in another and different sphere altogether. The doctrine of election, turning on the notion of an absolute unconditional decree in the mind of God, is made to be the principle, and only really efficient cause, we may say, of the whole work. God having of his mere good pleasure determined, from all eternity, to save a certain fixed number of persons belonging to the human family, and not to save any besides, is supposed then to have ordered the entire plan of redemption in subordination to this purpose. All the provisions of his grace, including the fact of the Incarnation itself, the atonement made by Christ's death, the benefits of his resurrection, the mission of the Holy Ghost, the establishment of the Church, the Bible, the ministry of reconciliation, and the holy sacraments, are conditioned and limited, according to this view, by the settled and foregone conclusion which it is proposed to reach by their means; becoming under such aspect, a sort of outward mechanical apparatus merely in its service. The result is an ultra-spiritualistic, shadowy idea of redemption, in which no real union is allowed after all to have place between the powers of heaven and the necessities of earth; and in full correspondence with this, a complete dualism is brought into the conception of the Christian life also, regarded as the subjective or experimental appropriation, on the part of believers, of the grace thus objectively provided on their behalf.[26] Human and divine factors are indeed both acknowledged, as entering in some way together into the process of conversion and sanctification; but no room is found for their free and harmonious cooperation. God becomes all, and man practically nothing; the consequence of which here again is, that religion becomes a scheme of mere abstract spiritualism, which carried out consistently, can hardly fail to turn it at last into a cloud-like phantom or hollow shadow, the counterpart in full of its own profoundly kindred error, the christological dream of the ancient Gnostics.

For the application of this system to the exposition of the New Testament, we could have no better example than Dr. Hodge's *Commentary on the Epistle to the Ephesians*. It proceeds upon the Calvinistic hypothesis, as now described, from beginning to end. So far as we can see, too, he does not shrink from acknowledging this hypothesis in its only fully consistent form, the supralapsarian conception we mean, as held by Calvin himself, though not generally by his followers.[27] According to that conception, as is well known, the decree of election, issuing in the salvation of the elect as the last end of God's works, so far as man is concerned, is taken to precede and govern in the order of being, not simply the idea of redemption, but the idea also of the fall itself; the amount of which is that God, having in mind his own glorification in the salvation of the elect and perdition of the non-elect, determined first the creation of the race, and then its fall, in order to make room for what was his ulterior purpose in that other form. Dr. Hodge does not, indeed, in so many words, adopt this supralapsarian theory; but it is the only view, we think, that suits what he says of the predestination of a fixed number of human beings, from all eternity, to everlasting life. It is certain, at all events, that this decree is made by him to be the principium of everything that is comprehended in the scheme of redemption itself and that all its arrangements

---

26. [Princeton theology held to a dualism of theology and piety; theology was the "objective" systematization of biblical teaching, which was then realized in "subjective" Christian experience (Loetscher, *Facing the Enlightenment and Pietism*, 26, 76, 170–71, 226, 251 and Hoffecker, *Piety and the Princeton Theologians*, 26–27, 70–71).]

27. [It has been customary among students of John Calvin to debate his view of predestination as either "supralapsarian" or "infralapsarian," that is, does election take place before the Fall or after. See John Calvin, *Institutes of the Christian Religion:* III.23.7, and *A Treatise on the Eternal Predestination of God* (1552).]

and provisions, accordingly, are considered as being circumscribed and limited by it in their force. They are universally for the elect only, and no part of the fallen world besides. Their scope and efficiency are absolutely bounded by the range of this narrow circle, unalterably settled in the Divine mind from all eternity, and cannot be said to extend beyond this really in any direction whatever. Predestination in this sense, and no other, is the "primal fountain," we are told, "of all spiritual blessings," as involving for the saints their "election to holiness before the foundation of the world."[28] The mystery of the Incarnation thus took place only for the elect, whom it was determined beforehand thus to save. Aside from them it would not have occurred at all; and for the rest of the world it has in fact no saving purpose or power of any sort. The rest of the world is not in a salvable state; for the economy of the Gospel is such, that the principle of its grace, considered here as an absolute decree in the Divine mind, cannot be said to reach even potentially those who stand outside the circumference of this decree. Salvation, as a possibility only, has just as little significance for them, as it would have if they belonged to another world entirely. Power to become the sons of God, the great privilege and prerogative of as many as receive Christ (John 1:12), belong exclusively to the elect. All others are doomed to hopeless impenitency and unbelief. Alas, what *should* they believe, if this view of the Gospel be itself the very truth of God which they are bound, under pain of damnation, to receive? For any of the non-elect to believe that Christ died for *them,* or that he is willing now to save them, must be, according to Dr. Hodge's scheme, to believe what is absolutely and eternally untrue. To agree at all with the actual truth of things, *their* faith must own and confess precisely the reverse. All this, we know, sounds monstrous enough. But we hold it to be a perfectly fair, unvarnished representation of the theology, which Dr. Hodge has brought with him as the compass and pole-star of his observations at St. Paul's Epistle to the Ephesians. The doctrine of election, as he holds it, involves beyond the possibility of logical escape, the notion of a corresponding partiality and limitation in all the arrangements of grace. Make such a decree the principle of salvation, and it must necessarily reduce the means of salvation throughout to the measure of its own action and intention. It will be no longer true, that Christ died for all men, made atonement for all, triumphed over death for all, and now reigns head over all things to the Church for all, having sent forth his ministers to preach repentance and faith to all, that they might be saved. Regarded as a merely external administration indeed, Christianity may claim and appear also to possess such universality of character. But looking to its proper spiritual economy, we find all to be different. In God's mind, it is a plan to save the elect only; the agency of his Spirit goes along with it, to make it certainly efficacious for this end; beyond this it carries in it neither purpose nor power of grace for any of the children of men.

 Such a predestination to eternal life, moreover, must necessarily draw after it, in the case of those who are its subjects, whatever is required to go forward in their

28. [Hodge, *Commentary on the Epistle to the Ephesians*, xvii.]

personal experience, in order that they may be prepared finally for this glorious result. The beginning and end of revelation, for every predestinated saint, are joined together with unalterable necessity from the start. No room is left thus to conceive of any real power on the part of men themselves, either to defeat or make sure their heavenly calling. What may seem to be attributed to human agency in this way by the Scriptures, must be regarded as having place in show only and outward appearance. The decree of election rules all, and turns the subjective side of redemption, as well as its objective side, into a sort of unreal parade, in which shadows are set before us continually for actual substances and really existing things. Dr. Hodge takes it for granted everywhere, that those whom St. Paul addresses as the "called of God in Christ," are such as have been individually and separately predestinated to salvation from all eternity, and that it is of course impossible for them in such view not to be saved. This does not imply that they can be saved in their sins, or without means and conditions; but it does unquestionably mean, that whatever may be needed in such form for the final result, is made infallibly certain by the same decree that fixes the certainty of the result itself. Predestination involves as its necessary indissoluble sequences, in the case of every individual to whom it extends, effectual calling, justification, sanctification, the resurrection of the just, and full glorification finally in heaven. There is no room in the theory for distinguishing between what is potential only and what is actual. Election to certain blessings, is taken to include as a matter of course the consequence of coming into their possession and fruition. The "elect" addressed by St. Paul, according to the *Commentary* before us, are "the actual recipients of the blessings spoken of, viz: holiness, sonship, remission of sins, and eternal life."[29]

Out of this way of looking at the subject arises of necessity a corresponding view of the Church. It is confessedly the body of the "elect," in the New Testament sense of that term. It is made up plainly, in St. Paul's view, of those whom he addresses as "saints," as the "called of God," as those who are "sanctified in Christ Jesus," as those whose vast privileges he describes as being in their measure a sort of counterpart of the resurrection and exaltation of Christ himself. It is a conception for him plainly, which is of one and the same measure precisely with these titles and representations. Settle it then that the true Scriptural sense of such terms is what we find it assumed to be always by the system before us, and we may see at once how the notion of the Church must shape itself to agree with the requirements of the case. It can no longer be considered as an outward and visible organization at all, except in an imperfect and improper sense. In its true nature, it can be regarded only as an invisible constitution, the community of the righteous as they are known to God. Such is the view presented to us very explicitly by Dr. Hodge. Election, he tells us, does not regard "any external community or society as such" (p. 29). Again we are told, that if election is to holiness, it follows that "individuals, and not communities or nations are the objects of it" (p.

---

29. [Hodge, *Commentary*, 30.]

DOCUMENT 3: "HODGE ON THE EPHESIANS" (1857)

35). Again, commenting (in his usual style of begging dogmatically the whole question he pretends exegetically to settle) on the words which is his body, he says:

> This is the radical or formative idea of the Church. From this idea are to be developed its nature, its attributes, and its prerogatives. It is the indwelling of the Spirit of Christ that constitutes the Church his body. And, therefore, those only in whom the Spirit dwells are constituent members of the true Church. But the Spirit does not dwell in church officers, nor especially in prelates, as such; nor in the baptized, as such; nor in the mere external professors of the true religion; but in true believers, who therefore constitute that Church which is the body of Christ, and to which its attributes and prerogatives belong (pp. 87–88).

The following is still more distinct:

> The idea of the Church which underlies this paragraph (Eph. 2:19–22), is that which is every where presented in the New Testament. The Church is the body of Christ. It consists of those in whom he dwells by his Spirit. To be an alien from the Church, therefore, is to be an alien from God. It is to be without Christ and without hope. The Church of which this is said is not the nominal, external, visible Church as such, but the true people of God. As however the Scriptures always speak of men according to their profession, calling those who profess faith, believers, and those who confess Christ, Christians; so they speak of the visible Church as the true Church, and predicate of the former what is true only of the latter. The Gentiles while aliens from the Church were without Christ, without God, and without hope; when amalgamated with the Church, they became the habitation of God through the Spirit. Such many of them truly were, such they all professed to be, and they are, therefore, addressed in that character. But union with the visible Church no more made them real partakers of the Spirit of Christ, than the profession of faith made them living believers (pp. 123, 124).

How exceedingly arbitrary all this is, and how little it agrees with the plain text of St. Paul himself; it is not our business just now to show. We bring it forward simply to exemplify the view which Dr. Hodge takes of the Church, from one end of his *Commentary* to the other. It agrees in full with his conception of the nature of Christianity, as being essentially a scheme of pure abstract spiritualism, starting in the election of certain individuals to salvation, and having no real significance or force beyond the carrying out of this purpose, which, at the same time, it cannot fail infallibly to reach. Under no such aspect can the Church be regarded as an outward and visible organization, carrying in it as such the powers of a higher world. Indeed it can be no *organization* at all; except in the character of a mental notion merely employed to generalize what are held to be the common attributes of its constituent members, as they are known certainly to God, though with no certainty to the world or to one another.

It answers only to the invisible process of redemption, as it lies behind the dramatic show with which it is made to play its part in the outward world, and not at all to this show itself. These two conceptions fall asunder completely. There is no inward connection between them. The invisible fact and the visible fact come to no organic union whatever. They do not meet together in the idea of any single constitution, but present to our contemplation always what must be regarded as two Churches in truth instead of one. The scheme in this view is grossly dualistic.

Such dualism subverts really the old doctrine of the Church, as it entered into the faith of the first ages, and continues to challenge the faith of the world still in the Apostles' Creed. It converts its whole being into a shadow, which, while it seems to promise much, means at last literally nothing for the process of man's salvation. Neither the true Church, in the sense of Dr. Hodge's distinction, nor the Church which is such in name only and outward show, can be said to add anything really to the "mystery of godliness," as otherwise ordered and made sure for its own ends. Neither the visible nor the invisible Church can be regarded in the light of a constitution, intervening with any real force between heaven and earth, and serving as the necessary form of all actual correspondence between them in the way of grace.

So far as the visible Church is concerned, this is at once plain. The system makes it to be, in and of itself, a mere profession of Christianity, a simply human association, a name and form at best and nothing more. If the presence of the Spirit go with it at all, it is there as something outwardly and mechanically joined with the other conception, and not as really belonging to it in any proper sense whatever. There is nothing indeed which the system is more ready to denounce, than the imagination of any sort of virtue or force for the purposes of salvation in the forms of religion as such; an imagination, indeed, which all may easily enough see to be both dangerous and absurd, if the premises of this judgment relating to the nature of the Church itself be allowed to go unquestioned. Grant that the visible side of Christianity in such view, its outward profession and forms, its whole constitution as a Church, carries in it no necessary relation whatever to its invisible privileges and powers; and it needs no farther argument certainly to prove that it must jeopardize then all the interests of piety, to lay stress on any such visibility and externalism, as having in themselves anything to do really with the proper kingdom of God, which is described as being within men, and as being "not meat and drink, but righteousness, and peace, and joy in the Holy Ghost."[30] The dualistic stand-point of the system in question, shuts it up to this judgment, and renders it, we may say, logically impossible for it to look at the subject in any other light. It is ever already, accordingly, to disparage all trust in the forms of religion, and to insist on the claims of its inward life and spirit, as something wholly independent of every such external aid. It is the foe constitutionally of the churchly, the priestly, the sacramental in religion, under every form and shape. Dr.

---

30. [Rom 14:17.]

Document 3: "Hodge on the Ephesians" (1857)

Hodge himself loses no opportunity of striking at these conceptions, wherever they come in his way; and often, indeed, allows himself to go out of his way for the purpose.

But the invisible Church of this dualistic theory is no more suited than its notion of the visible Church, for the office here in question; and just as little account is made of it in fact under any such view. It adds nothing to the conception of Christianity, as apprehended without it. It is in truth nothing more than this conception itself, thus previously full and complete. It is at best the comprehension only of the "elect," whose salvation is a fact already secured under quite another aspect and view, and who thus bring with them in their character of saints all that is made to belong to them in its communion.

What has been now said may serve sufficiently to show the general nature of the Calvinistic hypothesis, on which Dr. Hodge relies so confidently for the right interpretation of the Epistle to the Ephesians. It is sufficient also to show, we think, how unequal his *Commentary* must necessarily be to the task of meeting and solving what we have already seen to be the fundamental exegetical problem brought to view in the structure of the Epistle itself. The hypothesis does not answer at all to the terms and conditions of this problem, as it has been already stated and described. It does not even seek to reconcile and unite the two apparently discrepant views of Christianity that run through the Epistle. It throws itself upon one of these views in a great measure exclusively of the other; and in this way violently breaks the knot which it has no power to unloose. It does well in asserting over against Arminianism the claims of grace as forming in the work of redemption an order of life and power distinct from nature and above it; but doing this in such a way as practically to sunder the two spheres altogether, it falls into a like one-sidedness in the opposite direction, making so much of God's agency as to turn the activity of man in fact into mere dumb show. With such a character, how can it possibly do justice to the text of the New Testament, or serve as a mirror to reflect the mind of St. Paul? Looking at the theory then as it is in itself, and comparing it with the plain demands of the case, we have the most perfect right to anticipate not any more particular investigation, and to say beforehand that the *Commentary* before us cannot possibly give us the true scope and sense of the Epistle it pretends to expound. The difficulty is not with the learning or ability of its distinguished author. These may be all that could be expected or desired. It lies in the preconceived scheme of thought which he feels himself bound to apply to the text, as the necessary norm of its meaning; but which is found to be in truth so foreign from the genius of the text itself, that no amount of learning can ever be able to interpret this faithfully and fairly by its means.

If this general *a priori* judgment in regard to the work at large be at all correct, we may take it for granted that it cannot fail to be corroborated and confirmed by an examination of it in its details. It is only what might be anticipated, therefore, when we look into it, and find its actual course of exposition attended with embarrassment and contradiction from the very start.

Take first of all the topic of election, which is found to be of such cardinal significance for the interpretation of the whole Epistle. With the merits of the doctrine itself in its Calvinistic form, as held by Dr. Hodge, we are not here immediately concerned. We have nothing to do with it now as a question of metaphysics or of general theology. What we have before us is a simple point of exegesis, which is not to be settled by any such speculation one way or the other. We ask not, whether the Calvinistic dogma, in itself considered, be right or wrong; but whether it be really and truly what was in the mind of St. Paul in writing this Epistle to the Ephesians, so as to be still the proper key to the actual sense of the Epistle itself. That is now the only question; and it is one which we find ourselves at no loss whatever to answer. The election of grace on which so much stress is laid by St. Paul, and which is made by him here and elsewhere to underlie the whole conception of the Christian Church, is *not* just of one and the same order with the "absolute decree" of Calvinism, regarded as determining the destination of every man to glory or perdition from all eternity. To settle this point, it is not necessary that we should be able to explain in full the relation of the two forms of thinking to each other, nor even that we should have it in our power to comprehend precisely the actual view of the Apostle at all points. It is enough to see that the suppositions and assumptions which are involved in the one hypothesis cannot be brought by any strain of logic to agree with what is plainly postulated and required by the other. No rule can be more sure or easy of application than this; and we need no other, for fully deciding the question here in hand.

The Calvinistic theory of election, presented to us in the *Commentary*, connects the beginning of salvation for all who are predestinated to life indissolubly with its end. There is no room to conceive of it coming short of its ultimate purpose in a single case. In addressing then "the saints and faithful in Christ Jesus" at Ephesus, St. Paul is to be regarded, according to this view, as having in his mind's eye directly those in whom this absolute decree had already begun to work surely towards its own end, and no others. None besides may be thought of as having any true denizenship in the kingdom of God. The conception of that kingdom is held to be necessarily of one and the same measure, with the actual operation of this absolute decree in those who are its subjects. They alone have part really in the "vocation" of the Gospel; and for them this heavenly calling is itself the guaranty and pledge, most surely, of everlasting life.

But now it must be plain, we think, for any unsophisticated reader, looking into the Epistle itself, that its theory of distinguishing grace, whatever it may be, is something widely different from this, something which refuses to coalesce with it altogether, and that demands absolutely quite another construction of Christianity. The "elect," whom St. Paul addresses, whom he describes as "called to be saints" and as "sitting in heavenly places in Christ Jesus," and who form for him the idea of the Church which is "the body of Christ, the fulness of him that filleth all in all,"[31] are not at once, to his mind, such as have been predestinated by an absolute decree, from all eternity,

---

31. [A patische and paraphrase of phrases from Eph 1 and 2.]

to everlasting salvation, and are now regarded as moving forward by the power of it, with unerring certainty, to this pre-ordained result. We have plain evidence of the contrary in every part of the Epistle. The difficulties it offers in the way of Dr. Hodge's scheme, are of the most unyielding kind; and they come up in every chapter, we had almost said in every paragraph and verse; so that recourse must be had everywhere to arbitrary and unnatural suppositions, to set them aside. The Epistle goes throughout on the supposition (common, we may add, to the entire New Testament) that those whom it addresses as Christians, chosen and called of God to the high and glorious privileges of the Church, might still fail to "make their calling and election sure."[32] This single fact, too plain to be disputed by any honest and unprejudiced mind, is sufficient to settle the question under consideration. It shows conclusively that the "elect" in the sense of St. Paul, are not the same with the "elect" in Calvin's sense; and that the New Testament conception of the Church is something much wider than any theological view, by which it is made to be the invisible comprehension simply of that favored class whom God has predestinated to everlasting life, and in whose case thus the work of salvation once begun has no power ever to fail.

"Those who were once enlightened," we learn from Heb. 6:4–6, "and have tasted of the heavenly gift, and were made partakers of the Holy Ghost, and have tasted the good word of God, and the powers of the world to come," may after all so fall away that it shall be impossible to renew them again to repentance. Much ado has been made by some with this passage, on account of its broad opposition to the Calvinistic theory of grace, and strange shifts have been resorted to for the purpose of bending it from the plain natural sense of its own words; as though it formed a sort of solitary exception to the general tenor of the New Testament teachings on the same subject. But the truth is, the only singularity of the passage consists in the immediateness and strength of the terms it employs, to express the general thought with which it is charged. The thought itself, so far as its material substance is concerned, forms the very hinge, we may say, on which the instructions and warnings of the Epistle to the Hebrews most manifestly turn from beginning to end. Throughout it goes upon the supposition, that there is such a thing as sinning wilfully and fatally after men have received the knowledge of the truth (ch. 10:26–29); that those who have been "illuminated," and who have passed through many trials joyfully in the service of Christ, may yet "cast away their confidence," and so lose all the benefit of their previous good confession (v. 32–35); that those who have believed, and need only patience and perseverance to win the crown of life, may still "draw back unto perdition" (v. 36–39); that as the ancient Israelites came short of the land of promise, so Christians now may come short of the heavenly rest (ch. 3:7–12); that the apostacy of the Old Testament people of God forms a fair and legitimate example for the warning of his people under the New Testament (ch. 4:1–3); that there is full opportunity and occasion, therefore, for exhorting these last to "take heed," to "fear," to "labor," lest any of them should be "hardened through

32. [2 Pt 1:10.]

the deceitfulness of sin," and so "fall after the same example of unbelief" (3:12–14; 4:1, 11). The great object of the Epistle indeed is to fortify the Hebrew converts to whom it is addressed, against the peril of falling away from their Christian profession and hope; a peril which is regarded not only as conceivable, but as absolutely imminent and hard at hand, creating just cause for earnest fear, and needing to be met with the most constant watchfulness and care. It deserves to be well considered, moreover, that the point of apprehension throughout is made to be, in the case of these converts, not the reality of their conversion itself as a past or present fact, but wholly and only its endurance in time to come. The question is not whether they had been already truly joined to Christ, whether they had experienced at all the power of the new truth, and so possessed in themselves the proper evidences of being in a state of grace, and having the inward life of religion as distinguished from its outward profession and form; but simply, when they should continue faithful and true to the privileges of their actually existing condition, which is presumed, as a matter of course, it would appear, to include in it all that is needed for their salvation. All depends on this perseverance. "We are made partakers of Christ, if we hold the *beginning* of our confidence steadfast unto the *end*" (3:14). We must not be slothful, but "followers of them who through *faith* and *patience* inherit the promises" (6:12). "Let us *hold* fast the profession of our faith *without wavering*; for he is faithful that promised" (10:23). Such is the general tenor and burden of exhortation from one end of the Epistle to the other; involving the assumption everywhere that the Christians for whom it was written belonged really and truly to the "household of faith," and yet had no security whatever of being finally saved for this reason. An assumption, it is hardly necessary to say, with which the Calvinistic notion of the Church can never be made to agree by any ingenuity or art.

Two different ways indeed have been tried, to get clear of the difficulty; but they deserve to be considered miserable *evasions* only, and nothing more. Only to state them, is to expose their dishonesty and want of force. One of them consists in a resort to the most arbitrary imagination, that the case towards which these warnings are directed is *hypothetical* only, without the possibility of its ever becoming actual and real. *"If they shall fall away,"* expresses a contingency, possible enough on the side of believers themselves, against which in such view, accordingly, it is right that they should be solemnly warned; but which is, at the same time, on God's side, made to be graciously impossible, in the case of all who, as the objects of his election in eternity, are the only real subjects of his salvation in time. So from first to last, the Epistle to the Hebrews is to be regarded as an argument and warning powerfully turned towards a form of danger, represented as urgent and dreadful, which nevertheless the inspired writer himself (not less knowing in the matter, we may suppose, than Calvin), well understood to be for the really elect, and therefore really "illuminated" (the only true membership of the invisible and only true Church), a fiction simply of the common understanding, and no proper reality whatever! It is difficult to conceive of any exegesis, more monstrous than this. The other evasion, however, carries with it just as little title to respect. It consists in supposing, that the possibility of apostacy contemplated in the Epistle holds good only of such as own the claims of religion in an outward way, without being brought savingly under its power; and that this, therefore, is the only case, which was really before the mind of the sacred writer in the strong language he allows himself to use on the subject. He is to be considered thus as writing in such strain, not really for the elect (in Calvin's sense), but for the nonelect; who, strictly speaking, had no saving grace, nor even so much as the possibility of it, to fall away from; no heavenly birthright to sell for any price, great or small; no faith whatever from which to draw back to perdition; but who might be warned against the guilt and danger of apostacy notwithstanding, in form merely and for the sake of effect, as having it in their power to fall away at least from the semblance of grace, and to give up a hypocritical profession of religion for no profession at all! The imagination is purely absurd. It stands before us, without a shadow of reason to shield it from contempt. The Epistle is addressed throughout, not to the world at large, but to those who are regarded and spoken of as believers gathered out of the world into the bosom of the Christian Church; not to such under any divided view, as having been partly true saints and partly saints only in name and form, with an eye now to the one class and then again to the other, but to their whole society collectively taken; and those so addressed, are presumed to be in this collective capacity or character, "holy brethren, partakers of the heavenly calling,"[33] possessing by their Christian profession a real, and not simply nominal, interest in the privileges of the Church, its opportunities of grace, its full powers of salvation; while at the very same time, and under the same general view, they are presumed again to be exposed most really to the possibility of losing all and perishing finally through unbelief.

And so with the Epistles of the New Testament in general. They look, in all their communications, directly and exclusively to the Church as distinguished from the world, to the congregation of those who are denominated saints, and described as the chosen and called of God in Christ Jesus. They keep themselves continually to this rule. They have to do only with "them that are within" (1 Cor. 5:12), and not at all with "them that are without." With them that are within, moreover, they have to do plainly in their collective character. It is not to a part only they speak, a still narrower circle mentally described within the limits of this first outward distinction. Not a particle of evidence do they show, in favor of any such arbitrary supposition. They speak to bodies of men, separated from the rest of the world in a visible, external way; and to these, as such, they refer without hesitation the lofty titles, the high privileges, the heavenly immunities and prerogatives of the Christian Church. Yet of those who are regarded as partaking of this glorious distinction, in such general view, do they again go on with just as little hesitation, to predicate, at the same time, directly and indirectly, the real possibility of sin, in forms involving an entire forfeiture of every advantage they

33. [Heb 3:1.]

had come to possess. However it may be with the Calvinistic doctrine of election, it is certain that the election and vocation here brought into view, carry with them no sort of guaranty whatever for the final salvation of their subjects.

The "elect" of St. Peter, chosen according to the foreknowledge of God the Father, through sanctification of the Spirit, unto obedience and sprinkling of the blood of Jesus Christ" (1 Peter 1:2), "begotten again unto a lively hope by the resurrection of Jesus Christ from the dead" (v. 3), "kept by the power of God through faith unto salvation" (v. 5), "redeemed from their vain conversation received by tradition from their fathers, not with corruptible things, as silver and gold, but with the precious blood of Christ, as of a lamb without blemish and without spot" (v. 18, 19), who had "purified their hearts in obeying the truth through the Spirit" (v. 22), who were "a chosen generation, a royal priesthood, a holy nation, a peculiar people," appointed and set apart to "show forth the praises of him who had called them out of darkness into his marvellous light" (2:9), the "elect" of St. Peter, we say, who hold so high a place in his mind, and into the mystery of whose vocation even "the angels desire to look" (1:12), are still to his inspired view compassed about with all sorts of temptation and danger, requiring them to "pass the time of their sojourning here in fear" (v. 17), and need to be exhorted against all sorts of deadly sin, in a strain which clearly implies everywhere the apprehension of its full *possibility*, as something to which the privileges of their Christian state formed neither bar nor let in any sense whatever. It is not enough in his view, that those whom he addresses had "obtained like precious faith with himself through the righteousness of God and our Saviour Jesus Christ" (2 Peter 1:1); nor that "his divine power had given unto them all things that pertain unto life and godliness, through the knowledge of him that had called them to glory and virtue" (v. 3); nor that "having escaped the corruption that is in the world through lust," they had it in their power by the "exceeding great and precious promises" of the Gospel to be "partakers of the divine nature" (v. 3 [4]). All this only opens the way for the successful cultivation of the Christian graces and virtues (v. 5–7), and so it is added:

> If these things be in you, and abound, they make you that ye shall neither be barren nor unfruitful in the knowledge of our Lord Jesus Christ. But he that lacketh these things is blind, and cannot see afar off, and hath forgotten that *he was purged from his old sins*. Wherefore the rather, brethren, give diligence to *make your calling and election sure;* for if ye do these things ye shall *never fall:* for so an entrance shall be ministered unto you abundantly into the everlasting kingdom of our Lord and Saviour Jesus Christ.[34]

If these words mean anything whatever, their plain sense undoubtedly is, that those who were elected and called to salvation, in St. Peter's sense, and who had been purged also from their old sins, were capable, nevertheless, of reverting again to their former state, and of so falling as never to enter heaven; the very case, indeed, of some he

---

34. [1 Pt 1:8–11, emphases Nevin's.]

speaks of as "having escaped the pollutions of the world through the knowledge of the Lord and Saviour Jesus Christ," and being "again entangled therein and overcome," so that "the latter end was worse with them than the beginning" (2:20). In full conformity with this view, accordingly, all ends with the exhortation: "Ye, therefore, beloved, seeing ye know these things before, beware lest ye also, being led away with the error of the wicked, fall from your own steadfastness" (3:17).

In like manner, the "elect" again of St. Paul are plainly represented to us in every direction, as being highly exalted indeed by their position in the way of opportunity and power to be saved; nay as possessing in such form the grace of incipient salvation itself; but never as being set apart to salvation in full, with infallible certainty, and beyond the possibility of failure, in the Calvinistic sense. The very opposite of this, on the contrary, is presumed in every sort of way. Throughout his Epistles, precepts and exhortations and warnings of the most solemn kind, which we have no right surely to regard as the empty skiomachy of one who beats the air, bear witness to the earnest apprehension he had of the liability of Christians to be overtaken with errors and sins involving a complete defection from the Christian faith; while complaints of heresy and corruption actually at work in the Churches furnish ample evidence, mournful and sad, that this apprehension was by no means without ground. What strange forms of seemingly incompatible carnality and worldliness, do we not find mixing themselves with the Christian profession of the Church at Corinth, composed of "them that were sanctified in Christ Jesus and called to be saints"? Theirs, it is signified to us, was no common election. "I thank my God always on your behalf," writes the venerable Apostle,

> for the grace of God which is given you by Jesus Christ; that is every thing ye are enriched by him, in all utterance, and in all knowledge; even as the testimony of Christ was confirmed in you: So that ye come behind in no gift; waiting for the coming of our Lord Jesus Christ; who shall also confirm you unto the end, that ye may be blameless in the day of our Lord Jesus Christ. God is faithful, by whom ye were called into the fellowship of his Son Jesus Christ our Lord (1 Cor. 1:4–9).

And then follows, almost in the same breath, a severe reprimand of their divisions and contentions; in reference to which he says subsequently:

> I brethren, could not speak unto you as unto spiritual, but as unto carnal, even as unto babes in Christ. I have fed you with milk, and not with meat; for hitherto ye were not able to bear it, neither yet now are ye able. For ye are yet carnal; for there is among you envying, and strife, and divisions, are ye not carnal and walk as men? (3:1–3).

And this is only the beginning of censure. The case grows worse as we proceed; and forms of evil come into view, as really existing, or at any rate, as really conceivable in this organization of saints "called unto the fellowship of Jesus Christ,"[35] which it is hard in truth to reconcile with our common ideal of a primitive Apostolical Church, and which for the honor of Christianity we might almost wish to have been either unnoticed altogether, or at least noticed in a more guarded and qualified way. There was no security in their communion, it seems, with all its celestial privileges, from the presence of even gross sins. A man that was called a "brother," one among the number of the "κλητοι αγιοι,"[36] might be nevertheless "a fornicator, or covetous, or an idolator, or a railer, or a drunkard, or an extortioner" (5:11); a monstrous case of course which is noticed only as calling for discipline and exclusion; the very supposition of which, however, is sufficient to show how real and near at hand for the Apostle's mind the whole bad possibility was of which we are now speaking, and how wide a range also he was willing to concede to it in his theory of the Christian Church. Here is another passage which sounds strangely, bearing on the same point:

> Why do ye not rather take wrong? Why do ye not rather suffer yourselves to be defrauded? Nay, ye *do* wrong, and defraud, and that your brethren! Know ye not that the unrighteous shall not inherit the kingdom of God? Be not deceived; neither fornicators, nor idolators, nor adulterers, nor effeminate, nor abusers of themselves with mankind, nor thieves, nor covetous, nor drunkards, nor revilers, nor extortioners, shall inherit the kingdom of God. And such were some of you: but ye are washed, but ye are sanctified, but ye are justified in the name of the Lord Jesus and by the Spirit of our God (6:7–11) [Nevin's emphasis].

And yet with all this purgation from their old sins, environed still, it would seem, with the danger of again coming under their power, and needing to be sharply warned of the fact, in terms that strike the ear certainly as better befitting the "children of disobedience" than the "household of faith"! Take another example:

> Know ye not that your bodies are the members of Christ? Shall I then take the members of Christ, and make them the members of an harlot? God forbid. [. . .] Flee fornication. Every sin that a man doeth is without the body; but he that committeth fornication, sinneth against his own body. What! Know ye not that your body is the temple of the Holy Ghost which is in you, which ye have of God, and ye are not your own? (6:12–20).

Only reflect on the opposite terms of this bold hypothesis, and then consider how much is signified by the *possibility* it serves to set before our view.

It would be easy to multiply exemplifications of the same general thought still farther from both the Epistles to the Corinthians. But the argument does not require it; and so we stop. It would be easy, moreover, to take St. Paul's other Epistles, one after another, and to show that they are all constructed throughout on precisely the

---

35. [1 Cor 1:9.]
36. [Trans. "called to be saints" in 1 Cor 1:2.]

same view of Christianity. But neither is this now necessary. The matter is abundantly plain, for all who care to study it in the light of the observations already made. These Epistles are all for Christians, for those who are considered and spoken of collectively as the chosen and called of God; and yet it is continually taken for granted in them, notwithstanding, that it was most perfectly possible for these very same persons to walk unworthily of their vocation, to forfeit their privileges, to part with their glorious birthright, to turn the grace of God into licentiousness, to make shipwreck of the faith, and so to come short eventually of everlasting life. Cases of such defection, as having actually occurred, are brought into view largely and without the least reserve; examples of unfaithfulness looking towards it are set before us under all imaginable aspects and forms; while the danger of it, as something not simply imaginary but most real and close at hand (the "easily besetting sin" of Heb. 12:1), is everywhere powerfully and irresistibly implied by cautions and persuasions, admonitions and exhortations, prohibitions and precepts, which must be considered absolutely void of meaning in any other view.

We repeat then what we have said before. The doctrine of election in the common sense of the New Testament, and as we have it proclaimed alike by St. Peter and St. Paul, is not the doctrine of election which is set before us in the theology of John Calvin. This is our thesis; and for the present (let it be well kept in mind), nothing more than this. Our business now, as has been already said, is not with the merits of the Calvinistic dogma absolutely considered. The argument for it in its philosophico-theological form, as set forth for example by Schleiermacher, is one certainly which it can never be easy to meet.[37] But the question now before us, is not one of philosophy or general theology. It is a question purely of exegesis. What we deny, is not the truth of metaphysical Calvinism as such, but its identity with the idea of election as it is found to underlie the conception of the Church in the sense of the New Testament. The two forms of thought, we say with the greatest confidence, are not the same. We hold it, therefore, for a fundamental fault in this *Commentary* of Dr. Hodge, that the difference between them is altogether overlooked, that St. Paul's doctrine of the "election of grace" is arbitrarily taken to be precisely of one measure with the doctrine of predestination to eternal life as held by Calvin, and that this last is then used as a key throughout, instead of the first, to open and expound the deep meaning of the Epistle to the Ephesians.

The consequences of so radical a mistake cannot fail, of course, to extend very far. They must affect the complexion of the entire *Commentary*, and may be expected seriously to vitiate the value of its expositions at every point. Our limits, however, will not allow us to pursue the subject any farther at the present time. We hope to take it up again hereafter, in another article. This will give us an opportunity of examining more

---

37. [Gockel, "New Perspectives on an Old Debate: Friedrich Schleiermacher's Essay on Election," analyzes an early essay and ends with a brief comparison to Schleiermacher's discussion in *Der Christliche Glaube* {*The Christian Faith*}.]

fully the true import and bearing of St. Paul's idea of election; as it will make it necessary for us also, to go somewhat particularly into the consideration of his doctrine of the Church; the proper parallel of that other idea, by the help of which alone it is possible to satisfy the opposing conditions of the great exegetical problem which runs, as we have already seen, through all his Epistles, so as to bring into their exposition the feeling of order, harmony and light. The true doctrine of the Church here is for the Calvinistic and Arminian theories, what the true doctrine of Christ's person was in the first centuries for the dreams of the Gnostic on the one side and the dreams of the Ebionite on the other,[38] the glorious everlasting synthesis under a real form of what they have no power to unite except in the way of shadow.

J. W. N.
Windsor Place, Lancaster county, Pa.

---

38. [While the early church believed and worshiped Christ as fully God and fully human, it took about 150 years (from 300 451) to articulate that faith as doctrine. In the process, they rejected two extremes, that of the Ebionites ("poor men") who believed that Jesus was a great teacher, worthy to be followed, but merely a human being, and that of the Docetists, from the Greek word *dokesis*, meaning "appearance," who believed Jesus was a celestial being who only appeared to be human. Docetism was a spin-off of Gnosticism, from the Greek word *gnosis*, meaning "knowledge." Gnostics believed that the material world was so corrupt that an entirely good being like God would have been incapable of inhabiting it. For modern scholarly summaries, see Pelikan, *Emergence of the Catholic Tradition*, 24, and Pétrement, *A Separate God*, 144–56.]

Hodge on the Ephesians: Second Article[1]

In resuming this subject, it seems proper to bring into view again, in the way of brief recapitulation, the leading topics or heads of argument discussed in our previous article.

The New Testament Epistles in general proceed throughout on the supposition of two different sides in Christianity, which, to a certain extent, oppose each other, and yet are quietly presumed always to be equally essential to its true constitution. In one direction all stress is laid upon its supernatural distinction, the fulness of divine grace which is comprehended in it for the salvation of its subjects. In virtue of this, they are represented as having a present interest in the privileges of Christ's redemption, which sets them high above the common level of human existence, and involves for them potentially all that is required in order to everlasting life. All the blessings of the new creation in Christ Jesus are regarded as already theirs, with a form of real possibility, such as we have no right to conceive of as existing for the world in any other circumstances, or under any different view. This is one aspect of the case. In another direction, however, we are met with such a representation of the simply human and earthly side of the same Christian state, as seems at times completely to obscure the glory of the other conception, and to bring all down again to the range of the most common every day experience. The powers and possibilities of a higher world, are found to be strangely at the mercy of the sins and frailties of the present world. The opportunities of grace show themselves as liable to be neglected, frustrated, or abused, as the corresponding opportunities of nature. Thus it is, that heavenly and earthly, divine and human, move hand in hand together throughout the whole economy of the Gospel, as it is here offered to our contemplation. So in the case of the Epistles of the New Testament generally; and so particularly, we may say, in the case of this Epistle of St. Paul to the Ephesians. It is palpably constructed on such a double or twofold view of Christianity, from beginning to end.

This being the case, it follows that no theological system or scheme can be relied upon as sufficient here for the purposes of exposition, which either fails to recognize at all the true and proper structure of the Epistle in this view, or brings with it no

1. [J. W. N[evin], *Mercersburg Review* 9 (April 1857) 192–245.]

power to do fair and full justice to both sides alike of the peculiar hypothesis on which it is thus found to rest. The solution must answer to the nature of the problem, which requires to be solved. The key must agree with the wards and turns of the lock it is employed to open. The commentary must be as wide as the text it pretends to explain, meeting its requirements with equal readiness and ease all round, and satisfying them in a natural and harmonious way.

From the nature of the subject, there is room thus for exposition to become false and inadequate here in two general ways. The simply human and earthly side of Christianity may be allowed to throw into the shade entirely its proper supernatural significance and force; or the wrong may be reversed, by making all of this latter interest, at the cost of what rightly belongs to the first. In either case, we shall have an imperfect onesided theory of religion that can never answer to unfold the full meaning of the sacred text. These two kinds of theological obliquity may be characterized by the terms Arminian and Calvinistic, as serving at once to express their general bearing.

The Arminian tendency makes no earnest account of the supernatural side of Christianity, the order of grace as distinguished from the order of nature. It confesses indeed the presence of the supernatural in its own way; but under the view only of such a relation to the constitution of nature as virtually resolves it into a mere abstraction, belonging properly at last to the life of nature itself. No room is left thus for the conception of another economy, different from mere nature, above it, and yet joined with it in the way of inward lasting union, in the bosom of which the powers of salvation are to be regarded as permanently comprehended, under a form not known in the whole world besides. The distinction between the Church and the world on the outside of the Church, loses thus all proper reality, and resolves itself into a simple word or name.

Such a scheme can have no power of course to do justice to the double aspect, under which Christianity exhibits itself to our view in the Epistles of the New Testament; and it is very easy, accordingly, to convict of palpable and gross failure any Commentary, which may pretend to expound these Epistles by its aid.

The opposite Calvinistic tendency, however, is not for this reason any more worthy of regard or trust, in the same exegetical view. It affects to do justice to the strong terms in which the supernatural side of Christianity is spoken of; but in doing so, it wrongs its proper natural or human side. The work of redemption is taken to be, not for the human race, as such, but for a certain portion of the race elected from all eternity to such distinction; and in this view it is regarded as the irresistible execution or carrying out of God's decree for this purpose, in favor of those who are thus predestinated to everlasting glory. In this way, the transaction of salvation is not so much a real historical process in the world itself, as the playing into it rather of supernatural forces, which are supposed to be at work above and beyond it, and yet come not really to any true union with its proper life. Whatever of human activity may seem to be concerned in it, must be considered as phenomenal more than actual and real, the mechanical echo or reflection simply of the divine activity that sets all in motion from behind the scenes. The two worlds thus come to no organic conjunction. There is no bridging over really of the deep chasm which lies between them. Natural and supernatural, human and divine, are held apart for the imagination, so as to exclude entirely the conception of any intervention, serving to mediate between them, and having power to bring them together in a real and constant way. It is taken for granted, that the action of the higher world upon the lower can be direct only, reaching over into this last under its own natural constitution, immediately and at once, without the help of any other constitution whatever. So we lose again the true idea of the Church; and for the conception of grace in its legitimate character, we are put off with what seems to be too often little better than the notion of magic.

This Calvinistic theory rules the thinking of Dr. Hodge. His *Commentary on the Ephesians* lives, moves, and has its being in it, from the first page to the last. It is an attempt throughout, to construct the sense of the Epistle according to this scheme. He does not extract his scheme, in the first place, from the text. It can hardly be said, that he pretends to do any thing like that. Most clearly, be brings it along with him to his work, as something already settled and fixed. The Calvinistic theology is to his mind one and the same thing with the doctrine of the Gospel; how may it be imagined then that St. Paul, rightly interpreted, should fail to agree with it in any of his Epistles? Thus it is, that the scheme, as an established preconception, is allowed to anticipate and forestall for the thoughts of the Commentator the general meaning of his text, and goes before him shaping the exposition of it everywhere into conformity with its own requirements. It is presumed, that St. Paul had in his mind exactly the same view of religion that is embodied in the writings of Calvin; that he was familiar with the same theological positions and distinctions; and that these, as a matter of course, were continually before him when he penned his Epistles; so that they must be considered to furnish now also the only key by which they can be properly understood or explained. The *Commentary* before us is a vigorous trial of this exegetical rule upon the Epistle to the Ephesians. The author shows himself in general true to his system throughout; not shrinking to follow it out, as it would seem, even to the full length of supralapsarianism itself.[2] The principle of the whole process of redemption is taken to be God's decree of election, in favor of a definite number of persons ordained from all eternity to salvation. Under such view, the process can have no reference really to those who are beyond the range of this decree. It carries with it the certainty of salvation for the elect, but includes no possibility of salvation, no actual provision of grace in order to salvation, for any others. All the arrangements of grace are at once bounded and circumscribed by the measure of the decree in whose service they stand, and can never have any force truly beyond the range of operation with which it is

---

2. [If a person is elected to salvation *before* (supra–) the fall of Adam, then as Nevin says in the next sentence, it seems that "the whole process of redemption" is "put together" (so to speak) as a means to the end of the salvation of the elect, and no one else.]

carried forward invincibly to its appointed end. The fall, it would appear, took place in subordination to this decree, to make room only for the restoration of the elect, while it served to doom all men besides to hopeless destruction. At all events, Christ became man, and died, not for the world at large, as the Scriptures seem to assert, but for the elect exclusively and alone. The promises are for them only. They alone can make any valid use of the means of grace; since to all others they are means in form and show only, and not so as to carry along with them any intrinsic significance really for the ends towards which they are made to look. The articles of the Creed are required necessarily to narrow themselves throughout to the same particularistic view.

Knowing the *Commentary* to be constructed on this scheme, we have a right to consider it a failure even before any more particular examination; just as we might come to a similar judgment by anticipation, in the case of a commentary pretending to take the full measure of the Epistle, from the opposite stand-point of Arminianism in its vulgar rationalistic form. No such one-sided view can possibly do justice to its twofold constitution. The true conditions of the problem to be solved are either misapprehended or ignored from the very start. How then should the solution be expected to succeed? In such circumstances, any commentary must, in the very nature of the case, prove wholly unequal to its proposed task. No ability or learning can help it.

The work before us corresponds in fact with this unfavorable presumption. As an exposition of the Epistle to the Ephesians, we cannot help feeling that it is lame and imperfect throughout. It fails to reach the deep sense of the Epistle, and comes short altogether of its grand and magnificent scope.

One general example and proof of its insufficiency meets us immediately, in the way it takes for granted everywhere that the idea of election, which plays so prominent a part in the Epistle, is of one nature precisely with the dogma of election as held by Calvin. We have taken some pains to show, that this imagination is wholly gratuitous and groundless. The two conceptions do not correspond at all. In saying this, no judgment whatever is pronounced upon the merits of the Calvinistic dogma, in itself considered. In its own form and place, it may be entitled to respect. The question here is not at all concerning the light in which it should be regarded as a point of metaphysical theology; but only concerning the use of it for exegetical purposes, in the exposition of the New Testament. Are the references to the idea of election in the New Testament such, as a general thing, that they may be fairly construed in the known and established sense of the Calvinistic dogma; or are they so circumstanced and conditioned as to require plainly a different interpretation? On this point, there is no room really for any serious doubt. The New Testament doctrine of election, as it meets us, for instance, in the Epistles of St. Peter, and rules continually the thinking and writing of St. Paul, is something essentially different from the doctrine of election which is presented to our view in Calvin's Institutes. The proof of this is found sufficiently in one single consideration. The Calvinistic election involves, beyond the possibility of failure, the full salvation at last of all those who are its subjects; there is no room to conceive of their coming short of this result, in any single instance, made certain as it is in the form of a specific purpose and predetermination in the divine mind, from all eternity. Election and glorification, the beginning and the end of redemption, are so indissolubly bound together, that they may be considered different sides only of one and the same fact. The "elect," in Calvin's sense, have no power really to fall from grace, or to come short of everlasting life. But, plainly, the "elect" of whom the New Testament speaks, the "chosen and called of God" in the sense of St. Peter and St. Paul, are not supposed to possess any such advantage. On the contrary, it is assumed in all sorts of ways that their condition carries with it, in the present world, no prerogative of certain ultimate salvation whatever. They may forget that they were purged from their old sins, lose the benefit of their illumination, make shipwreck of their faith, and draw back to everlasting perdition. They have it in their power to throw away the opportunities of grace, just as much as it lies in the power of men continually to waste in like manner the opportunities of mere nature. Their salvation is after all hypothetical, and suspended upon conditions in themselves, which are really liable to fail in every case, and which with many do eventually fail in fact. Hence occasion is supposed to exist, in the sphere of this election itself, for all sorts of exhortation and warning to those who are the subjects of it, having the object of engaging them to "make their calling and election *sure*."[3] The tenor of all is: "Walk worthy of your vocation. Only such as endure unto the end shall be saved. So run, that ye may obtain."[4]

Plainly, we repeat, the two conceptions are not the same. The difference here brought into view is such as to show unanswerably, that the Calvinistic dogma is one thing and the common New Testament idea of election altogether another. The Calvinistic election terminates on the absolute salvation of its objects; that forms the precise end and scope of it, in such sort that there is no room to conceive of its failing to reach this issue in any single case.

The New Testament election, as it enters into the thinking of St. Peter and St. Paul, terminates manifestly on a state or condition short of absolute salvation. Whatever the distinction may involve for those who are its subjects, in the way of saving grace, it does not reach out at once to the full issue of eternal life. The fact it serves to establish and make certain for them, is of quite another character and kind. It sets them in the way of salvation; but it does not make their salvation sure.

All this is so clear, that we may well be surprised to find no account whatever taken of it by Dr. Hodge; while it is at the same time of such far reaching import, that his want of attention to it must be considered as forming at once a fatal objection to his whole *Commentary*. He confounds here, from the very start, two materially different conceptions, in a way that cannot fail to bring uncertainty and confusion into every part of the Epistle he seeks to explain. Those whom St. Paul addresses as the subjects of God's election and vocation in one view, he considers to be addressed as

3. [2 Pt 1:10.]
4. [Eph 4:1; Matt 24:13; 1 Cor 9:24.]

the subjects of such election and vocation in quite another view. For the Pauline idea of election, he substitutes at once, as though there were no room to imagine any sort of difference between them, the idea of election as held by Calvin; and then proceeds, accordingly, to measure the mind and sense of the Apostle, from first to last, by this hypothetical theory alone, reducing all to conformity with it as he best can. What must be regarded as in fact a fundamental mistake, is made thus to condition and govern throughout the formation of his work. St. Paul writes to the "saints at Ephesus" under one view; Dr. Hodge has them in his thoughts under another view altogether. The case which is before the mind of the Apostle, as the general object of his address, is not the case which is before the mind of the Commentator, as the general object of his exposition. It is not necessary to say, that Dr. Hodge's scheme of election is anti-scriptural and false. We pronounce no such judgment upon it here. It is enough for us to know, that whether true or false, it is not what was present to the mind of St. Paul, in writing this Epistle to the Ephesians. He was not thinking at the time of the metaphysical subtleties, since known as the theology of Calvin. These furnish, therefore, no true rule for the interpretation of what he has written. He wrote from a widely different stand-point. How is it possible then that Dr. Hodge, with all his learning and piety, refusing to see this plain fact, should be able to make us acquainted fully and fairly with the sense of the Apostle's text? Must it not be more or less travestied in his hands throughout? How shall it pass through such Procrustean exegesis (forcing all ruthlessly to the measure of its own iron bed), without being subjected to serious dislocations and wrested into all manner of false proportions?[5]

Before proceeding, however, to notice farther the difficulties and defects that grow out of Dr. Hodge's system of interpretation, it may facilitate the order of our discussion to consider here more particularly what that election of grace is (in distinction from the Calvinistic predestination to eternal life), on which the whole doctrine of the Church is made to rest, with St. Paul, in this Epistle to the Ephesians, as well as in his Epistles generally.

It determines, we have just said, not the certainty of final salvation for its subjects, but only the possibility of it, in such a form as places it really and truly within their reach, while it leaves it in their power, notwithstanding, to come short of it altogether. In this view, their condition is represented to be parallel precisely with that of the ancient Israelites, who were chosen and set apart by solemn covenant to the possession of certain great and glorious privileges, in the way of possible future good, which yet carried along with them no sort of guaranty whatever, as was proved by the event on a large scale, that what was thus possible should at last become actual and real. All were under the cloud of the Divine Presence, we are told (1 Cor. 9:1–5), and

5. [In Greek mythology, Procrustes had an iron bed on which he forced his victim to lie. If a victim was shorter than the bed, he stretched him by hammering or racking the body to fit. If the victim was longer than the bed, he cut off the legs to make the body fit the bed's length. In both options, the victim died. The "Procrustean bed" has become proverbial for arbitrarily forcing someone or something to fit into an unnatural scheme or pattern.]

all passed through the consecrating miracle of the Red Sea; so as to be baptized unto Moses in the cloud and in the sea. All partook moreover of the manna in the wilderness, and of the water that flowed from the rock. Their relation to God, as his covenant people, was most real. Its privileges were such as to exalt them far above every other people. All was ordained and designed, at the same time, to bring them into the full possession finally of far greater blessings, the natural and proper end of the covenant, to which none might hope to come beyond the range of its peculiar grace. "But with many of them God was not well pleased, for they were overthrown in the wilderness" (v. 5); and now they are held up, in such view, as examples of warning and admonition, for those who have been chosen and called out of the world to enjoy the opportunities and privileges of the Christian state, under a like real view (v. 6–11). Indeed no parallel is more familiar than this to the mind of the sacred writers; and it is of itself sufficient to show at once, what view they were accustomed to take of the grace which was supposed to be involved in the Christian profession generally, for those who were "called to be saints," and distinguished as the "faithful in Christ Jesus." It was, in their way of looking at the subject, such grace as made room for salvation, opened the way to it, secured a full right and title to it, rendered it in all respects practicable and possible, while it allowed full occasion still for the exhortation: "Let us fear lest a promise being left us of entering into his rest, any of you should seem to come short of it!"[6]

Here, however, all depends on having some right idea of what is meant by the real possibility of salvation, which is thus made to be the peculiar and characteristic distinction of the state in question.

It may be so taken, as to amount to little or nothing more than the relation of the world at large to the Gospel, so far as this has come to be published and known. There is a sense, of course, in which Christianity is for men in general, offering to all alike wherever it comes, the opportunity of having part in its glorious benefits. So much the Arminian has full right to assert, over against the false particularism of the Calvinist, which seeks to restrict this opportunity to one part of the human race exclusively, in such a way as to place all the rest of it beyond the reach of salvation entirely. The commission which commands the Gospel to be preached to every creature, and which makes the obedience of faith also to be incumbent on every one to whom it is thus preached under pain of eternal damnation, is amply sufficient of itself to prove that what all are so required to believe is really and truly for all a divine fact that may and should be believed. It is no empty word merely sounding forth the phantom of a sense which is not in it actually and in truth, but in all respects, as St. Paul terms it (1 Tim. 1:15), "a faithful saying," a word credible and "worthy of all acceptation," when we are told that "Christ Jesus came into the world to save sinners," and that God so loved the world as to give his only begotten Son (John 3:16), "that *whosoever* believeth in him shall not perish, but have everlasting life." We have no right to narrow the meaning and force of the Christian salvation a whit within these catholic limits. In its own

6. [Heb 4:1.]

nature, it is as wide as the power of the curse from which it proposes to set men free, as fully universal as the wants and necessities of our whole fallen race. Take men just as they are then, in the order of nature, all the world over, and wherever the Gospel is preached to them, we may say that in a most important sense it makes it possible for them to have part in its grace. Christianity is applicable to their circumstances, addresses itself to their wants, and verifies for them the full signification of that word:

> Say not in thy heart, Who shall ascend into heaven? (that is, to bring Christ down from above) or, Who shall descend into the deep? (that is, to bring Christ up from the dead). The word is nigh thee, even in thy mouth, and in thy heart; that is, the word of faith, which we preach: that if thou shalt confess with thy mouth the Lord Jesus, and shalt believe in thine heart that God hath raised him from the dead, thou shalt be saved (Rom. 10:6–9).

It may be supposed now, as we have already intimated, that this general relation of the world to the grace of the Gospel, forming what may be denominated the opportunity of salvation in the order of nature, the possibility of redemption as it extends to the world at large along with the diffusion of Christianity, includes really all that is comprehended in the gracious condition or state of which we are now speaking, as that distinction of Christians on which so much stress is laid in the New Testament. To such rationalistic extreme the Arminian habit of thought always tends, running its natural course through Pelagianism out to the open, bleak and dreary waste of Unitarianism itself. Men may be regarded, according to this view, as possessing in the bosom of regularly organized Christian societies or churches, certain advantages and helps for the cultivation of religion, which they cannot have to the same extent in the surrounding world; just as they may be assisted in any other pursuit by similar organizations voluntarily formed for the purpose; but it is not to be imagined, that they should come thus within the range and scope really of a new and higher form of grace altogether, "powers of the world to come,"[7] means and appliances of salvation armed with divine virtue and supernatural force, for the action of which no room is to be found in the whole compass of the world's life besides. The conception of the Church falls, in this way, to the reigning level of man's ordinary natural existence. It is one simply among the other forms of its proper social order, the result of its general relation to the powers of religion; just as the organization of a school in politics or science may be considered the product of the general spiritual tendency it serves to represent. So far as the actual efficiency of the heavenly forces of the new creation is concerned, they cannot be said to be in the Church in any other sense than as they are in the world at large. Their relation to the world generally is taken to be immediate and direct, needing no intervention in any such form to make room for their saving action on the souls of men. The very notion of any such mediating constitution,[8] indeed, is

---

7. [Heb 6:5.]
8. [That is, the church *mediates* the supernatural activity of God in the world *with* the natural

boldly repudiated, as something supposed to be fundamentally at war with the entire genius of the Gospel. The order of grace, in such view, is confounded with the order of nature; the wall of distinction between them falls to the ground; in such sort that there ceases to be, for faith, any order of grace whatever in the Christian economy. All resolves itself into the life of nature, acted upon through its religious powers by influences imposed to proceed from a higher world. Looking at the subject in this way, the distinction of the Christian profession, of which so much account is made by St. Paul, must be considered more nominal than real; and it becomes necessary, therefore, to allow, that much of his language in regard to it carries with it a certain hyperbolical sound, which needs to be toned down exegetically to a much more moderate key, in order that it may suit fully for our common thinking the actual nature of the case. In the hands of a Commentator, like Paley,[9] or Taylor of Norwich,[10] this is done to some purpose. The "saints" at Ephesus or Philippi, we are told, are only those who have been gathered outwardly into the bosom of the Christian Church. So much is clear. But no such merely outward state, as such, can be supposed to carry along with it really any supernatural grace. What St. Paul seems to say of it, therefore, in such view, must be looked upon as a sort of figure of speech merely, a mode of thought transferred from the relations of the Old Testament to the different relations of Christianity, in conformity with the mental habit of the Jewish nation, for the purpose of effect. Election, vocation, translation from darkness to light, exaltation to heavenly places in Christ Jesus, sonship in the family of God, sanctification itself in the primary sense of the term, mean nothing more here than the powerless fact, that those of whom these high sounding terms are used have been led to make an outward profession of Christianity, and are to be regarded as having so far gone before others in seeking to improve the resources of salvation which it offers for the use of all in its proper higher and more spiritual form. The great things which are spoken of their state are either shorn thus of all proper significance, or come to be referred to an ideal Christianity, whose actualization cannot be said to depend on the resources of this state in any exclusive sense whatever. The possibility of salvation which is secured to Christians in the Church, turns out to be at last nothing more than the general possibility of salvation which is set before men universally, wherever the Gospel comes with its message of grace and peace.

How little this agrees with the plain sense of St. Paul, we need not be at any pains to show. The Calvinist has a most perfect right, on his side again, to protest against it, as a view of Christianity which goes to destroy the idea of supernatural

---

structures of human activity.]

9. [English theologian and philosopher William Paley (1743–1805), *Horce Paulince; or the Truth of the Scripture History of St. Paul.*]

10. [William Taylor (1765–1836), an English Unitarian known more for translating German literature into English, promoted the study of the composition and history of biblical texts, i.e., higher criticism. For more on Taylor, see David Chandler, introduction to *William Taylor of Norwich.*]

grace altogether; although he can have no right, for this reason, to force upon us his own theory of partial redemption, as if that were the only and, therefore, necessary alternative of what he feels thus bound to reject. The possibility of salvation which is put forward as the general distinction of the Christian state in the New Testament, is neither one nor the other of these antagonistic views, but carries with it a form which plainly excludes them both. It is not for those only who are predestinated to eternal life in Calvin's sense, and so have no power to come short of it in the end; for it is everywhere taken for granted, that the state or condition in question includes no such certainty of salvation whatever. And yet it is just as much taken for granted everywhere, that the condition is one which offers, not to some only, but to all who have part in it, a form of grace which is not to be found in the constitution of man's life under any other view, and in virtue of which salvation is brought nigh to them with such a character of real and full possibility as is not known in the whole world besides.

Those whom St. Paul addresses collectively as saints, chosen of God to be holy, partakers of the heavenly calling and heirs of eternal salvation, are not regarded by him certainly as the possessors of a merely nominal and imaginary distinction, over against the world at large with which their state is thus broadly contrasted and compared. It is not in the way of compliment only or conventional form, most clearly, that he can be supposed to speak of it in such lofty terms. Nothing can be more plain than that for his mind the difference between their condition and that of the world around them, was most substantial and real, and of a kind to warrant in full all the strength of language he was accustomed to use in regard to it. His sense of difficulty, in setting forth the significance of the distinction, is not that his terms are too high for his subject, but only that they come not up to the proper greatness of it, as he finds it overwhelming his own thoughts. It is no simply outward separation alone, no merely nominal peculiarity of position, which in the view of the Apostle goes to make up the true idea of the Christian profession, the state into which men are brought by entering the hallowed precincts of the Church. This state, as he looks upon it, sets all who are in it, whether the privilege be properly improved or not, in a relation to God which cannot be said to exist at all for others. The possibility of salvation here is made to assume a far higher form, than all it is ever found to be in the world at large. It is no longer the mere capability of being saved, but in a most material sense salvation already begun. The difference of relation to the powers of redemption is not merely in degree, but actually and truly in kind. A new order of life has been entered, the order of grace as distinguished from the order of mere nature. In this respect, the state includes a strictly supernatural character. Those who are in it stand, by virtue of their position, in correspondence with the powers of a higher world, the mysterious forces of the new creation in Christ Jesus, in a way not possible to men in any other condition. They are brought within the range and sweep of that victorious dispensation, which having run its course first in the person of the Saviour himself, is now revealing its presence in the world, through the Spirit, for the final and complete salvation of his people. To this salvation they have already a full title. It is theirs by covenant and promise, and they have full opportunity to come at last into its possession.

Such clearly is the conception of the Christian state, in its distinction from the general condition of the world, as it dwells in the mind of St. Paul. And this conception forms for him precisely the idea of the *Church*; the sense of which enters so largely into all his Epistles, but most of all we may say into this Epistle to the Ephesians; underlying as it does here the universal course of his thought, and forming in truth the key note around which it seems to proceed throughout, as a grand and magnificent anthem belonging not so much to earth as to the skies.

Answering to the view now described, the Church is regarded by St. Paul as a real constitution of supernatural origin and force, existing in the world under an outward historical form, and comprehending in it the opportunity and possibility of salvation as they are to be found nowhere else.[11] It finds its symbol or type in the Ark, which served in the days of Noah to save those who sought refuge in it from the waters of the deluge. So far as it lay in the power of the unbelieving and disobedient generally, at that time, to give heed to the Divine warning and betake themselves to the hope which was set before them in this form, it might be said that there was a possibility for them to be saved. But the possibility of salvation for those who had already entered the Ark, as we can see at once, was of a very different kind. It was not such indeed, in its own nature, as to make it absolutely necessary for them to be saved. There was no room, it is true, for any question in regard to the full sufficiency of the Ark for this purpose. But it was possible for those who were in it, to frustrate for themselves its merciful purpose and design. They might forsake it through unbelief; or staying in it, they might neglect the needful conditions of life, so as to come short finally of the proper end of their probation. Notwithstanding all this, however, their state was already one of glorious miraculous privilege, as compared with the condition of the world at large. It placed them in a new order of existence, and brought them into living actual communication with the scheme of grace which God had been pleased to provide for the deliverance of his people. It was in such view this deliverance itself, already in sure progress towards its appointed end. In these circumstances, those who were in the Ark might be spoken of easily enough as possessing from the first the full and entire salvation which was really comprehended in its constitution for their benefit; although this was not yet reached, and might possibly never be reached by all of them in fact; since that must depend, in the nature of the case, on their own persevering use of the means they enjoyed for this purpose. Still all might be said to be theirs, as soon as they passed from the sphere of nature here into the sphere of grace. They were rescued from the general condemnation of the world. They were made secure from its impending destruction. They were prepared to outride the flood. They might be said

---

11. [The thesis that pervades all of Nevin's work. He develops it in this, and the next four, paragraphs.]

even to have a present footing on the shores of the new earth, which they were called to seek through its waters.

Behold a true figure of the Christian Church (1 Peter 3:21), as it appeared to the mind of St. Paul. It stands as contrasted with the world in its natural character, under the most real view, as a different order of life altogether. The world in its natural character is fallen, alienated from the life of God, and literally under the power of Satan; who is styled, for this reason, "the god of this world" (2 Cor. 4:4), and "the prince of the power of the air, the spirit that now worketh in the children of disobedience" (Eph. 2:2). The redemption of man, in these circumstances, called for the intervention of grace under a wholly new form of existence. This was accomplished by the mystery of the Incarnation. Here the "Word became flesh;" in such a way as to bind heaven and earth together in a new mode of human life, which comprehended in itself supernaturally the power of surmounting and overcoming the evils that press upon this life in its natural and merely Adamic form. Christ came into the world, not simply to make known the will of God, and to preach righteousness, as the last and greatest of all the prophets; but primarily and mainly to actualize God's will, to create righteousness, to bring grace and truth for men into being. The salvation of the world stood, first of all, in his own person. It was there as a real outward constitution, an act of self-revelation on the part of God, set over against the order of nature, the presence of a higher economy brought down into the midst of it from above, and making room within its bosom for all the grace that is comprehended in the idea of the Gospel. "In him was life; and the life became the light of men."[12] He was himself the way to the Father, the absolute truth, the resurrection and the life. It is in this deep sense originally, that the Gospel is represented to be "a new creation;"[13] for it is in fact no modification merely of the old Adamic order of man's life, but the introduction into the world really and truly of a new and higher mode of being, through the coming of our Lord and Saviour Jesus Christ in the flesh. The case required, however, that this new creation should not remain an isolated fact in Him, who was thus constituted its original ground and foundation. Hence the process of redemption, in the ordinary sense of the term, including the whole conflict of Christ with the powers of darkness, the satisfaction which he rendered to the broken law of God, his sufferings upon the cross, his voluntary bowing to the stroke of death, his descent into hades, his resurrection from the dead, and his glorious ascension into heaven; all designed to complete the full sense of the mystery which lay hid in his person, by advancing his Mediatorial life to its proper position of actual victory and superiority over the whole world of sin and death, that it might become thus for men generally, through the mission of the Spirit, the principle and fountain of life after its own kind, thenceforward to the end of time. Such is the order of salvation, as we find it embodied in the Apostles'

---

12. [John 1:4.]
13. [2 Cor 5:17.]

Creed.[14] The constitution of grace in distinction from the constitution of nature, as it appeared originally in Christ's single person, was never designed certainly to be a mere temporary fact, passing out of the world entirely when he was "put to death in the flesh," only in order that he "might be quickened in the Spirit," and so enter into his glory, and take possession of his kingdom in its true and proper form.[15] No thought could well be more remote than this from the habitual thinking of St. Paul. The constitution of grace, to his view, becomes fully established in the world, only after Christ's glorification; and then it is identical for him with the idea of the Church. He sees in the Church always, accordingly, a peculiar and distinct order of existence, an economy of life absolutely different from the constitution of the world under every other view, in which is comprehended the actual presence of forces and powers for man's salvation that are strictly supernatural; not belonging at all to the world in its merely Adamic life, and not to be measured by the capabilities of this in any way; but such as are derived wholly and entirely from the new creation in Christ Jesus, carried out to its proper completion in his glorification at the right hand of God. He reigns there as "head over all things to the Church;" which in this very view is denominated "his *Body*, the fulness of him that filleth all in all;"[16] as being the form of his continual presence in the world, as well as the organ and medium of his grace through all time. Here he works with a power, which goes altogether beyond the strength of nature, transcending its whole fallen constitution, and producing results that cannot possibly be reached in any other way. The Church is the Home of the Spirit, and the true Ark of Salvation; offering to men under a real form the supernatural resources, by which alone it is possible for them, so to "pass the waves of this troublesome world that finally they may come to the land of everlasting life."[17]

So apprehended, the Church is found to be, in a most important sense, the necessary medium of salvation for men. How should it be otherwise, if it be indeed the constitution of grace itself, the only form in which the powers of the new creation are at work in the world; while all beyond resolves itself into that mere life of nature, from the weakness and curse of which it is the object of the Gospel to set men free? To say that no such intervention is needed to make room for the course of the Christian salvation, is virtually to deny and reject the truth of all that has now been said concerning the difference between the order of nature and the order of grace, and to hold that men may be saved absolutely in the order of nature itself without any order of grace at all; which is such an error again, as necessarily involves at last, when carried out to

14. [See especially "Thoughts on the Church" below, 153–60.]

15. [1 Pt 3:18.]

16. [Eph 1:22–23.]

17. [Excerpt of a prayer in "Ministration of Public Baptism of Infants" in *The Clergyman's Companion in Visiting the Sick*, which was included in the *Works of William Paley*, 268. The *Clergyman's Companion* includes the offices of public and private baptism so as to be "convenient for clergy in the course of their parochial duty."]

its legitimate end, the denial and rejection of the whole mystery of the incarnation. If the grace by which salvation is made possible be in the world only as a supernatural system, flowing from Christ, and if this system be itself the Church, related to him as the body to the head, it follows forthwith that there can be no ordinary salvation out of the Church, that it is the first duty of all to seek refuge in its bosom from the wrath to come, and that those who do so are at once made to have part in such full power and possibility of being saved as may be said to be in fact salvation already begun. So much, accordingly, is involved everywhere for St. Paul, in his established idea of the Church. He has no difficulty whatever in assuming continually, that it sustains to the world a relation corresponding in full with all that the Ark was, in the days of Noah, to the men of his generation.

Apprehended as it is by St. Paul again, the Church has necessarily an objective organic life. It is in this respect a system or constitution parallel in full with the constitution of the world, under its simply natural form. It is made up of manifold forces and powers, working with a vast array of outward historical results, through successive ages, which are yet all bound together as one general movement, and capable of being referred to a common principle or source. That principle is Christ. The Church starts from him, and stands in him always, as its perennial undying root. Whatever of grace, power, opportunity and possibility, there may be in it, as distinguished from the universal range of man's life on the outside of it, all proceeds from the new order of existence which was introduced into the world by his incarnation, and in virtue of which he now reigns at the right hand of God. It is a sphere of being, which refers itself back organically to the principle of the new creation in such view, even as the sphere of nature, with all its powers and possibilities, refers itself back organically also to the principle of the old creation, advanced to its highest form in the "living soul" of Adam.[18]

Such in general is St. Paul's conception of the Church. It unites in itself at once the two sides of the peculiar and truly enigmatical hypothesis, on which we have found all his Epistles to be constructed; doing full justice to both, and causing their seeming contradictoriness to disappear; for which very reason also it offers to us the only satisfactory solution of their sense, the only key by which it is possible to expound them in any full and harmonious way.

It is easy to see, that no like idea of the Church is at all attainable for either of the one-sided tendencies, which allow themselves, as we have seen before, to turn the true synthesis of the Christian mystery into a false antithesis, by separating its factors, and then exalting one at the sore cost and sacrifice of the other. It is very certain, on the contrary, that these schemes must lead necessarily, each in its own way, to a different notion of the Church altogether; and it is very certain, moreover, beforehand, that no such different notion can ever be made to square exegetically with the true meaning

---

18. [1 Cor 15:45. This formulation is continuous with *The Mystical Presence*, MTSS ed., 149–51.]

of St. Paul's Epistles, but must serve rather to involve the exposition of them in endless and hopeless embarrassment.

Neither the Arminian nor the Calvinistic extremes can make true earnest with the proper objective and historical character of the Church, regarded as a constitution of grace in distinction from the constitution of nature. Neither of them can do justice to the idea of its organic nature, the unity and continuity of its being, considered as the power of a new creation in Christ Jesus. With neither of them can it ever come to a true acknowledgment of the position which properly belongs to it in the supernatural economy of salvation, as a part of the "mystery of godliness,"[19] itself a mystery, and in such view fairly and of right an object of faith, as it is made to be in the Apostles' Creed. For neither of them is the Church, in any sense, what the Ark was in the time of Noah, the bearer actually of the redemption which it offers to those who are invited into its bosom, the very organ and medium of grace, the home of the Spirit, the sphere of celestial powers, through whose intervention alone the blessings of the Gospel are made to be available and possible truly for any of the children of men. Both schemes are careful in fact to denounce the idea of all such interposition and mediation in any form, as interfering with what they take to be the proper freeness and directness of Divine grace, and as tending in their apprehension to rob religion of that character of inwardness and spirituality, which forms its highest distinction, and which it is held to admit only in the form of an immediate personal transaction between every man and his Maker.

In the case of the Arminian or Pelagian theory (having its natural end in Socinianism),[20] all this is at once plain. It brings the whole economy of salvation, regarded as a process upon the earth, down into the order of nature, in such a way as to leave no room truly tor any order of grace whatever. Grace with it is at best the presence of supposed heavenly forces, coruscations of power from a higher world, playing over into the world of nature in a purely magical way; which remains in such view throughout the real field of action where all is carried forward and brought to its conclusion. The Church cannot be considered thus as any thing more, than a particular province of the general life of man, defining and taking in his religious relations, just as his social relations are variously embodied and expressed in other provinces of the same life, without its being imagined for a moment that these form in any separate view the actual ground of their being.

The Calvinistic theory, sublimating as it does the idea of grace, and laying all stress on what it conceives to be the strictly supernatural side of religion, would seem to offer room, on first view, for a much more honorable notion of the Church. Who

---

19. [1 Tim 3:16.]

20. [Socinianism is a system of doctrine named after two natives of Siena, Lelio Sozzini (1525–1562) and his nephew Fausto Sozzini (1539–1604). The surname appears in a variety of forms, but the Latin, Socinus, is currently used. This antitrinitarian system denies the full deity of Christ, predestination, original sin, total depravity, the atonement as a penal satisfaction, and justification by faith alone. See Mulsow and Rohls, ed., *Socinianism and Arminianism*.]

can fail to be impressed by the well-known, lofty and solemn terms, with which Calvin himself approaches the topic in the last book of his *Institutes*? "Coming to speak now of the visible Church," he says, [Bk IV,] chap. I, §. 4.,

> ... let us learn from the single title *Mother*, how much lies for us in the knowledge of it; since there is no other entrance for us into life, unless she conceive us in her womb, unless she give us birth, unless she nourish us from her breasts, unless finally she hold us under her tutelage and care, until having put off our mortal flesh we shall be as the angels (Matth. 22:30). For our infirmity will not allow us to be discharged from school, till we shall have finished the whole course of life as pupils. Add, that beyond her bosom no remission of sins is to be hoped for, and no salvation.

All this sounds like a true echo of the ancient faith, as it might have been pronounced with unfaltering voice by St. Augustine or St. Cyprian, the faith of the universal Church in the beginning, according to the plain sense of the Creed. It is, however, in truth, the old doctrine in sound only, and nothing more. Calvin's conception of the Church, after all, is by no means the same with that contained in the Creed; and it is easy enough to see, how his theological system is at war with this, and leads necessarily to a wholly different view. This comes out fully with Dr. Hodge.[21] He too has much to say of the Church; and is forced to allow it a prominent place in his *Commentary*; as how indeed could it be otherwise, in endeavoring to explain an Epistle like that to the Ephesians, which is so full of it from beginning to end? But the article, in his hands, is conditioned by the Calvinistic notion of election and predestination, in such a way as to bear almost no resemblance whatever to the light in which it was regarded by St. Paul. A passage, quoted from his work, may assist us in coming to some right apprehension of this point.

"The purpose of election," he tells us (pp. 30–31 [32]),

> is very comprehensive. It is the purpose of God to bring his people to holiness, sonship, and eternal glory. He never intended to do this irrespective of Christ. On the contrary it was his purpose, as revealed in Scripture, to bring his people to these exalted privileges through a Redeemer. It was in Christ, as their head and representative, they were chosen to holiness and eternal life, and therefore in virtue of what he was to do in their behalf. There is a federal union with Christ which is antecedent to all actual union, and is the source of it. God gave a people to his Son in the covenant of redemption. Those included in that covenant, and because they are included in it—in other words, because they are in Christ as their head and representative—receive in time the gift of the Holy Spirit and all other benefits of redemption. Their voluntary union with Christ by faith, is not the ground of their federal union, but, on the contrary, their federal union is the ground of their voluntary union. It is,

---

21. [As noted earlier, it is probably not fair to blame Calvin for Hodge's peculiar interpretation.]

therefore, in Christ, i. e., as united to him in the covenant of redemption, that the people of God are elected to eternal life and to all the blessings therewith connected.[22] Much in the same sense, the Israelites are said to have been chosen in Abraham. Their relation to Abraham and God's covenant with him, were the ground and reason of all the peculiar blessings they enjoyed. So our covenant union with Christ is the ground of all the benefits, which we, as the people of God, possess or hope for. We were chosen in Christ, as the Jews were chosen in Abraham. The same truth is expressed in 3:11, where it is said that the carrying out or application of the plan of redemption is "according to the eternal purpose which He purposed in Christ Jesus our Lord." God purposed to save men in Christ, He elected them in him to salvation.

So Dr. Hodge expounds theologically the clause: "According as he hath chosen us in him before the foundation of the world" (1:4). All this means plainly, that the economy of redemption starts in God's absolute unconditional decree of election, terminating first of all on a certain definite number of the human race, singled out as individuals, without any respect whatever to the mode and manner of their salvation; for whom, and in whose behalf exclusively, it is then purposed to provide a Redeemer, who should be constituted from all eternity, in God's mind, their federal head and representative, having authority to undertake for them in the covenant of redemption, and power to execute in full afterwards the terms of this covenant, by accomplishing all that their salvation required; in which view they may be considered to have been chosen in him to holiness and eternal life before the foundation of the world; just as he forms now actually in time the instrumental medium, through which the purpose of election in their case is carried forward to this its necessary end. Christ, in this view, is not first in the order of the decree, but only second. He is not the primary and main object of it, but only a subordinate provision brought in for the purpose of carrying it into effect.

Now the first thing that may well strike us with surprise here is, that this view does not correspond at all with the case which is brought forward by Dr. Hodge himself as its proper parallel, the relation namely of the Israelites to Abraham. "We were chosen in Christ," he says, "as the Jews were chosen in Abraham."[23] Very true. But if so, then most certainly not in the sense of this Calvinistic decree. To bear out any such analogy as that, the Abrahamic covenant must be supposed to have sprung primordially from an unconditional eternal purpose, on the part of God, to separate and call to the peculiar benefits of this covenant a certain fixed portion of mankind, chosen

---

22. [For an explanation of Hodge's federalism, see Evans, *Imputation and Impartation*, 196–208. In its simplest form, federalism asserted that both original sin and union with Christ are imputed to persons by way of a "covenant" (Latin *foedus*). Humanity had violated the original covenant of works and could only be saved through a covenant of grace. Layman provides an overview of this Reformed tradition as the context for the origins of Nevin's thought in the general introduction to *Born of Water and the Spirit*, 4–10.]

23. [Hodge, *Commentary*, 31.]

simply as so many individual units of the race, and without any reference whatever to their subsequent nationality as Jews; in the service of which decree then, Abraham himself was also preordained to be the instrument both of their national existence and of its covenant blessings; so that they might be said to have been chosen in him to Judaism and its privileges, before all time. Only so would the case offer a fair and true parallel with the other representation. But who seriously believes anything like this to be the actual signification of the Abrahamic constitution? Who does not feel rather, that the whole subject is caricatured by being placed in any such monstrous light?

Looking at the Abrahamic Constitution in its true light, we have before us here, in fact, two altogether different forms of election. We may distinguish them as mechanical and organic. The scheme set before us by Dr. Hodge is strictly of the first character; the reigning Biblical scheme is altogether of the last. The difference between the two conceptions is so important, that we may well be at some pains to have it clearly in mind.

If a man should suppose a law in nature to be of one measure exactly with its phenomenal results, the numerical comprehension of these and nothing more, a mere term to express and set forth the general truth of their existence as so many separate facts, it would be an example of a mechanical notion coming short entirely of the real nature of its object. The case calls for an organic conception. Such a law is not the product merely of its own results (a contradiction in terms), nor yet an instrument simply for bringing them to pass; but the very power itself of their existence.

To bring the matter nearer to the case in hand, take now the common relation of a tree to its branches, blossoms and fruit. If these should be supposed to exist in any certain quantity and form aside from the tree itself, and there to be joined to it in an outward way, causing it to appear as the instrumental bond and bearer of their collective life, the conception would be again purely mechanical; whereas the actually existing relation itself, as all may easily see, is organic; the tree being in fact the true ground and foundation of all the life that is comprehended in its branches, blossoms, and fruit; to such extent, that they cannot exist at all, nor be so much as conceived even to exist, except through its presence and power.

Make such a case, in the next place, the object of God's decree; which must be considered in truth to extend to all his works; and we may readily see how there is room here again for the same difference of conception, accordingly as the decree may be taken to agree with one or the other of these views. What the tree is really, it must be considered in any right view to be ideally also in God's eternal purpose and plan. The order of its being, in both modes, must be intrinsically the same. The decree looks to the branches, blossoms, and fruit, only through the tree, which forms the whole ground of their being and life. They are viewed as being in fact a single constitution. To will their existence, is to will, not secondarily but primarily, the existence of the tree itself. In such sense only, may they be said to be chosen in it to what is at last their actual destination. The election, by which this is secured, is organic. Dr. Hodge, however, to be consistent with his own theological theory, would need to reverse the order of the conception altogether. The branches, the blossoms, the fruit, are to be considered as all predetermined to their existence in time, in the first place, just so many, neither more nor less; and then, next in order, and for the purpose of bringing this to pass, must be supposed to follow the preordination of the tree, fitted and contrived to serve as an instrumental medium for reaching the end in view. This is the mechanical notion of election. The two schemes, in this case, may be distinguished without any great difficulty; and it is by no means hard to say, which of them is entitled to the most respect.[24]

Take now, finally, the natural constitution of the human race, flowing from Adam; which is so often referred to in the New Testament, and especially by the Apostle Paul, as forming a general parallel with the new order of life in Christ. All proceeds from God's eternal purpose or decree; and we may say of men universally, that they have been chosen in Adam before the foundation of the world, to become what they are actually afterwards in time. It makes all the difference in the world, however, in what sense this election may be taken. Conceive of it under the mechanical character which Dr. Hodge assigns to the corresponding election of grace, and it must be held to mean, that the decree starts with the purpose of calling into actual existence, under a human form, a distinctly settled number of possible beings, irrespectively altogether of any intervening condition, and then falls upon the expedient or device of making the whole process centre in Adam, as it does now in fact; a view that is not likely to be entertained seriously here, we think, even by Dr. Hodge himself. The organic conception alone falls in rationally with the demands of the case. So apprehended, the decree coincides with what we are irresistibly constrained to regard as the world's actual constitution. The relation of Adam to men generally is seen to be an organic law; through the presence and power of which alone they come to be what they are; and aside from which, therefore, there is no room really to conceive of their existence at all. To be the object of God's purpose then in any way whatever, they must be regarded by it from eternity in this form and no other. The Divine decree terminates on the whole race immediately and at once; as a constitution derived from Adam, and holding in him continually as its natural root.

Such unquestionably is the eternally established order of the Adamic constitution, as it presented itself to the view of St. Paul; and with this corresponds in full also, we are bound to believe, his doctrine of election as applied to the new creation in Christ. The decree of creation, so far as the human race is concerned, looks to men as being in Adam, that is, as having part in the conditions, and qualities of humanity, the order or sphere of life that grows forth from him as its organic principle and root.

---

24. [I.e., the organic scheme says the tree is "elected" *in order to produce* the branches, blossoms, and fruit; the mechanical scheme reduces the tree to a mere "means to the end" of producing the branches, blossoms, and fruit, which are "elected" apart from the tree. See Nevin, *The Mystical Presence*, MTSS ed., 142–49, 183–85.]

He is the law, in which is comprehended the whole real possibility of their being. They are elected in him, as far as they are ever to exist at all, to whatever of worth and significance there may be in the simply natural life, into which they are introduced only by being born of his blood. And just so Christ is considered to be, only in a far deeper way, the principle and root of the new and higher order of life, which is supposed to be comprehended in the Church, as distinguished from the world. The "faithful" are held, by the very conception of their faith itself, to be in Christ; and with this order must be allowed to correspond also, in their case, the decree of salvation. It is strictly organic. It looks to them only through Christ. They are chosen to salvation, not as being out of him and beyond him in the order of nature, but as being in him, and so in the order of grace.

It may be said, indeed, that even under this view it must be owing to God's purpose and election at last, that some are brought to be in Christ, and so to have part in the constitution of grace, while others fail to enter it and perish; just as it may be said also, that the specific results of any organic law in the sphere of nature are all numerically foreknown, and so necessarily foreordained, in the Divine mind, from all eternity; that every particular tree, for instance, and every particular herb and plant, produced by the law of vegetation, must be viewed as being chosen out of all possible entities, and determined to the order out of which it then actually grows and proceeds; or that, in the case of any single tree, its countless leaves, and buds, and blossoms, are all numerically willed to exist, and fixed to their several places, and ordained to their various individual contingencies and fortunes, from all eternity, in the same way. All this may be said; and we are quite willing to allow, that the metaphysical argument for predestination, when thrown into this broad and universal form, is one which it is by no means easy to meet. Three things, however, are to be observed in relation to it.

In the first place, this metaphysical view of foreordination,[25] as it may be supposed to lie back of all organization, deciding and fixing in every case its precise contents and results, is not the view of St. Paul presented to us in the Epistle to the Ephesians. We do not say that it is one which he was not prepared to understand or acknowledge, in its proper place. That is another question. What we mean is, that it was not in his mind at all, not present to his thoughts in any way, in writing this Epistle; and that it cannot be used, therefore, as a true key to its sense.

In the next place, the conception in question does not offer itself as one that is peculiar in any way to the sphere of religion. It looks to the universal constitution of the world.[26] So far as it goes, the order of grace is viewed as being the real counterpart and parallel of the order of nature. That is just what it is made to be in the thinking

---

25. [To assess the development of Nevin's doctrine of election and moral responsibility, see the 1833 sermon, "Election Not Contrary to a Free Gospel" (available on Google Books); as well as his primary ethical essay from his Mercersburg period, "Human Freedom," (rewritten in a briefer form as "Faith, Freedom, and Reverence").]

26. [A point Nevin made in "Election Not Contrary to a Free Gospel," 213.]

of St. Paul. The one is to him as really as the other an objective constitution, having in itself its own laws and powers, and working organically for the accomplishment of its own ends. With what may be supposed to lie behind all this in either case, the metaphysical conception of the Divine decree, he does not allow his mind to concern itself in any way whatever.

In the last place, it makes a vast difference, whether this metaphysical conception be allowed to form directly one notion of election as in the mechanical scheme, or be simply thrown as an impenetrable mystery behind it, according to the organic view. In the first case, it becomes absolutely unconditional, having regard to no conceivable relations or qualities whatever; as being itself necessarily the ground and reason of all such distinction; in which view, we can think of nothing more perfectly abstract. In the other case, it is at once conditional; eyeing all existences from eternity as they actually are in time; seeing the whole always in its parts, and the parts in their whole, as well as in the relations they bear mutually among themselves; determining and fixing things concretely; the only way that can be said to answer truly at last to their being; the only way, indeed, in which they can ever be really and truly the object of either purpose or thought at all.[27]

Such is St. Paul's idea of election, we repeat, as applied to the economy of the Christian Church. It is not mechanical but organic; not abstract, but concrete. It has to do with men, not in the general view simply of their common natural humanity, but under the conception of their being Christians, such as have come to stand, through the obedience of faith, in the bosom of the new order of life which is revealed in the Church; without any reference immediately to the way in which this may be supposed to have come to pass. What the Apostle has immediately in his eye, is not so much the election of men into Christ, as their election in him; the heavenly prerogatives, the glorious privileges, possibilities, opportunities and powers, that are comprehended in the new creation of which he is the Alpha and Omega, and to which they are chosen in fact by being embraced in its organic sphere. Just as, by being in the vine, its branches may be said to be elected and chosen in it to all the fruitfulness, which is made possible for them in this way, and in this way alone.

The grand object of the whole purpose is primarily and fundamentally the Lord Jesus Christ himself. All else is seen as having place only in him and by him. What fills the soul of the Apostle with adoring admiration, is the thought of the glorious constitution of grace in his person, considered as present to the mind of God from all eternity, and as forming in truth the ultimate scope of all his counsels and dispensations towards the human race, though in the unsearchable depths of his wisdom it was not allowed for ages to come fully into view. Through all the graces of nature, made

---

27. [The key to Nevin's reading of predestination, which permits him to theoretically assent to a more traditional view, is that the divine decree is eternal and unitary, but it can be "broken down" into its temporal moments; i.e., one can "unpack" the experienced events that constitute the "organic" whole of election.]

subject to vanity by reason of sin, its gloomy forebodings, and wild utterances of despair; through the long night of expectation that went before the Flood and followed after it; through the clouds and darkness, which shrouded the mysterious presence of Jehovah during the whole period of the Old Testament; this was the end, towards whose revelation, in the fulness of time, the universal plan of the world had been directed from the beginning, and in the advent of which alone was to be reached finally the full resolution of its inmost sense. All looked in this way to the new constitution which was to be ushered into the world by the glorious fact of the incarnation, carrying with it redemption and victory over the powers of sin and hell, for all who should come into its bosom, and use faithfully its grace. And now God's eternal purpose was fulfilled. The mystery of ages was no longer hid, but open. Christ had come in the flesh; and by his death and resurrection room was made for the Church which now stood among men accordingly, and was destined to do so to the end of time, as the comprehension of the unutterable blessings which had been procured for the world by his mediation. Into the bosom of this Divine economy, both the Apostle himself, and those to whom he writes, had been already brought. There was nothing doubtful or uncertain, to his mind, about the reality of their privilege in this view. They had submitted themselves, with the obedience of faith, to the authority of the Christian constitution, coming into its supernatural order by the holy sacrament of Baptism; and they were regarded as being, for this reason, certainly in the sphere of redemption, with a full title to all its privileges and powers. The Apostle does not allow himself to be disturbed for a moment, by the consideration that some of them, in all probability, were not what their profession called for, and that it was possible for such to come short of salvation altogether. He sees in them all notwithstanding, the subjects of a true heavenly distinction. Use it as they might, their Christian birth right was a present boon, the value of which was not to be expressed by any earthly arithmetic. They were elected in Christ to everlasting life; called and set apart in him to be saints; brought out of the order of nature, where neither sanctity nor salvation were possible, and placed in the order of grace, where there was room and power for both. What if some prove false to their vocation, faithless to the covenant of life in Christ Jesus? "Shall *their* unbelief make the faith of God without effect?"[28] Shall it be said that there was no reality in God's purpose here, no actual meaning in the election of grace on his part, because men fail to "make their calling and election sure,"[29] and, it may be, turn his grace itself to the purposes of licentiousness and sin? God forbid: yea, let God be true, though every man be found a liar (Rom. 3:4).

As viewed by St. Paul, the being of the Church, the power of Christianity, is not just the aggregate of actual piety which may be found among Christians at a given time; but something far wider than this; even as a true law of life in any case, forming objectively a new and distinct sphere of existence must ever go far beyond the measure

28. [Rom 3:3, Nevin's emphasis.]
29. [2 Pt 1:10.]

of its actual products, quantitatively considered, being always in truth of endless force and fulness in its own order. It is a constitution, as real as the constitution of nature, starting from its own principle, and carrying with it a whole world of powers for its own purposes and ends. It is of itself a supernatural, or more than merely natural, condition and state, over against the vanity and misery of the world in every other view; and simply to be in it therefore, is to be εν τοις επουρανίοις εν Χριστω,[30] with an emphasis of meaning that comes up fairly to the full strength of the expression itself. It is the sense of all this, reigning in the heart of the Apostle, that gives form and tone to his whole address directed to the "saints at Ephesus." In view of this, they are congratulated as the chosen of God, whom he has been pleased to "bless with all spiritual blessings in heavenly places in Christ." With reference to this, he prays that their understanding may be enlightened to know what was actually comprehended in the Christian calling, "the riches of the glory of God's inheritance in the saints, and the exceeding greatness of his power towards them that believe."[31] On this, as a foundation, he rests the whole plan and scope of the Epistle, all its instructions and all its exhortations, from beginning to end.

With his Commentator, Dr. Hodge, all is different. He has in his mind another notion of election altogether; and along with this, consequently, an altogether different notion of the Christian Church. Such a notion in fact as really destroys the very being of it entirely, in any form answering to the idea of St. Paul. Christianity with Dr. Hodge is the product of a purely mechanical decree on the part of God, terminating at once in the eternal salvation of its objects, considered under the most abstract view, without the intervention of any really objective and concrete constitution of grace whatever. Of course, then, it can be only for the "elect" in this miserably narrow sense; having as little to do with others, as though they belonged to a different world altogether. It is easy to see, in these circumstances, what must become of the Holy Catholic Church. It must resolve itself into an abstraction or an empty form. Regarded as the comprehension of those who are really so in Christ, as to be sure of final salvation, the case of the elect only, it takes necessarily the first character, being in truth but the generalization of this fact as it dwells in the knowledge of God. Regarded as the "body of those who profess the true religion,"[32] and nothing more, it just as necessarily takes the second character, being at best an outward show and name only employed to represent something which it is not in fact. The first conception is that of the invisible Church; and it is the only one which deserves from these premises to be considered valid; as it is the only also, indeed, with which Dr. Hodge pretends to make earnest, as answering

---

30. [Eph 1:3. Trans. "in the heavenly places in Christ."]

31. [Eph 1:18–19.]

32. [The Westminster Confession, Chapter 25:1–2, describes the invisible church as "the whole number of the elect, that have been, are, or shall be gathered into one, under Christ the Head thereof; and is the spouse, the body, the fulness of Him that fills all in all," and the visible Church as "those throughout the world that profess the true religion."]

at all to the "glorious things which are spoken of Zion"[33] in this Epistle. The other notion is that of the Church visible or empirical; which, however, is not considered to exist necessarily under such view, in the form of any general organization, nor even in the form of any number of particular organizations as such; but if we are to believe Princeton, may be in the world without any organization at all, "so long as professors of the true religion exist" (*Bib. Rep.*, Oct., 1856, p. 696),[34] being the collective body only of such as own this faith in any and every way. So all runs out here again also into a sheer generalization, a mere word or notion simply employed to bring a certain class of persons outwardly under a common view. The whole theory, at the same time, is perfectly dualistic. It gives us in fact two totally different notions of the Church instead of one; for there is no sort of common life really between the two spheres which are thus baptized with a common name, as though they were opposite sides merely of the same fact. There is not so much as the shadow of an organic relation, joining them together, and making them unitedly the subject of any common predicates whatever. Each has its proper being really on the outside of the other; and each moves in its own separate orbit, much as it might do if the other had no existence at all. Such duplication, however, brings with it here no gain, but only wide and heavy loss. With its show of two Churches, the theory in effect leaves us none—none, we mean, that can be said to possess in any way the true and proper attributes of the Church, or to fulfil its needful offices and functions in the economy of redemption; none answering in such view to the place which is assigned to the article in the Apostles' Creed; none that could possibly have satisfied the mind of St. Paul. In neither view does it come before us in the character of a real constitution or order of grace, whose existence is at once objective, historical, organic, and concrete. In neither view can it be said to come between God and men, like the Ark of old, as the necessary organ and medium of their salvation. Nothing of this sort, indeed, is pretended or imagined on the part of those by whom the theory in question is held. It is one of the last things precisely, which they have any disposition to admit.

So far as the doctrine of Dr. Hodge is concerned, there is no room here for any mistake. Not only does it flow necessarily from his theological system; not only does it lie before us plainly expressed in this *Commentary*; but he has taken special pains besides to make the world acquainted with it, in different articles on the subject published in the *Biblical Repertory*. Many, we believe, have been dissatisfied with these articles, even in the Presbyterian Church itself. By some they have been considered well-nigh scandalous, seeming as they do to betray the cause of Protestantism completely into the hands of its foes. It must be allowed, at all events, that the ground they take is exceedingly low. It is not saying too much to affirm, that Dr. Hodge has no faith whatever in the article of the Church, in the only sense in which it was held to be in the beginning a necessary part of the Christian Creed. We make the affirmation

---

33. [Ps 87:3.]
34. ["The Church—Its Perpetuity," *Biblical Repertory and Princeton Review* (October 1856), 696.]

sorrowfully, but at the same time deliberately, and with the fullest conviction of its truth. The only marvel to our mind is, that one so wise should not himself clearly perceive the fact, or that one so good should be able to do so and not be seriously troubled with the perception. He holds what he calls the doctrine of the Church in a certain sense of his own, and considers himself at liberty then to profess the old formula of the Christian faith with this in his mind; as though in doing so, he placed himself really on the same platform of belief. But to what can any such merely verbal correspondence amount, where there is no consent after all, in so material a point, with the actual meaning of the symbol itself? To receive the Creed truly can only be to receive it in its own original and proper sense. That Dr. Hodge, with the Puritan world in general, does not do.[35] The sense which rightfully belongs to the article of the Church in the early Creed is by no means doubtful or obscure. It simply echoes what we may easily know (if we *will*), to have been the universal faith of the true Christian world in the first ages. It is in truth determined also by the position of the article in the Creeds themselves. Between this sense and the low Puritanic conception of Dr. Hodge, the difference is very wide indeed. The Church, in the old view, constitutes an essential part of Christianity; belongs to the "mystery of godliness;"[36] is truly and properly an object of faith; includes in itself as such the presence of supernatural powers under a natural form; stands in the world indestructibly as the body of Christ and the home of the Spirit; and challenges the obedience of all men to its high claims in such view under pain of eternal damnation. All this is comprehended unquestionably in the article: "I believe in the Holy Catholic Church," according to the order it holds in the Apostles' Creed. For the whole mystery of salvation, as it takes its rise in the miraculous conception and birth of Christ and flows onward to his resurrection and ascension, is there represented as afterwards descending upon the world, through the "coming of the Holy Ghost," in the constitution of the Church; which is then immediately made to be again the comprehension of its powers, and the orb of its whole celestial action, from the one baptism for the remission of sins onward to the resurrection of the body and the life everlasting. Need we say, that the Church, in which Dr. Hodge professes to believe, is of another order altogether? Under neither of its dualistic aspects, as they have come already under our consideration, can it be in truth the object of any such faith. His theory furnishes no clue for understanding at all its position in the Creed; as the whole architecture indeed of this grand and venerable symbol belongs plainly to another order of thought, and to be fairly comprehended must be seen and studied from a wholly different point of view.[37]

But our business is not now primarily with the faith of the Primitive Church and the true sense of the Apostles' Creed. It may be said, that we are not bound here by the opinions of the first Christian ages; that their doctrine of the Church was extravagant

---

35. [See Nevin, "Puritanism and the Creed," scheduled for vol. 8 of MTSS.]
36. [1 Tim 3:16.]
37. [Nevin attempts to explain this "architecture" below in "Thoughts on the Church," 157–62.]

and false; and that there is no good reason therefore why it should not be revised and improved at pleasure in the modern Puritanic and Baptistic form. Let what we have just said on this subject pass then as merely spoken by the way. What we charge upon this low scheme of the Church at present is, that it is plainly at war with the doctrine of St. Paul. The Epistle to the Ephesians is constructed throughout on precisely the same view of the Church that is made to challenge our faith in the old Christian Creeds; whereas it wholly refuses to fall in naturally with the scheme of Dr. Hodge, and is put to exegetical torture only in being forced, however skillfully and adroitly, into any such sense.

In the Epistle, the organic view of Christianity reigns throughout. With the *Commentary*, all is mechanical and abstract. In the Epistle, Christ is held to be the real root of the Church; which is then spoken of continually as an actual constitution in the world, proceeding from his person. With the *Commentary*, the notion of God's absolute decree is made to be the only principle of salvation; and the Church is nothing more at last than the fact of its execution in the case of the elect, a word or at most a mere thought employed to generalize its actual results.

The difference, in this view, between the spirit or soul of the text, as we may term it, and the spirit of the exposition, is of a kind to be felt almost everywhere. Take, for example, what is presented to us as the "analysis" of chap. 1, vs. 3–10. The Apostle blesses God, we are told, for the spiritual gifts bestowed upon his people. Of these, "the first in order, and the source of all the others, is election," vs. 3–6, the second is "actual redemption through the blood of Christ," vs. 7–8; the third is "the revelation of the divine purpose in relation to the economy of redemption;"[38]—as if all lay really in the form of any such logical mechanism! As if these were to be considered so many separate kinds of grace externally brought together, instead of being taken to represent, as they do in truth, the proper wholeness and full concrete unity of one and the same grace. So it follows then in the particular exposition: Election first, a system purely abstract, and as such full and final in its own form. Then redemption on the outside of this to serve as an instrumental medium for carrying it into effect—another system, full also and final in its own form. And then, lastly, the revelation of all this, on the outside of both the other blessings, to make room for their subjective apprehension on the part of believers—still a third system, again full and final in its own form. It does not seem to come into the mind of Dr. Hodge, that both the election and the revelation of which the Apostle speaks are in Christ himself; that the mystery of election is in very truth the mystery of his incarnation and its glorious results; and that the true revelation of the Gospel is no written word or doctrine merely, no report made concerning Christ in any simply external way, but the very presence rather of what Christ actually is, under the view now stated, in his own person. Just as any living object in the world of nature, a plant for instance, may be said at once to actualize its own idea,

---

38. [Hodge, *Commentary*, 26.]

the thought from which it springs, and also to make this the matter of intelligence and knowledge as it can never be in any other way.

A still worse specimen of analytical logic, is presented to us in the *Commentary* on chap., 1, vs. 17–19, taken in connection with the verses that follow. "There are three leading petitions," it is gravely declared,

> expressed in the prayer here recorded. First, for adequate knowledge of divine truth. Second, for due appreciation of the future blessedness of the saints. Third, for a proper understanding of what they themselves had already experienced in their conversion.[39]

The first petition, according to this scheme, ends in the middle of the 18th verse, and is to be considered a prayer for spiritual illumination in general. The residue of the verse, "That ye may know what is the hope of his calling, &c," forms then a new petition;

> having prayed that the Ephesians might be enlightened in the knowledge of God and of divine things, the Apostle here prays, as the effect of that illumination, that they may have a proper appreciation of the inheritance to which they have attained.[40]

Lastly v. 19, "he prays that his readers may have right apprehensions of the greatness of the change which they had experienced." The mere statement of the scheme may enable us to presume, in what style it is carried out. "The hope of his calling," means the hope which true Christians "are now, on the call of God, authorized to indulge."[41] There are two things which the Apostle desires they may know; first, the nature and value of this hope; and secondly, the glory of the inheritance in reserve for them. The "exceeding greatness of God's power towards them that believe," mentioned in the supposed third petition, is made to refer wholly to their experience of conversion, regarded as a past fact. "Grotius,[42] indeed, and commentators of that class," we are told, "understand the passage to refer to the exertion of the power of God in the future resurrection and salvation of believers." But this is summarily denied. "It evidently refers to the past and not to the future."[43] Then most characteristically:

> The Apostle never compares the salvation of believers with the resurrection of Christ, whereas the analogy between his natural resurrection and the spiritual resurrection of his people, is one to which he often refers. This is the analogy which he insists upon in this immediate connection. As God raised Christ

---

39. [Ibid., 71.]
40. [Ibid., 74–5.]
41. [Ibid., 75.]
42. [From 1641 to 1644, the Reformed Dutch jurist and theologian Hugo Grotius (1583–1645) wrote the nine-volume *Annotationes in Novum Testamentum*.]
43. [Hodge, *Commentary*, 76.]

from the dead and set him at his own right hand in heavenly places; so you that were dead in sins, hath he quickened and raised you up together with him. This analogy is the very thing he would have them understand. They had undergone a great change; they had been brought to life; they had been raised from the dead by the same almighty power which wrought in Christ. There was as great a difference between their present and their former condition, as between Christ in the tomb and Christ at the right hand of God.[44]

This, we say, is characteristic. Dr. Hodge, it would seem, has no sense for the proper wholeness of Christianity, as a fact reaching over in a real way from Christ to his people, and including in their case the entire process of redemption from the first germ of life in the soul to the full resurrection of the body at the last day. It does not occur to him, that the idea of Grotius need not necessarily be so taken as to exclude his own; that the two things thus compared and opposed sustain to each other the most intimate inward relation; that the only true conception of Christianity must be allowed to involve them both at once, with all that lies between them, as going together to make up the concrete fact in which it consists. The bodily resurrection of believers, as it is to take place when Christ shall come in his glory, is not considered to be the continuation strictly of the process which begins with their new birth this side the grave[45]—the last result of that "law of the spirit of life in Christ Jesus,"[46] by which they are made free from the law of sin and death even in this world; and it is only metaphorically, moreover, that their spiritual resurrection itself is represented as answering in any way to the natural resurrection of our Lord and Saviour Jesus Christ. The relation resolves itself, when all is said, into a mere "analogy"!

Afterwards, indeed (p. 81), the representation is somewhat improved. Commenting on the words: "According to the working of his mighty power which he wrought in Christ when he raised him from the dead" [ch. 1:] v. [19–]20, Dr. Hodge tells us they evidently mean two things. "First, that the power which raises the believer from spiritual death is the same as that which raised Christ from the grave" (just as one might say, we suppose, that the power put forth in the creation of Adam was the same as that employed in creating the angel Gabriel).

Secondly, that there is a striking analogy between these events, and an intimate connection between them. The one was not only the symbol, but the pledge and procuring cause of the other. The resurrection of Christ is both the

---

44. [Ibid., 77.]

45. [Nevin thought the "bodily resurrection of believers" *is* "the continuation strictly of the process which begins with their new birth": *Mystical Presence*, MTSS ed., 149, 152–54; Nevin and Hodge, *Coena Mystica*, 90–1, 148. For Nevin's Christological framework consult (in vol. 4 of MTSS) "New Creation in Christ," 39–45; "Wilberforce on the Incarnation"; "Jesus and the Resurrection," 139–49.]

46. [Rom 8:2.]

type and the cause of the spiritual resurrection of his people, as well as of their future rising from the grave in his glorious likeness.[47]

This is well so far as it goes. But it falls immeasurably short of the whole truth, as it was before the mind of St. Paul. The causal relation allowed in the case remains after all instrumental only, mechanical, and outward. As for any proper apprehension of the true organic nature of the connection that holds between the resurrection of Christ and the spiritual life of his people, it would seem to be wanting altogether. Only so can we explain the truly surprising observation made on p. 82; where we are told that, the immediate subject of discourse in this chapter being the blessings of redemption conferred on believers, "the resurrection and exaltation of Christ are introduced incidentally by way of illustration;" and that having dwelt for a moment on the nature of this exaltation, and on the relation of Christ to his Church (in the way of digression, we suppose), the Apostle then, at the beginning of the following chapter, "reverts to his main topic!"

How differently all shows itself, when we take the right position for looking at it, and then simply allow the text to speak for itself. It is only strange how any one can commune with the spirit of this grand and magnificent passage at all, and not have the organic idea of Christianity and the Church irresistibly forced upon his mind. It is this precisely which imparts to the whole subject, in the mind of the Apostle, that character of greatness, which no language seems to him sufficient fully to express. What fills him with overwhelming interest, is the sense of the new creation, the mystery of godliness in its proper universal form, as it proceeds from Christ and runs its course in the Church. To his glowing contemplation, past, present, and future, rush together here with the power of a single glorious fact. The prayer with which he starts is not made up of three logically different topics, in the sense of Dr. Hodge; but wrestles throughout with one and the same general object of thought, only thrown rapidly into different aspects, till the whole loses itself at last in a sort of triumphant song of praise to the risen and glorified Christ, from whom the entire order of salvation proceeds. What he desires is that those who have been brought to stand within the economy of grace through the obedience of faith may have their understanding enlightened to know, more and more, how much is comprehended in this high and glorious distinction for the purposes of life and salvation; as being not nominal merely, but replete with power; as serving to set them truly in communication with heavenly agencies and forces; as carrying with it potentially all the supernatural blessings of the new creation, from "the washing of regeneration and renewing of the Holy Ghost"[48] away onward to the "resurrection of the body and the life everlasting." It was much to understand and appreciate the privileges of the Jewish covenant, in its distinction from the general life of the world; for even the Jewish covenant was by no means outward merely and

---

47. [Hodge, *Commentary*, 81.]
48. [Titus 3:5.]

nominal; but here is something which goes immeasurably beyond all that. Where Judaism had to do with shadows and types only, Christianity has to do with the very realities themselves to which these shadows and types referred. It is a constitution, which without any sort of figure may be said to carry in its own bosom actually the "powers of the world to come"[49]—powers more than natural, having their principle in Christ, and able with him to triumph over the whole present world in every other view. All this of course, can never come within the range of mere natural observation and knowledge. How should any such intelligence transcend the order of its own life, so as to become truly cognizant of that which is above it and beyond it altogether? The presence of such grace in the Church, as being not the shadow only of good things to come but their very image (αυτην την εικονα των πραγματων, Heb. 10:1), is by its very nature such a mystery as can be really apprehended only by faith. Nor is it easy for believers themselves to maintain a steady practical sense of the mystery, over against the suggestions of the mere carnal reason; while the general apprehension of faith also is not of itself enough, to bring them at once to anything like a full and complete knowledge of all that is included in the mystery which they are thus enabled to own; even as it is not enough to be set down by the power of sense in the actual midst of the world of nature, that one may be prepared to take in at once the full sense of the manifold facts, relations, powers, and possibilities which go unitedly to make up the conception of its vast and mighty organization. Therefore it is that the Apostle, here and elsewhere, makes it the burden of his prayer for Christians, that they might be able to comprehend what was actually at hand for them in that new world of grace into which they had been introduced by their faith in Christ; that they might have some just sense of the relations of love and peace in which they were brought to stand with God through the merits of his well beloved Son; that they might learn to think largely enough of the exceeding greatness of God's power embodied in the economy of redemption, not simply as means by any particular effect already wrought in themselves, but more especially and mainly as taken in connection with the whole range of its action in the Church, and the glorious resurrection life of Christ in which it has its origin and source. For it is no outward analogy only, that holds between the life of Christ in this view and the mighty working of God in the Church. This last is nothing more nor less than the organic force of the new creation itself, in virtue of which Christ rose from the dead. To know what it is then in believers, and especially to know what the Church is in whose mysterious constitution it finds its enduring home in the world, we must consider what it has been and still is in the Saviour himself. The power which appeared in his resurrection, and by which he now reigns "head over all things"[50] at the right hand of God, is that which he puts forth by his Spirit also in the Church.

49. [Heb 6:5.]
50. [Eph 1:22.]

Document 3: "Hodge on the Ephesians" (1857)

It might be interesting, as it would be easy also, to pursue still farther this sort of comparison, by bringing into view other examples of plain discordance between the true sense of the text and the sense assigned to it in this *Commentary*; all going to illustrate and confirm what we have already said of the different theories of religion and different conceptions of the Church which are involved in the case. But the length to which our article has already run, admonishes us to forbear. We may say in general, however, that wherever the text lays stress on any point under a churchly view, it is sure to be wrested by Dr. Hodge into some other aspect altogether, to suit the requirements of his own most mechanical and unchurchly scheme. The view, for instance, which is taken of the Christian ministry by St. Paul in chap. 4:8–16,[51] making it to be a strictly divine constitution derived from the ascension of Christ, and designed to carry forward the purposes of his glorious exaltation in the Church—a view which involves necessarily the idea of Apostolical succession, and of a true mystical force in the solemnity of ordination—fades with Dr. Hodge, we may say, almost into thin air. The ordinance of Baptism, which he allows to be the object of reference in chap. 5:26–27,[52] is laboriously shorn in his hands of its true sacramental character altogether. As a matter of course again, in the exposition of chap. 5:30–32,[53] no proper justice is done to the mystical union and the doctrine of Christ's presence in the Lord's Supper. Here, however, it must be acknowledged there is an evident sense of difficulty, and no small amount of confusion, in the effort which is made to get through the deep meaning of the text.

On the subject of Calvin's view of the Eucharist, our author now says without any reserve:

> Calvin did not hold that Christ's body was locally present in the Lord's Supper, nor that it was received by the mouth, nor that it was received in any sense by unbelievers. He did hold, however, that the substance of Christ's glorified body, as enthroned in heaven, was in some miraculous way communicated to believers together with the bread in that ordinance. He, therefore, understands the Apostle as here referring to that fact, and asserting that we are members of Christ's body because the substance of his body is in the Eucharist communicated to us (p. 341).

This is just the view ascribed to him in the *Mystical Presence*.[54] Dr. Hodge, however, rejects the whole idea of any such mystery, and denies besides that the passage here in question includes any allusion whatever to the Eucharist.[55]

---

51. [Beginning Hodge, *Commentary*, 212. Hodge's exposition of v. 11 begins on p. 222.]
52. [Ibid., 318–25.]
53. [Ibid., 337–52.]
54. [Nevin, *Mystical Presence*, MTSS ed., 47–51, 57–65.]
55. [Hodge, *Commentary*, 342.]

But what now, leaving the Lord's Supper out of view, is Dr. Hodge's own theory concerning the union of believers with Christ, as answering to the declaration: "We are members of his body, of his flesh, and of his bones?"[56] The passage in which we have his reply to this interrogation offers too rich a specimen of his philosophical and theological style of thinking, not to be quoted here in full.

"The doctrine taught," we are told,

> is not community of substance between Christ and his people, but community of life, and that the source of life to his people is Christ's flesh. In support of this interpretation it may be urged: 1. That it leaves the passage in its integrity. It neither explains it away, nor does it make it assert more than the words necessarily imply. The doctrine remains a great mystery, as the Apostle declares it to be. 2. It takes the terms employed in their ordinary and natural sense. To partake of one's flesh and blood, does not, in ordinary life, nor according to scriptural usage, mean to partake of his substance, but it does mean to partake of his life. The substance of which the body of any adult is composed is derived exclusively from his food and from the atmosphere. A few years after the formation of Eve not a particle of Adam's body entered into the composition of her frame; and yet she was then as truly as at the beginning, bone of his bone and flesh of his flesh, because derived from him and partaker of his life. For the same reasons, and in the same sense, we are said to be flesh of Adam's flesh and bone of his bones, although in no sense partakers of the substance of his body. In like manner nothing is more common than to speak of the blood of a father flowing in the veins of his descendants, and of their being his flesh. This means, and can only mean, that they are partakers of his life. There is no community of substance possible in the case. What life is no one knows. But we know that it is not matter; and, therefore, there may be community of life, when[57] there is no community of substance. There is a form of life peculiar to nations, tribes, families and individuals; and this peculiar type is transmitted from generation to generation, modifying the personal appearance, the physical constitution, and the character of those who inherit it. When we speak of the blood of Hapsburghs, or of the Bourbons, it is this family type that is intended and nothing material. The present Emperor of Austria derives his peculiar type of physical life from the head of his race, but not one particle of the substance of his body. Husband and wife are in Scripture declared to be one flesh. But here again it is not identity of substance, but community of life that is intended. As, therefore, participation of one's flesh does not, in other connections, mean participation of his substance, it cannot be fairly understood in that sense when spoken of our relation to Christ. And as in all analogous cases it does express derivation or community of life, it must be so understood here (pp. 344–346).

56. [Eph 5:30.]
57. [Hodge, *Commentary*, 345 says "where".]

Document 3: "Hodge on the Ephesians" (1857)

We may be peculiarly constituted; but to our mind, we are free to confess the mysticism of Olshausen[58] is like the light of day, and as the genial breath of summer, in comparison with the hard, dry obscurity of this wonderful statement. We do not pretend to understand it, as applied to the subject in hand. It sounds to us absolutely unintelligible. Is the life of a man, then, no part of his substance? Are these two things extraneous each to the other? Or taking a man's body aside from his soul, does the "substance" of that stand only in what is derived "from his food and from the atmosphere"?[59] The law of life, the organic power, by which alone such material aliment is received, assimilated to its nature, and made to live in its constitution—is this indeed no part of its true substantial being? So Dr. Hodge would seem to think, if we may trust here the sound of his own words. For his argument allows nothing between the idea of life in its most spiritual form, and the idea of simple matter, which he takes to be synonymous with substance; and having satisfied himself that participation in the life of any one does not imply participation in his substance, under such view, that is, in the very matter of which his body is composed as such, he proceeds at once to draw what is in fact a far wider conclusion—this, namely, that it involves no participation whatever in the bodily side of his existence under any view. Making the body thus to be its own bulk of matter simply, and nothing more. As if such a man as Olshausen ever dreamed of taking the idea of corporeity (*Leiblichkeit*) in any such grossly Capernaitic sense[60]—but we drop the subject.

The two schemes before us, as they involve totally different conceptions of the Church, lead also to materially different notions of faith. With St. Paul, the Church, regarded as a real constitution of grace in the world through which only the resources of Christ's resurrection life are made available for the purposes of man's "deliverance from this present evil world" (Gal. 1:4), is of course at once an object for faith, as really as Christ's resurrection itself. It is a constituent part of Christianity, answering truly to the position which is assigned to it under such view in the primitive Creeds.

It is no abstraction, no mere generalization, resolving itself at last into the mental notion by which it is apprehended; but in some form the objective presence of a true concrete fact, whose authority men are required to own in an outward practical way, as well as with the inward homage of the spirit. This practical acknowledgment forms thus an important part of the true idea of the Christian faith; nay, we may say, it is the very form in which all such faith necessarily begins. For if there be any constitution of this sort really in the world, the first duty of all men must be plainly to acknowledge its supernatural claims, and to place themselves within its bosom, in order that they may

---

58. [Hermann Olshausen (1796–1839), influenced by both Friedrich Schleiermacher and August Neander, wrote *Kommentar über sämmtliche Schriften des Neuen Testaments* [Trans. *Commentary on the complete text of the New Testament*]. It first appeared at Königsberg in 1830, and was translated into English in 4 volumes (Edinburgh, 1847–1849)].

59. [Hodge, *Commentary*, 345.]

60. [A reference to John 6:24–65, which took place in Capernaum. The Jews misinterpreted Jesus' self-description as the "bread of life" in a "grossly" physical or carnal sense.]

be saved; and it can never be anything better than folly for them to talk of believing and obeying the Gospel at other points, while they refuse to comply here with that requirement, which in the very nature of the case must be taken to underlie and condition all requirements besides, as offering the only way in which it is possible for them to be fulfilled; just as it would have been the folly of madness itself, for any in the time of the Flood to have professed faith in the Ark, and firm trust in its offers of grace, whilst they continued obstinately to stay on the outside of its walls. In this light, the sense of the Apostolical commission becomes plain. It ordains a constitution, not in the world before, flowing directly from Christ's glorification ("all power is given unto me, &c."), through the Apostles ("go ye *therefore*, &c."), organized and set off from the world at large as a distinct sphere of life ("preach—make disciples—baptize")[61]; to which accordingly, all men are required to yield the "obedience of faith," not simply by consenting to what they may hold to be the truth of its doctrines in their own minds, but by actually bowing to its claims, and coming into its bosom, through the sacramental sign and seal of baptism. Hence also the stress laid on the significance of this sacrament throughout the New Testament (as being the entrance or birth of men into this heavenly constitution, the laver of regeneration, the washing away of sins, the counterpart of salvation by Noah's ark and the passage through the waters of the Red Sea), all in full conformity with what is well known (by such as choose to know), to have been the universal way of thinking and speaking about it in the first Christian ages.[62] In the Epistle to the Ephesians, as elsewhere, St. Paul's idea of faith is plainly conditioned always by this reference to the Church, regarded as Christ's "body," the necessary organ and medium of the whole Christian salvation. It never enters into his mind, certainly, that any proper use of his instructions and exhortations could be made by those who were not in the Church; that there could possibly be any room to talk of faith, spirituality, charity, and good works generally, in the Christian sense, so far as any were concerned who still in this way showed themselves "disobedient" to the heavenly vision of the Gospel, by refusing to come within the range of its power. He writes for Christians, for the baptised, for the faithful in Christ Jesus alone. All others with him are "children of disobedience," and for this very reason still under the power of Satan, whose kingdom is thus assumed to be commensurate in full with the universal order of the world's life on the outside of the Church (Eph. 2:2). All this of course the *Commentary* now under consideration has no power to see or acknowledge; because it moves in a wholly different sphere of thought. The Puritanic notion of faith is really independent of the doctrine of the Church altogether.

"The word απειθεια," Dr. Hodge tells us on Eph. 2:2,

> means unwillingness to be persuaded, and is expressive either of disobedience in general, or of unbelief, which is only one form of disobedience. In

---

61. [Matt 28:18–19, Nevin's emphasis.]

62. [Three years later, Nevin attempted to show this continuity in the thought of St. John Chrysostom in "The Old Doctrine of Christian Baptism."]

> this case the general sense is to be preferred, for the persons spoken of are not characterized as unbelievers, or as obstinately rejecting the Gospel, but as disobedient or wicked.[63]

This exegesis cuts the true nerve of the thought completely, and altogether obscures the primary sense of faith and unbelief as they were conceived of by St. Paul. "Disobedience," with him, is emphatically unbelief, considered not simply as an obstinate rejection of the Gospel in the Puritanic sense, but as the general opposite of that faith which brings men actually to bow to the authority of the Church. This is the radical sin of the world (John 16:9), its true and proper condemnation (John 8:19); just as faith, on the other hand, under the like practical view is the root of salvation, the mother of all other graces and virtues belonging to the Christian life.

It is everywhere taken for granted by Dr. Hodge, in the common Puritanic style, that the presence and power of the Spirit, which all acknowledge to be the medium of Christ's presence now in the world, are in no way bound to the Church, regarded as a fixed objective constitution in any view; that he works in the world at large; that faith in Christ may be complete, without reference to anything beyond the abstract thought of Christ himself, as having died to save sinners; that the Church indeed is only a name, used to denote collectively those who are considered to be already Christians under a different aspect altogether. No opportunity is spared of dealing what is held to be, in this view, a home thrust at the "Church system," as being supposed to obscure the proper freeness of the Gospel, and also to contradict the true conception of God's grace, by making it to depend on something beyond itself. "The only essential and indispensable condition of participation in the benefits of redemption," it is declared

> is union with Christ. And this union is effected or brought about, *by the Gospel.* It is not by birth, nor by any outward rite, nor by union with any external body, but by the Gospel, received and appropriated by faith, that we are united to Christ, and thus made heirs of God (p. 166).... *We* have this access to God; we believers; not any particular class, a priesthood among Christians to whom alone access is permitted, but all believers without any priestly intervention, other than that of one great High Priest who has passed through the heavens, Jesus the Son of God" (p. 175).... This is the great question which every sinner needs to have answered: How may I come to God with the assurance of acceptance? The answer given by the Apostle, and confirmed by the experience of the saints of all ages is: By faith in Jesus Christ. It is because men rely on some other means of access, either bringing some worthless bribe in their hands, or trusting to some other mediator, priestly or saintly, that so many fail who seek to enter God's presence (p. 176) [emphases original].

The general drift of all this is abundantly plain. It is the key on which the unchurchly spirit is ever ready to harp. To what, however, does it amount at last? A mere

---

63. [Hodge, *Commentary*, 102.]

play upon words, and nothing more. All depends, of course, on faith in Christ. So much was allowed even by the ancient Gnostic, as it is allowed now also by the Unitarian. But the question is always, What does such faith necessarily involve? His real coming in the flesh, we say at once, against the Gnostic. Even the Puritan will admit, however, that this again involves his life of sorrow, his death upon the cross, his resurrection, and his ascension to the right hand of God. And now the question comes, With what reason does *he*, the Puritan, require us to stop just there with our idea of what necessarily belongs to faith in Christ, and to shut off all that follows in the Creed as something to which it need not reach. As if it were possible to believe really in the Lord Jesus Christ on to the point of his glorification, and yet not take account of what this was to prepare the way for, the mission of the Holy Ghost, and the constitution of the Holy Catholic Church. It is at best only begging the whole matter in debate, when this mutilated notion of faith is held up to our view as being all that is comprehended in the Formula: "Believe in the Lord Jesus Christ, and thou shalt be saved."[64] In the sense of the Creed, beyond all controversy, such faith includes necessarily an acknowledgment of the Church, under the very view that Dr. Hodge so heartily dislikes; and St. Paul here, we have no hesitation in saying, agrees with the Creed.

Many thoughts, well worthy of attention, offer themselves here for consideration, growing out of the general subject of our discussion and bearing on the doctrine of the Church, which, however, it would carry us altogether too far to notice now in any sort of detail. If we have succeeded at all, in bringing into view the form in which this great doctrine was held by St. Paul, and the place it occupies in his writings, it must be at once plain that it is not easy to lay too much stress upon the significance which properly belongs to it in the Christian system. It is found to take its position at once very near the centre, and not simply in the outward circumference, of the general scheme of salvation; in a way which answers exactly to the order of the Creed, and serves to justify in full also the method or plan of its construction. The very first object of faith, following the mission of the Holy Ghost, must be in the nature of the case (if Christianity be no mere abstraction, and no modification simply of the life of nature, but really and truly a new order of existence in the sense of St. Paul), just what it is made to be in the Creed. Not the Bible, but the Church; not any particular doctrine, such as human depravity, for instance, or the atonement, but the fundamental fact of Christianity itself, on the ground of which only it is possible to hold any doctrine whatever with true Christian faith. The argument for the Church, in this view, is very broad. It lies in the organic structure of Christianity itself. Once fairly apprehended, as we have it in the Creed, this is found to involve the article as a necessary part of its general conception or scheme. We may say, indeed, that the article of the Church forms the very keystone of the grand and glorious arch, with which the mystery of the new creation is represented in the Creed to span the chasm, otherwise impassable,

---

64. [Acts 16:31—Nevin substituted "in" for "on"; a proof-text of the evangelical piety of Nevin's era.]

which separates between earth and heaven, creating thus a way for the ransomed of the Lord to pass over. Only to suppose it gone is to turn the arch itself into a Gnostic vision. The argument for the Church, we say, is comprehended mainly in the organic constitution of Christianity itself; and this is the form precisely, in which it is made to challenge our faith, and our obedient regard, in the New Testament. The doctrine of the Church is in the New Testament just as the other articles of the Christian faith are there; not so much in the way of single naked texts, as under the general and broad view of necessary comprehension in the Christian system regarded as a whole.

That is a most lean use of the Scriptures at best, which affects to keep itself in any case to isolated texts, and overlooks the vastly more important significance of what lies in the organic relations of the facts themselves with which the whole revelation is concerned. What are the few testimonies which assert in an immediate and direct way the doctrine of the Trinity, or the doctrine of the Saviour's Divinity, in comparison with the vast body of evidence for both, which is involved in the representations and assumptions of the Gospel in its universal view? They underlie in fact the whole thinking of the New Testament, the entire universe of its gracious revelations, just as they are made to bear up the whole structure of the Creed.

And so it is with this article of the Church. There are single and separate texts which may be quoted in proof of its being, its attributes, and its claims to regard; more than we are able to produce in such form for the doctrine of the Holy Trinity; more than we have for the inspiration and divine authority of the Sacred Scriptures. But it would be a great mistake to think that the Scriptural argument for the article lies wholly, or mainly, in any such passages. The true force of this argument comes into view, only when we are brought to see how the truth of the article is everywhere assumed and taken for granted in the New Testament, as something necessarily involved in the very constitution of Christianity, and as little to be separated from the conception of the mystery in any case, as form from substance, or body from soul. Of this we have a broad and striking example in this Epistle of St. Paul to the Ephesians. Strong testimonies occur in it for the doctrine of the Church, in the direct textual form; testimonies that may well embarrass the Puritan mind, so utterly foreign are they from its whole habit of thought. But these texts are, after all, only a small fraction of the evidence, which is really contained in the Epistle for the doctrine in question. That is found, not so much in what the Apostle directly asserts on the subject, as in what he presumes to be true of it, from the salutation with which his Epistle begins to the benediction that brings it to a close. The idea of the Church runs as a silent hypothesis, or underlying assumption, through all his teachings and exhortations. It may be said to be fairly woven into his whole scheme of religion. All that he says is conditioned and ruled continually by the thought, that those whom he addresses stood not in the general world, but in the bosom of the Church; and that their position in this view served to place them actually, and not by figure of speech only, in correspondence with the powers of a higher world, under such form as was not possible elsewhere, while it was sufficient here to justify in full the strongest language he employs in regard to their privileges and hopes. This is in fact a constant practical recognition of the article in question, as it stands in the Creed; and a recognition of it also under the same general view, as being not simply an arrangement added to Christianity from without, but a true organic part of its actual substance and proper heavenly constitution, making it to be fairly and of right an object, not of opinion merely, but of faith, for all men in all ages of the world.

J. W. N.
Windsor Place, Lancaster county, Pa.

DOCUMENT 4

"Thoughts on the Church" (1858)

Editor's Introduction

In 1857 the *Provisional Liturgy* was published by Lindsay and Blakiston,[1] concluding a lengthy political and ecclesiastical process that began in 1849 when Nevin, Schaff, and a dozen or so others were commissioned by the German Reformed Church to develop a liturgy for ordinary occasions of public worship. Once completed, Nevin was relieved but not "hopeful as to the success of the work."[2]

Nevin was given responsibility for developing the service of "Ordination and Installation" of ministers for inclusion in the *Provisional Liturgy*. Much of the service comes from secondary sources, such as the *Mayer Liturgy*, the *Book of Common Prayer*, and the *Catholic Apostolic Liturgy*.[3] In fact, Nevin wrote "compilation" across the top of the first draft.[4] This statement, however, was Nevin's personal contribution to the liturgy:

> The office is of divine origin, and of truly supernatural character and force; flowing directly from the Lord Jesus Christ himself, as the fruit of his Resurrection and triumphant Ascension into heaven, and being designed by him to carry forward the purposes of his grace upon the earth, in the salvation of men by the Church, to the end of time.[5]

Nevin's service was included in the *Provisional Liturgy* and, some years later, approved with minimal changes for inclusion in the *Order of Worship* of 1866, an official publication of the German Reformed Church. Its regular use provided an instrument by which Nevin cast his vision for the church and her ministry well past his death.

In 1858, coincidentally the year that marks the end of the general religious awakening in North America,[6] Nevin wrote "Thoughts on the Church." He began the article from Windsor Place where he stayed while his new home in Lancaster was being

---

1. *Acts and Proceedings of the Synod of the German Reformed Church . . . , October,* 1859, 115.
2. Appel, *Life and Work of John Williamson Nevin,* 503.
3. Maxwell, *Worship and Reformed Theology,* esp. 185–243.
4. Ibid., 237.
5. Ibid., 238; see the longer excerpt in Nichols, ed., *Mercersburg Theology,* 346–47.
6. Murray, *Revival and Revivalism,* 331–53.

Document 4: "Thoughts on the Church" (1858)

constructed; he completed it from his new residence.[7] He published "Thoughts on the Church" in two issues of *The Mercersburg Review*. A modern editor, however, might have encouraged the author to publish the article under a different title, such as the "The Church Question," in that it provides the platform from which Nevin develops twenty distinct but related ideas about the church, each of which he has addressed in previous writings. That same editor might also lobby for the title "The Church and the Creed" as Nevin's understanding of the essential relationship between the two finds a prominent place in the document.

Theodore Appel describes "Thoughts on the Church" as Nevin's *pia desideria* (pious desires), written in seclusion.[8] With that description, Appel calls to mind the classic statement of German Pietism by Jacob Spener (1635–1705).[9] His *Pia Desideria*, often translated "Heartfelt Desire for God-pleasing Reform," served that movement as both a devotional work and a textbook on church renewal. By describing Nevin's "Thoughts" as such, Appel encourages readers to approach this work, not only as a resource for "silent personal meditation,"[10] but as a collection of Nevin's essential convictions about the church.

The two articles combined begin with an introduction and end with a conclusion. In between, Nevin offers twenty "thoughts on the church."[11] They do not break new ground for Nevin. Instead, they systematically summarize the essentials of his answer to the church question. For Nevin, the Apostles' Creed provides the answer to the church question. It affirms that the blessings of the Gospel are imparted to each individual through union with Christ, a union that takes place by and through the ministry of the church. Faith in Christ, then, requires faith in the church. The two are inseparable. Furthermore, even "the Bible, great as it is in the scheme of Christianity, could not be substituted for the Church."[12]

---

7. Appel, *Life and Work of John Williamson Nevin*, 551; see also D. G. Hart, *John Williamson Nevin*, 173–74.

8. Appel, *Life and Work*, 551.

9. Philipp Jakob Spener (1635–1705), known as the "Father of Pietism." See Shantz, *Introduction to German Pietism*.

10. See the second paragraph in the text below.

11. Nevin separated each section with a dash. In this edition, the dash has been replaced by sequential Roman numerals. The editors have added short headings for the benefit of the reader.

12. See below, 161.

Thoughts on the Church [First Article][1]

[Introduction]

THOUGHTS—not formal argument or discussion. What the case requires, is not immediately and first of all a full regular construction or theory of the doctrine of the Church; much less a direct plea for any existing church organization. Back of all this lies the region of first principles and elementary ideas, by whose right determination alone it can ever be possible to bring any such theory or scheme to fair and proper trial. Of what account can it be to dispute concerning the power of the sacraments, or about points of ecclesiastical order, where the parties in controversy have no common conception whatever of the nature of the Church itself, but set out in their thinking with regard to it from wholly different points of observation? The great matter, in every such case, is to get attention fixed on first truths, without regard for the time to the polemical issues with which they may be concerned in actual life. There must be of course always an intimate living connection between what is first here and what is secondary; the practical issues involve necessarily their own theoretical principles, the ideal elements out of which they grow. But still the two things, as all may easily perceive, are not by any means the same. They are capable of full separation at least for thought. Many hold their practical notions with great zeal, without seeing at all the theoretical first truths which lie at the ground of them, and without having courage it may be to own the authority of any such truths when confronted with them face to face. Their principles are for their thinking implicit rather than explicit; in the mind, if we may so distinguish, but not in the understanding. And just so, on the other hand, it is possible to make ideas and principles here the subject of thoughtful contemplation, without running them out at once into any particular practical system. We do not mean to say, that the ideas themselves may cease to be practical. They are no metaphysical abstractions. They go at once into the depths of the Christian life; and to commune with them at all in a real way, is to have necessarily the most solemn and profound sense of their practical importance. But this does not preclude

[1]. [J. W. N[evin], *The Mercersburg Review* 10 (April 1858) 169–198.]

the possibility of their earnest consideration, as a separate preliminary and preparation for their being carried forward subsequently to any results in which they may find their proper practical conclusion. And just such preparation it is most of all, we may say, that is needed to open the way towards the true and right settlement of any of these results.

Thoughts, we say again; not words merely for the indolent, nor dreams for the sentimental, nor empty speculation for the curious. Thoughts for the *thoughtful*; for such as have a will to think, and at the same time some power to think; for such as know the solemnity of the subject, and feel the necessity of looking at it with an earnest and manly spirit; for such as have their mind set on real things in the world of religion, more than upon names simply and outward traditional forms. What such need in any case, is not so much full discussion as fruitful suggestion, hints for reflection, material for silent personal meditation. They take not their thinking at second hand, but are ready nevertheless to honor and welcome any thought which may serve as an occasion to put them on thinking for themselves in the right direction. A single idea with such may be of more account, than a whole volume of elaborate argument with many; because it shall be found to carry with it a truly creative force in their minds, giving rise to other ideas, and gradually making room for the presence of a new spiritual world. Our present article is for this class of persons. We write for the religiously thoughtful; not as offering to take the work of thought out of their own hands; nor yet as pretending to set before them any particular church scheme, rounded at all points and ready for their use; but only for the purpose of assisting and guiding their own thoughtfulness on that great subject under consideration, that it may be exercised to the best purpose and with the best effect.

[I. The Primacy and Unity of the Church Question]

The Question of the Church is in its ground and principle *One*. To a superficial thinker this may not be at once apparent. On first view, there might seem to be rather a number of church questions meeting in no common ground. At one time, the matter in dispute is episcopacy; at another time, it is the power of the sacraments; then again, it may be the use of a liturgy, the observance of the Church Year, or the stress which it is proper to lay on the forms and ceremonies generally of religious worship. It soon becomes evident, however, on serious consideration, that all these points, different as they may seem, involve here in some way the presence of a thought or idea more general than themselves, through the power of which they come together at last in the form of a single great question. These are after all subordinate and secondary issues only, the whole significance of which lies in the sense of a far deeper and more comprehensive issue that continually conditions them from behind.

The sense of this may be indeed more an instinct, than any clear apprehension; still it is always at hand, where any true interest is taken in these subordinate questions.

Hence, it is never difficult to know how the parties on any one such question will form themselves, when the subject for consideration comes to be another. The lines are still drawn always as between the same churchly and unchurchly tendencies; and no one is at a loss to anticipate in each case beforehand in what way the distinction must fall. This distinction therefore is not made by any of these subordinate issues, nor yet by all of them taken together; but it forms the rule and measure rather by which *they* come to exist. It is not a particular view of the sacraments that makes a man to be churchly or unchurchly; but it is his sense of the Church, on the contrary, that gives complexion and character to the view he may have of the sacraments. The church feeling thus is older and deeper in the order of nature than the sacramental, or the liturgical, or any other of like partial kind and form. The partial interest in each case refers itself spontaneously to the general interest in which it is comprehended, and bears witness in doing so to the unity of the whole subject. There is, accordingly, on all sides, a sort of intuitional sense of such ultimate unity or oneness reaching through the various questions that are agitated in regard to the Church, which may be said to go much beyond what is generally dear for the understanding.[2] All these questions are felt to resolve themselves finally into one, which is the *Church Question* in the full and proper sense of the term.

[II. The Significance of the Church Question]

This general issue, in which all secondary questions in regard to the Church come finally together, is not imaginary only and unreal, or of only slight and unsignificant account. Some affect at times to look upon it in this light, making it to be at best a question of mere forms, or a controversy about empty fancies and dreams. They will have it, that it argues both a want of religious earnestness, and a want of sound judgment and good sense, to take much interest in the subject, or to have any serious difficulty whatever with its pretensions and claims. But this style of thinking can never satisfy long any truly thoughtful mind. It cannot be said to satisfy really the class of persons by whom it is assumed as a convenient affectation; for they show always

---

2. [By now Nevin understood that "the Church Question" was to be grasped (as we would say today) "holistically." In the middle of his crisis of 1852–53, he wrote: "I see well the necessity of something far beyond mere logic or natural evidence, to bring [?] the mind to a clear apprehension of the true mystery of the Christian Church, and a full and firm acquiesence in it for the purposes of salvation. Meditation [?] and prayer, rather than any dialectic process, must bring to a solution at last the great problem with which I feel myself confronted here now every day, and I may almost say every waking hour. The most powerful impressions of truth are those which come from flashes, sent out as it were from the invisible orb of the whole idea, rather than from this or that particular reflection or argument presented to the understanding in detail (Letter to J. A. McMasters, 26 February 1853, microfilm in the Lancastriana Collection, Philip Schaff Library, Lancaster [Pennsylvania] Theological Seminary; original in the Brownson Archives, Notre Dame University Library)." Nichols paraphrases this text in *Romanticism in American Theology*, 215; a full quote is given in Layman, "Revelation in the Praxis of the Liturgical Community," 124–25.]

an instinctive sense of the significance of the Church Question, which is not to be silenced or kept down by any judgment of this sort. If the case were in truth even for themselves what they pretend to make it, they would not be so easily moved as they are by what they consider its provocations. The question is felt all round to involve far more than any dispute concerning mere names and outward forms. However near the surface of Christianity the immediate matter of debate may seem to be in any particular case, the parties in controversy have the sense really of a general interest at stake which reaches ultimately to the very ground of the Christian life itself, and is held sufficient to justify a measure of zeal and intolerance that would bear no sort of proportion otherwise to the occasion calling it forth. Only in this way can we understand the spirit, which is found to rule in general the agitation of the Church Question, and which comes into view more or less in the discussion of every topic that runs into it as its necessary end. Difference here is felt to imply a deeper and more radical separation, than any which results from the ordinary theological divisions of the Christian world, and one that is more readily resented as a sort of direct antagonism allowing no compromise or reconciliation. The relation of the two opposing interests is one of broad, open exclusiveness and intolerance. It is such as leaves no room for mutual sympathy or common understanding. In this respect it goes beyond the distinction of mere sect in its usual form, and is felt to carry with it a deeper and wider meaning than is comprehended in the occasions and causes by which our religious sects generally are held apart. It is not co-ordinate and parallel simply with the difference that holds for instance between Calvinists and Arminians, between Congregationalists and Presbyterians, or between Methodists and Baptists. The questions and interests that divide such sects, however important they may seem to be when separately considered, are all felt to be of less fundamental moment than the issue which is brought into view by the idea of the Church, and are readily made to give way when it is felt necessary to take common ground over against its claims. All this goes to show the radical nature and multitudinous bearings of the Church Question. It enters necessarily into the very conception we form of Christianity, and may be said to exercise a moulding influence, and conditioning power, over the whole structure of the Christian faith.

[III. The True Character of the Person Asking the Church Question]

Some proper sense of the true character of the Church Question in the view now stated, some power to perceive and acknowledge in a fair manner its claims to respect, must be considered to be an indispensable preliminary condition to any right inquiry or just judgment concerning its merits one way or another. The want of such appreciation, the absence of such positive insight into the reality and magnitude and true religious earnestness of the problem to be here solved and settled, is an argument at once, wherever found, of full disqualification for the task of taking it in hand; and goes with good reason, we may add, to create a presumption of wrong against the cause in whose service it appears. For in the nature of the case, the disqualification must be *moral*, and not simply natural. Not to be able to see at all the solemn interest of the subject, is necessarily in some degree also not to be willing to see it. There is a measure of insincerity and affectation always, we have reason to believe, in any such assumed posture of indifference or contempt towards what all feel notwithstanding to be of the deepest meaning for Christianity. Children feel it; it enters as an instinctive sentiment into all unsophisticated piety; the sense of it reveals itself, as we have already seen, even in those who pretend to make light of it, by the intemperate spirit with which they are sure to meet the subject wherever it comes in their way. There is that in their interior consciousness here, which gives the lie palpably to what they say with their lips and try to think in their hearts. Such being the case, we repeat, they are not qualified to sit in judgment on what they undertake thus magisterially to condemn. They lack the conditions of the hearing ear and the seeing eye. We have a right to distrust their cause, for the very reason that it allows, and seems to favor, a spiritual posture which we may easily know to be so dishonest and false.

Paganism in its first conflict with Christianity, affected in this way an entire superiority to the whole question which this last offered for its consideration. It could not condescend to meet it in any earnest and serious style. The story of the Gospel was treated as a Jewish dream, too foolish and absurd to deserve the least respectful attention; and the religion of those who embraced it was held to be a fair occasion for unbounded mockery and scorn, as being fit only for such as had taken leave of their senses. So Paganism talked, and so, no doubt, Paganism tried also to believe, persuading itself that its view of things was the fruit of actual knowledge and conviction. But it is easy to see now that this was not the case; and that for a thoughtful mind even then there might have been found a strong presumption for the Christian cause in the very posture and spirit of the unbelieving power by which it was thus superciliously opposed. For Paganism had no power to sustain itself quietly and steadily in this affectation of contempt towards Christianity, as it might surely have been able to do, if the new religion had been in fact so worthy of being laughed at as it pretended to think. There was that in its own consciousness, which after all gave the lie to its professed indifference, and compelled it in spite of itself to feel that it was at issue in this case with a force which threatened nothing less than its own destruction. However particular points of the Christian controversy might seem to offer easy and fair opportunity for caricature and overwhelming explosion, for biting wit or triumphant sneer, there was still an evident feeling all the time that the subject did not end in any such points, that all these particular questions resolved themselves mysteriously into the presence of a deeper general question lying behind, and that this had to do in truth with the universal life of the world as it then stood. Paganism knew in this blind way at least, in the midst of all its levity, that Christianity was a great power, an earnest power, a power that had a right to challenge its solemn apprehension and dread. It was the sense of this precisely, which made it impossible for it to treat Christianity in the way it could treat other religions. They might be tolerated, even where they were despised. But for Christianity there could be no toleration. Over against its claims, there was no room for equanimity or patience. Hence the strange spectacle of that which was ridiculed as the most unmeaning of all religions, being the most ready object nevertheless of wrath and persecution on the part of those who made themselves superior to it in such style. No one can consider such a relation, without perceiving at once that it implied weakness and wrong on the side of Paganism, and a lack of power to cope fairly with the strength of the interest it sought to crush. Its want of ability to meet the claims of Christianity in an earnest and serious manner, its superficial levity in a case whose profound interest at the same time it was compelled to confess in the secret depths of its own mind, made it certain in the circumstances that it could do no justice to the Christian argument, and that any judgment it might pronounce upon it was far more likely to be wrong than right.

And so in any case, where a deep moral interest is involved, where a question of momentous practical bearings is to be settled, there must be some proper sense of the true earnestness of the subject, some sympathy with it, and some power to perceive and appreciate its claims to respect, before there can be any fitness or right to sit in judgment upon it; and no verdict or conclusion reached in regard to it without such previous qualification, can ever deserve to be held of any account.

The case now before us comes fully within the scope of this rule. Where there is no power, because at bottom there may be no will, to see and acknowledge the true solemnity of the issues involved in the Church Question, there can be no right to make them the subject of judgment, no title to be heard respectfully in pronouncing upon them any opinion or sentence. Those who think to dispose of the whole subject by any summary process of contempt, as though it were without all reason and sense and fit only for derision or condescending pity, do but betray the intrinsic weakness of their own position, and give room for a just presumption against the cause they represent. Their levity and frivolity here are out of character and out of place. Whether they choose to know it or not, the matter under consideration is both profound and earnest; and it argues religious unsoundness, to approach it, or to touch it, in any other than the most thoughtful and serious way.

[IV. The Judgment of the Ages on the Church Question]

The presumption against all such easy and wholesale judgment becomes still stronger, when it is considered that the views, which are thus summarily charged with madness and folly, have exercised in fact the widest and most powerful influence in the Christian world through all ages. One would suppose it might serve to tame somewhat the confident tone of those who allow themselves to think and talk in this way, only to know that by far the largest part of Christendom at the present time is ruled, both practically and theoretically, by the authority of just that system of ideas in regard to the Church, which they are accustomed to revile and deride as resting on no ground of reason whatever. But the case becomes a great deal stronger, when it is remembered that the same system of thought has in fact prevailed, with overwhelming authority, in every age of the Church from the beginning. There is no mistake with regard to this point. It is just as plain as it is possible for it to be made by the evidence of history. We read the full proof of it in all the movements of Christian antiquity. Right or wrong, reasonable or unreasonable, the very idea of the Church which is now denounced in the quarter of which we are speaking as no better than a silly dream, is that precisely which is found to pervade the reigning mind of the Church catholic from the century of the Apostles down to the century of the Reformation. It meets us in the old Creeds; it speaks to us from every page of the Christian Fathers; it breathes through all the ancient Liturgies; it enters into the universal scheme of the early Christian Faith. The very points in it which strike the party in question as most grossly obnoxious to vilification and reproach, were admitted and proclaimed without the least feeling of reserve. Points, for example, that such a man as Mr. Spurgeon, the popular juvenile preacher of London, can find no terms too strong to stigmatize as the perfection of brainless puerility, had power notwithstanding to command the reverence of entire ecumenical synods, and were received everywhere with unquestioning faith by the wisest and best men.[3] What is with him a subject only for heartfelt mockery, was a solemn heavenly mystery to the mind of an Augustine or a Chrysostom. He finds it easy to wade, where an Origen or a Jerome found ample room to swim.

We do not mean to say, that this sort of authority should of itself settle the question on which it is brought to bear. We are not pleading now the argument of prescription and use, in Tertullian's style,[4] in favor either of the Church system as a whole, or of any point which may be comprised in it as a part. The question is not, whether baptismal regeneration (in the old Christian sense as distinguished from the modern Puritanic confusion of terms), is to be held true, because it was notoriously the doctrine of St. Augustine, and of all the Fathers before him and after him; nor whether the idea of a real oblation of Christ's body and blood in the sacrament of the altar is to be owned and accepted,[5] because it most manifestly enters into all the ancient liturgies; nor whether the article of "one holy catholic Church," in its original historical mean-

---

3. [Nevin was clearly not a fan of Charles Haddon Spurgeon (1834–1892), the then twenty-four year-old Particular Baptist preacher from London who was criticized by more traditional Protestants for his dramatic flair while preaching. See Drummond, *Spurgeon: Prince of Preachers* for more on the one who was criticized for being a "pulpit buffoon."]

4. [In *De Praescriptionibus Adversus Haereticos*, 15–19, Tertullian (ca. 150–225) argued that only the churches that stand in succession to the apostles possessed the true teaching of Christ. For Tertullian the main issue was not the right interpretation of scriptures, but who possessed the right to interpret scriptures. See Naidu, "Reading and Interpretation of Scriptures in the Early Church" in *Transformed in Christ*, 18–82.]

5. [Nevin presented John Chrysostom's doctrine of baptismal regeneration in "The Old Doctrine of Baptism"; on the eucharist as a "real oblation" in the Fathers, see "Wilberforce on the Eucharist" (both essays in vol. 6 of MTSS).]

DOCUMENT 4: "THOUGHTS ON THE CHURCH" (1858)

ing, is to be considered a necessary object of faith, because it was made to be so, as every body knows, in the primitive creeds. Nothing of this sort is before us at present. All that we now mean to say is simply this: that let it fare with these great points as it may, the mere fact of their being so circumstanced as they show themselves to be in the view now mentioned, ought of itself to shield them from the flippant, not to say ribald tone and style, in which they are too often approached by the class of thinkers who find it most easy to dispose of them at the present time. Their method of resolving and settling this whole question, whose issues are so vast and great, without the least regard for the judgment of other ages, without the smallest respect for the opinion of hundreds and thousands of Christian men quite as wise and good, to say the least, as themselves, is altogether too sweeping, too presumptuously dogmatic, to be at all satisfactory to any earnest mind. Where the case can be disposed of in such style, there is reason at once to apprehend that it has never yet come to be rightly understood, or that the right moral conditions are not at hand for treating it with any sort of justice.

[V. The Accusers of the Church Question and the Spiritual Power of the Church Idea]

The presumption of wrong against this easy and light way of meeting the subject becomes still greater, when it is considered that the views which go to form the church system of Christianity, and which have such a weight of outward authority in their favor, find a wide and profound sanction also in the common religious nature and constitution of men. We have full evidence of this at once in the fact that they have been able, in the way we have just seen, to master the faith of the Christian world to so great an extent through all ages, drawing all doctrines and instructions in their own direction; a fact which is only made the more striking, if we allow it to be assumed that the true Christian scheme, in its original Apostolical form, was something wholly different from all this, diametrically opposed to it indeed, and that these views forced themselves into the Church therefore as an actual apostacy or falling away from that original scheme, against the will of Christ, and in full contradiction to the clear sense of the Scriptures. So much the enemies of the church system themselves are constrained to see and confess; and they try accordingly to turn the fact, in their shallow way, to the advantage of their own cause. Human nature, we are reminded, is carnal and corrupt, and always more ready to embrace a lie than the truth; and so, after the fashion of the somewhat famous *dictum,* "Every man is born an Arminian,"[6] it may be said also, Every man is born with a proclivity to the notions which go to make

---

6. [E.g., Edward Dorr Griffin, *Sermons Not Before Published on Various Practical Subjects* (New York: M. W. Dodd 1844), 116. The original version seems to have been "every Man is born a *Pelagian*" (John England, *A View of Arminianism Compared to Moderate Calvinism* [London, 1707], 5, emphasis original, quoting [Thomas] Fuller, *Church[-]History of Britain* [originally published 1655: see *Dictionary of the Christian Church*, 646]).]

up the church system as distinguished from Christianity in its proper spiritual and evangelical form. It is easy to see, however, that this amounts to no just solution of the difficulty whatever. The movement of Christianity in the direction now considered shows itself of quite too broad and profound a character, to be satisfactorily accounted for in this way. To understand it at all, we must refer it to a far deeper ground of life than any which is brought to view in the vanity and corruption merely of our fallen nature; which after all does not represent to us the deepest and last sense of our souls even in their present state. Such a fact as that which is offered to us in the almost universal reign of the church system, commencing so far back and reaching so far forward, bearing all things in its own direction, carrying along with it the deepest forces of the Christian life, hallowed by the prayers and sanctified by the sufferings of the best Christian ages, honored by the zeal of martyrs and the learning of fathers, conquering nations to the law of Christ and building into form the whole structure of their worship and faith—such a fact as this, we say, can never be rationally construed without recourse to the idea of a much deeper reason for it in the nature of man, than any which is found simply in its perversion through the power of sin. The whole phenomenon is of such an order, that in view of it we are bound to acknowledge a mysterious correspondence in some way between this style of religion and the inmost religious wants and impulses of the soul.

So much is apparent also, we may add, sufficiently so at least for all thoughtful persons, from the power it is found to exercise over many in modern times, under circumstances that might seem to be the most unfavorable to its influence. The reigning temper of Protestantism, in its present Puritanic form, is against it, not only having no sympathy with it, but absolutely intolerant of its presence. And yet in the bosom of this Protestantism itself, it seems to be a spirit which can never be effectually and finally laid. It is ever ready, sometimes in one form and sometimes in another, to raise its unpopular head, and enter its solemn protest, more or less loudly, against what it conceives to be the downward tendencies of the predominant unchurchly interest. In almost every denomination we have, if not an open, at least a sort of quiet and silent war, going forward between the less churchly and the more churchly, the point of controversy being the question of retaining or parting with some idea, or some practice, involving still as far as it may reach the old conception of the Holy Catholic Church. But in some cases, the issue reveals itself in a far bolder and much more earnest form. Of this sort is the Anglo-catholic movement in the Church of England, and the Old Lutheran movement in the German Church.[7] Nothing can well be more superficial, than the style in which it is pretended too often to account for such manifestations of the church spirit; nothing more inwardly helpless and imbecile, than the way in which it is attempted in most cases to meet them and put them down. Our business now, however, is not to speak in their direct defence; we leave them severally to their several

---

7. [For more on the Oxford Movement and other confessional movements, see Conser, *Church and Confession*.]

merits whatever these may be. But so much at least we have a right to say: the circumstances under which they come into view are such as absolutely preclude the idea of their being the product of ignorance, pride, self-will, dislike to spiritual religion, or any other bad natural power of this sort, and make it certain on the contrary that they stand connected with the inmost religious wants and most earnest spiritual longings of our general human life. Affection, sentimentalism, and pedantry, may indeed join themselves to such a movement, and be carried along with it in a sort of outward way; caricaturing the true sense of it, and making it offensive or ridiculous; as they may do, and have a tendency to do, in the case of any great religious movement whatever. But the true ruling force of the stream must be sought in depths far more profound.

It requires indeed only some proper communion with the subject in our own spirits, to perceive the truth of the general thought which we have now in hand. It is wonderful with what power church ideas make their appeal to the soul, when it is brought into the right posture and habit for perceiving their force. And this habit is anything but such as it might be supposed to be, on the theory of those who seek to resolve all sentiments of the sort into worldly and unspiritual motives. It does not come of logic. It is no fruit of the mere understanding. It owns no sympathy with the noise and rush of material interests, the common outward life of the present world. It is a habit rather, in which the mind is brought to fall back upon the depths of its own nature, and to converse with the spiritual things, not so much in the way of outward reflection, as in the way of inward intuition.

In some such style it is, that the unperverted thoughts of childhood are accustomed to go out towards the realities of the world unseen and eternal; and children, as we have had occasion to say before, have a natural receptivity for all churchly ideas; a truth which any one can easily verify, by remembering the experience of his own childhood, or by observing the childhood of others. What true child ever had any difficulty in admitting the idea of baptismal grace, or in acknowledging the mystical force of the Lord's Supper? So at every point children are peculiarly open to just those views and sentiments in religion, which enter into what may be termed the objective churchly side of Christianity, as we have it developed in the old Catholic Church. The only true order of faith for them is always the Apostles' Creed. No symbol, no catechism, ever speaks to them like that. They are disposed to believe in saints, and, to hold in reverence the memory of confessors and martyrs. They have an active sense for the liturgical in religion, for the mystical, for the priestly and sacramental. It costs no trouble to bend their first religious thoughts this way. Their earliest piety will not flow smoothly in any other channel.

And thus it is through life, where the child is allowed to remain still "father to the man" in any right sense, and where opportunity is still found for the religious sensibilities to work in their proper primitive form. The "testimony of the soul," on which Tertullian lays so much stress,[8] as being on the side of all religion, and as

8. [*O testimonium animae naturaliter Christiana* [Trans. *On the Testimony of the Soul*], written

bearing witness in particular to the claims of Christianity the absolutely true religion, goes unquestionably in favor also of Christianity under the churchly view, and lends countenance to the whole circle of thoughts and feelings in which this view may be said to have its natural and proper home. There is that in the inmost depths of our religious being, which echoes responsively to the voice of this special form of the Christian faith, wherever there is room for it to be rightly and fairly heard. Is it not here, in truth, we reach the ground and foundation of all religious art? All such art is churchly by its very constitution, and ceases to be intelligible where some sense of the Church comes not in as a key to explain its meaning. Puritanic ideas are for the understanding; Catholic ideas speak more directly to the heart.

Here again, however, we do not mean to make the voice of nature in this form an argument at once for the truth of every particular point of opinion or belief, that may be found entering into the general order of faith which is thus commended to our regard. As the testimony of the soul in favor of Christianity at large cannot be held sufficient to accredit all views that prevail in the name of Christianity; as many such views may be superstitious, fantastic, exaggerated and false, even while they seem to fall back upon that general witness, and to find in it their natural encouragement and support; so ought it not to be considered strange certainly if the same testimony of the soul, uttered in favor of the Church, should appear improperly used in many cases to recommend like superstitions and errors prevailing in the name of the Church. Opinions may belong to a certain order of thought, and find in it their easy natural home, without being for this reason after all any part of its legitimate life. There may be, we have a right to suppose, wrong interpretations of Catholic feeling, false ways of carrying out the applications of Catholic truth, just as we know there is room for like misconstruction and misapplication where other spheres also, whether of sentiment or principle, are concerned. We are not called upon here to discriminate between the true and the false in single particulars. Our argument is not now in behalf of any certain points. What we mean to assert is simply the authority of the church system in its general and whole view, its title to respect, its right to be acknowledged as a necessary side of the Christian faith.

[VI. The Church as a Living Idea]

The sense of the Church, as an article of faith, shows what power it carries with it for the interior life of the soul, by the way in which it is accustomed to work and make itself felt where it has once begun to prevail. It is then no barren opinion merely, no mechanical tradition simply, but the power of a living *idea*, which is not so much apprehended by the mind, as it seems itself rather to apprehend this, and to bear it along irresistibly in its own direction. The idea may not start at the centre; is more likely

---

in 198, is a defense of Christianity against the pagans.]

indeed to begin with some point in the general circumference of that great circle of thoughts which it pervades with its presence; but let the force of it be felt where it may first, it has a tendency always to grow and spread, reaching from one point to another, and settling itself always more widely and firmly in the mind. This serves to show the vitality of the idea. Those who have no sense for it, and with whom the consciousness of religion holds only in the unchurchly form, may look upon it, and speak of it, as a whim or caprice without any proper spiritual root in the soul; but the actual subjects of its power know better. They know it to be in themselves something both deep and living; it has for them the force of a real inward awakening; it is not so much an opinion with them as an experience; and the more it comes to prevail within them, the more impossible it becomes for them to rid themselves of its presence. Especially impossible is it for them to be engaged to any thing of this sort, at the bidding of such as show plainly that they have never really known in their own minds the nature and meaning of that which they oppose. The case is felt to be one, in which no such purely outside judgment can deserve to be held of any weight.

[VII. Even Sects Recognize the Church as the Power of Christianity]

A great argument for the idea of the Church appears in the fact, that all Christian sects find themselves compelled to do homage to it, indirectly at least if not directly, in spite even of their own natural disposition too often drawing them the other way. Sects are in their own nature hostile to the true conception of the Church; the sect spirit is constitutionally an unchurchly spirit. But notwithstanding this, we find among all properly Christian denominations some practical acknowledgment of the church system, as being necessary in some way to carry out and complete the full sense of the Gospel. There would seem to be in fact no escape from this, short of the giving up of Christianity altogether, and the resolution of it into merely natural religion. Christianity has no power, it would seem, to divest itself absolutely of that form of existence we call the Church. Hence no sect can avoid altogether the assumption of some church character, and the assertion of some of the elements of a true church life in its own favor.[9] There is a difference of course in the case; some sects go much farther than others in the unchurchly direction; while all of them, in their various ways, fall short of the full conception of the Church, thus laboring under inconsistency and contradiction. But none of these is able to ignore and repudiate the conception as a whole. The most unchurchly among them is under the power of a law here which is too mighty to be cast off entirely, and with however bad a grace must conform in some part to the demands of the very system against which it claims to be an earnest uncompromising protest. Every sect has to be, whether it will or not, some sort of a *church*. Even the Baptists hold themselves to be something more in this view than the American Bible

---

9. [Nevin, *One, Holy, Catholic, and Apostolic*, Tome 1, 223, 263–68.]

Society or Tract Society;[10] and the most rank Congregational Independency will not allow itself to be just of one order with a city Young Men's Association or a Village Lyceum.[11] Ever sect in its way sets itself up for a reliable and sufficient guide in the things of religion, an authorized exponent of the Divine will, the bearer of a true heavenly commission for the exercise of spiritual powers to which it would be nothing short of blasphemy to think of laying claim in any other view. Every sect arrogates to itself, in its own denominational range at least, religious functions that are in their very nature catholic; prophetical functions, priestly functions, kingly functions; the right of mediating between man and his Maker; the power of the keys; rights and powers generally, such as to be legitimate can flow only from a Divine commission, and such as cannot be honestly acknowledged at all therefore without being allowed to be as broad and universal as Christianity itself. The nearest approximation to a full and complete denial of the Church under the show of Christianity, comes to view among the Quakers;[12] but even with them some poor remains of the idea have been found necessary all along to preserve this show; and the elimination of these now more and more from their system, is the sure signal of its speedy resolution everywhere into thin air. Rightly considered, nothing can well be of more force to establish the maxim "No Church, no Christianity" than this compulsory witness in its favor on the part of the whole sect world, which may be considered in full conspiracy against it, and whose very life would seem to depend on its successful contradiction.

[VIII. The Essential and Necessary Form of the Idea of the Church]

In view of these manifold relations to the idea of the Church, and the power it is found to exert over the conception of Christianity in such various ways, it becomes the more important that we should be able to fix our minds on what may be considered the fundamental form of this idea, as distinguished from its operations and effects under a derivative and merely secondary view. In all religious bodies we meet with the idea of the Church, expressed in some elements which owe to it clearly all their meaning

---

10. [The American Bible Society (1816) and the American Tract Society (1825) were two of a plethora of interdenominational, nonprofit organizations that originated in early nineteenth-century America.]

11. [During the first half of the nineteenth century, residents in villages scattered throughout New England, as well as other parts of the nation, organized voluntary societies for the purpose of "elevated conversations" and "mental improvement." By 1840 more than 3,000 communities contained such a society. These societies were organized under a variety of labels—lyceums, young men's institutes and associations, library and debating societies. The majority of the societies called themselves "lyceums" after the society that Josiah Holbrook established in 1826 in Millbury, MA. See Donald Scott, "For the Purpose of Mutual Improvement: Lyceums, Debating Societies and Popular Entertainment" at http://resources.osv.org/explore_learn/document_viewer.php?DocID=1015.]

12. [The Society of Friends or Quakers, founded by George Fox who once said, "Christ is come to teach his people himself," affirm the possibility of direct, unmediated communion with the Divine. For more, see Nesti, "Early Quaker Ecclesiology".]

and force; while it is no less plain, that in many cases at least such elements are at hand only in an isolated and fragmentary way, without reaching to the unity of a true church system, and without being referred to their own necessary ground and principle, the idea of the Church itself. We are bound, therefore, to distinguish in the case between what is derivative and what is original and fontal, and to look steadily through the first, if possible, back to the last; and it is plain also, that in doing this our inquiry ought to be concerned primarily not with particular organizations claiming to be churches, the Presbyterian, for instance, the Episcopal, or the Roman Catholic, but with the thought of the Church itself, its purely ideal nature, as something lying back of all such organizations, and seeking actualization through them in some way answerable to its own essential requirements and demands.

The true sense of the Church Question, in this view, that which forms its proper nerve and gist, is not found really in those points around which the controversy is most commonly made to revolve. The first matter needing to be settled is not the right of any outward historical organization to be considered the Church or a part of the Church, but what the Church itself must be held to be in theory or idea; not the force and value of any institution or usage or order which may be set forward in any quarter as evidencing the presence of the Church, but what this presence in any case must be taken actually to involve and mean. If men have no common notion or conception of the Church, some taking it to mean much and others taking it to mean very little or almost nothing at all, it can never be more than a waste of time for them to dispute concerning the modes of its being or the proper methods of its action. Only when the *idea* of the Church has been first brought to some clear determination, can the way be said to be at all open for discussing either intelligibly or profitably such questions as relate only to the manner in which the idea should be, or actually may be anywhere, carried out in practice. That is always a most heartless sort of controversy about church points, where the parties at issue agree at bottom in disowning, or not perceiving, what forms in fact the true core of the subject in debate, and thus show themselves to be contending for an empty form and nothing more; as when the Baptist insists on the obligation of the sacraments against the Quaker, or the Congregationalist defends the baptism of infants against the Baptist, without any faith on either side in the old doctrine of sacramental grace; or as when the Episcopalian is violent for bishops, or for the use of a liturgy, against the Presbyterian, while for both alike all resolves itself into a question of mere outward appointment, and neither the Christian ministry nor Christian worship mean a particle more for the one than they mean for the other. Such questions, belonging to the periphery of the church system are of course important; but only as they are viewed in connection with the centre of the sphere in which they have their place. Disjoined from this in thought, they cease to have any meaning or force. What earnest mind can make much account of the question of infant baptism, if the whole sacrament be considered an outward sign merely without any sort of objective force? To what can the question of Episcopacy amount for any such mind, where the ministry is not held to be of strictly divine right, and the necessary channel of God's grace in the Church? It may be something relatively churchly to uphold the authority of the sacraments in opposition to the Quakers, to be in favor of infant baptism in contradiction to the Baptists, to go for Presbyterianism instead of Independency and Congregationalism, to press the distinguishing points of Anglican or American Episcopacy against all other denominations; but no such distinctions are sufficient of themselves to bring into view the absolute sense of the quality which is applied to them by the term churchly. To reach this, we must go farther back. The fundamental question is not of the sacraments, nor of a liturgy, nor of the church year, nor of ordination and apostolical succession, nor of presbyters, bishops, or popes; but, as we have said, of the nature of the Church itself, considered in its ideal character, and as an object of thought anterior to every such revelation of its presence in an outward way.

Is the Church really and truly a constituent part of Christianity, the necessary form of its existence or being in the world? Does it belong to the "mystery of godliness," the constitution of grace, in such a sense that this must stand or fall with its presence? This, if we look at it rightly, is the question of questions for the subject before us, that on which turns the whole significance of the controversy concerning the Church. This is that last profound issue, towards which, whether with full consciousness or not, all other issues in the minds of men on the subject of the Church flow naturally as to their proper end, and in the bosom of which alone it is possible for them to be brought to any final and full solution. Accordingly, as this question may be either affirmed or denied, all other questions appertaining to the church system will be found to retain or lose their interest. If the question be affirmed, and the only true and proper idea of the Church is held to be that which is expressed by such answer, it is easy to see how at once all points flowing from it, or depending upon it in any way, must acquire a corresponding solemnity of sense; how they must be considered no longer as things of curious and vain speculation merely, but as matters of deep practical import; how it must be felt, that instead of bearing to Christianity the relation simply of outward accidents or adiaphorous forms, they reach in truth to its inmost heart, and have to do with the deepest spiritualities of its life. Let the answer, on the contrary, fall the other way, so that the Church shall be held to be no necessary constituent of Christianity, but only an arrangement joined to it from without, and it becomes then just as easy to see, how at once all points connected with it must be shorn, to a corresponding extent, of their meaning and interest, and how it can never be any thing more than pedantry at best to lay any great stress upon them, or to make them the subject of earnest strife one way or another. It is a poor business surely to stickle for forms, where the whole idea is disowned which can make them to be of any force. Without faith in the mystery of the Church, as being the real bearer of heavenly and supernatural powers, to what can it amount to be zealous for the mere modes of its action, the mere circumstantials of its constitution? Then indeed to be churchly, is to be at the same time formal and superstitious, narrow and pedantic. Then the more men pretend to lean this way, the worse, since their religion in any such form must appear only the greater sham. The most ghastly of all shams is that which takes upon itself in fullest measure the form and show of what it pretends to be, without having in itself still the power of the central idea which is needed to breathe through the whole its proper life. What is the Christian ministry, what is ordination, what are sacraments, without the old conception of the Christian Church? Presbyterianism, without this conception, is a sham over against Congregationalism; as this itself is also over against the still more unchurchly position of Baptists and Quakers. But Episcopalianism without it must be held a worse sham than all.

No one can be said to know at all the meaning of the Church Question, no one is prepared to speak of it intelligibly or to purpose, who has not been confronted with it face to face in the radical form now mentioned, and who has not felt it necessary to meet it in this form with some definite and distinct answer. All dispute about the outward organization of the Church, about its proper rights and powers, about its historical movement, and its actual presence in the world under any particular profession and title at a given time, must be in a great measure unmeaning and profitless without this. The question *"What is the Church?"* is older in the order of nature than the question *"Where is the Church?"* and must be brought to some steady determination for our thinking, before we can have any right at all to pronounce in regard to this last any judgment whatever.

[IX. The Root of Controversy Over the Church Question]

What is the Church? What is the true idea or conception of it, in the economy of the Christian salvation? Does it belong to the essence of Christianity; or is it something accidental only to its proper being, a constitution made to inclose it in an outward way, and capable of being separated from it without serious damage to its life?[13]

This, we say, is the true *Church Question*, the root of that great controversy concerning the Church, whose ramifications reach so far, and whose multitudinous bearings are found to cover at last the entire field both of Christian doctrine and Christian

---

13. [At least in the twentieth century, Nevin's question became expressed as a distinction between the church's *esse* ("being") and its *bene esse* ("well-being," "benefit"). See e.g., Avis, *The Church in the Theology of the Reformers*, esp. 35, 46–7 (for some of the Reformers, discipline was only of its *bene esse*); Sykes, *Old Priest and New Presbyter*, 84 (episcopacy not of the *esse*). Bavinck, *Reformed Dogmatics* 4:273–325, gives an extensive discussion of the "essence" of the church (albeit without using the above terminology). Here Nevin thinks the question is more basic: is the church *itself* of the very being of Christianity? Compare Hodge, "Idea of the Church": "the Church, as defined in the [Apostles'] Creed . . . is not, however, presented as a visible organization, to which the form is essential . . . (249)." By this point in Nevin's thought, it should be clear, the notion that a "visible organization" was *not* "essential" to the church would have made no sense. *Hodge* made sense of it by understanding the "true" church as being the invisible body of the truly regenerate. The editors thank Joseph Minich for pointing out these sources.]

practice. Here is the fountain head of the difference, which like some mighty stream divides throughout the churchly system of religion from the unchurchly. Here is the beginning of the great gulf fixed between them, which serves to place them as it were in two opposite worlds. No other issue, within the Christian sphere itself, descends so deep or reaches so far. It enters into the very idea of faith, affects the sense of all worship, conditions the universal scheme of theology, and moulds and shapes the religious life at every point. It gives rise to two phases of Christianity, which are so different as to seem at last indeed, in their full development, more like two Christianities than one.

[X. The Essence of the Church Question Shown in the Apostles' Creed]

Is the Church of the essence of Christianity, the necessary form of its presence, the only medium of its grace, the true organ of its power, in the world? Whatever difficulty there may be about the proper answer to this question in modern times, for the Christian world in the first ages there was none. They answered the question at once in the affirmative, and considered it treason to the Christian faith to think of answering it in any other way. The full evidence of this lies before us in the Apostles' Creed; or rather, we should say, in all the primitive Creeds, for the Creeds of the early Church are in truth one; any differences among them being variations simply of the same theme, that touch not in the least the true unity of its sense. This theme takes in everywhere the idea of the Church; takes it in also under the very aspect of which we are now speaking, as being of the essence of Christianity, and not simply one of its outward adjuncts. The doctrine or fact of the Church is not in the Creed by accident. It is there, just as the fact of Christ's glorification is there, in virtue of its belonging really and truly to the movement or progress of the general mystery of godliness, which it is the purpose of the Creed to present as the great object of the Christian faith. In no other view could it have a place in the Creed at all, if we suppose this to be a true organic representation of what Christianity is in its fundamental conception, and not a loose throwing together simply of particular opinions without inward law or reason. The article of the Church is in the Creed, not just by wilful determination on the part of the framers of the symbol, but by the constitutional necessities of the Creed itself. It is the necessary outbirth of the Christian faith, keeping pace with the progress of its glorious object, just at the point where it comes into view. As Christ's glorification makes room for the mission of the Holy Ghost, so the mission of the Holy Ghost unfolds itself with necessary consequence in the constitution of the Holy Catholic Church. Blot out that article, and the whole Creed is mutilated and broken in its sense.

It may help us to appreciate the force of the article in this view, if we allow ourselves to suppose some other article made to stand in its place. Take, for example, the doctrine of the authority of the Bible, as being the inspired word of God and the only infallible rule of faith and practice. Suppose the Creed to run: "I believe in the Holy

Ghost, the inspiration of the Holy Scriptures, &c." It is very easy to see, that this would not fall in with the true organism of the symbol at all. The coming of the Holy Ghost, was not in order to the publication of the Holy Scriptures primarily, but in order to the founding of the Holy Catholic Church. For the thinking of the early Christian world, therefore, it was not possible to place the Bible before the Church in the order of faith. The Church was for them a fact deeper, and wider, and nearer to the proper life of Christianity, than the Bible. Not with any feeling of disrespect for the Bible of course; and not from any doubt of its being the inspired word of God, but because their sense of Christianity was such as to require this order rather than any other.

There is no room for any mistake in regard to the sense, in which the Church is made to be an article of faith in the Creed. This is determined by its connexions, as well as by the whole aim and purpose of the formulary itself. The Creed is intended to set forth the true fundamental facts of the world of grace, as it has come to be established in the midst of the world of nature. These facts in such view are all mysteries, objects for faith as distinguished from natural understanding. The Church thus is made to be a mystery, the presence of a supernatural fact in the world, which men are required to acknowledge as a necessary part of the Christian faith. It is made to be this, moreover, in such a way as to carry along with it, in its own place, the full power of the Christian salvation. The Church, in the Creed, stands out manifestly as the connecting medium between all that goes before and all that follows after. The grace which starts in Christ's birth, and flows onward through his life, his death upon the cross, his descent to hades, his resurrection, his ascension to the right hand of God, and the sending of the Holy Ghost, is the same that then discharges its full stream into the bosom of the Church, and that is poured forth from this again in the benefits of redemption, from the remission of sins onward to the life everlasting. Beyond all question, the Creed means to affirm the being of the Church, as an indispensable link in the scheme of salvation, and as something not accidental merely but essential to the constitution of Christianity.

In this view, it defines itself and fixes its own attributes. It is necessarily one, holy, catholic, and apostolical. It can be no real object of faith at all, except in this character and form. Its ministry is of divine right. Its sacraments convey grace. The scheme of the Creed, in a word, is churchly throughout; and it is not possible to understand it, or to have any sympathy with it, except from the posture of a true churchly faith. For the strictly Puritanic mind, it can never seem to carry a right sound.

[XI. The Church Question Answered by the Ancient Church]

If there could be any doubt concerning the proper sense of the Creed here, separately considered, it must disappear immediately in view of what may easily be known in other ways to have been the general faith of the early Church on this subject. As all the variations of the Creed proceed in one and the same strain, so also is this found to be in full harmony at the same time with the universal religious thinking of the time to which they belong. No one who has taken the least serious pains to qualify himself for an intelligent opinion in the case, can make any question in regard to this point. The idea of the Church which meets us in the Epistles of Ignatius, is the same that rules the polemics of Irenaeus, animates the zeal of Cyprian, and comes to its full systematic development at last in the theology of the great Augustine.[14] It is the idea, by which all institutions and arrangements, all offices and sacraments, all forms and rubrics, belonging to the Church, are made to be something subordinate to the living constitution of the Church itself, in virtue of which only they can be supposed to carry with them either grace or power. Faith in the Church, with these Fathers, was not just faith in bishops, or in an altar, or in the use of a liturgy; for bishops, and altars, and liturgies, were common among such as were held notwithstanding to have neither part nor lot in the true commonwealth of Christ. It terminated on what the Church was supposed to be as a divine mystery, back of episcopacy, and behind all sacraments, symbols, and forms, the force of which must turn necessarily at last on its own nature. The peculiarity of this old church faith is, that it goes right to the heart of the true Church Question, where many are altogether unwilling to follow it, who still affect to make great account of it for other points; infant baptism, for instance, baptismal grace, the mystical power of the Lord's Supper, or the three orders of the ministry; without perceiving that such points in fact mean nothing, save in union with the central life of the system to which they belong. The old faith went hand in hand with the Creed; saw in the Church the presence of a new order of life in the world, flowing from Christ's exaltation and the sending of the Holy Ghost; owned it for the body of Christ, and the home of the Spirit; ascribed to it for this reason heavenly prerogatives and powers; and found no difficulty accordingly in speaking of it as the ark of salvation, in whose bosom alone men might hope to outride safely the perils of their present life, and to be borne finally into the haven of eternal rest.

14. [In *The Gospel and the Catholic Church*, Michael Ramsey includes a chapter on the Church Fathers. Commenting on the importance of their era, he echoes Nevin's assertion: "It is important, not as a golden age, nor as a model for the imitation of Christians (as the Tractarians somewhat extravagantly claimed), but as an age when the whole Gospel found expression in the life and Liturgy of the one Body, with a balanced use of all the Church's structure and with a depth and breadth and unity which contrast strikingly with every subsequent epoch (140)." More recently, Robert Crouse, in "Problems of Ecclesiology: Patristic Perspectives," reminds us of the plurality of ecclesiological perspectives, a perspective Nevin may not have shared: "For St. Irenaeus, for instance, the church is primarily the *magisterium*, the authoritative witness to saving truth, in the face of gnostic error. For Tertullian (becoming a Montanist, and finally a Tertullianist), the church is the closely disciplined community governed immediately by the inspiration of the Spirit. For early Christian rigorists, in general, the church is the community of the perfect, while for the laxists, it is a means of healing imperfections. For Eusebius of Caesarea, the church is the redeemed empire, under the monarchy of the sacred emperor, while for the monks in the deserts of Egypt, the true church is to be found only in *contemptus mundi*, the rejection of the world. And so it goes: not just one, but a plethora of ecclesiologies." For other examples where modern scholars find pluralism when Nevin saw uniformity, see Nevin, "Wilberforce on the Eucharist," 138n15, 140n18, 154n48.]

We speak not now of the merits of this faith. We ask not, whether it was right or wrong. All we wish is to hold it up to view steadily as a historical fact. In this light at least, it deserves our solemn attention; and no one certainly can be supposed to deal fairly and honestly with the Church Question, who is not willing to look the fact full in the face, or who does not feel it necessary to come to some right understanding with it in his own mind. Take it as we may, we find no Puritanism in the ancient Church; but touches of it only among heretical bodies on the outside. We can hardly read a page of the old ecclesiastical literature, Greek or Latin, without falling on something, the proper sense of which involves necessarily, if it does not directly affirm, the churchly view of religion. The authority of the church system is felt to stretch itself over the whole field of thought and life. Strange, is it not, if it should have been after all as brainless and heartless, as it is the fashion with some to make it in these last days!

[XII. The Idea of the Church in the Creed Contrasted to Puritanism[15]]

A still farther argument for what we have seen to be the sense of the Creed in reference to the Church might be found, if it were needed, in the notorious unpopularity of the symbol among all unchurchly religious bodies, in proportion precisely to the measure of their alienation from the old idea of the Church. Here we have a fact again, make out of it what we may, which admits of no dispute, Puritanism has no sympathy with the Creed; no taste for it; no power to make any honest use of it as a symbol of faith. Its notion of Christianity runs not naturally into any such form, but left to itself seeks always a different course of expression. The Creed does not sit easily upon it; finds no hearty and full echo in its soul; is allowed by it, therefore, to fall quietly into general neglect. Why is it that our Protestant sects commonly, at this time, make no use of the Creed either publicly or privately? The question surely deserves some consideration. Such indifference to the oldest formulary of the Christian faith can not be without profound significance in some way. The Baptists of course have nothing to do with it; the Methodists make no account of it; New England Congregationalists consider it the fossil relic only of a by-gone age; Presbyterians, as a general thing, regard it with suspicion, or else ignore it altogether. Can this be merely accidental? Could it be at all, if there were not at bottom, in all these cases, a material variation from the system of religious thought in which the Creed is constructed?

The nature of the variation may easily be understood. It turns upon the conception of the Church, which enters essentially into the structure of the Creed, and conditions both the form and spirit of it throughout. The article of the Church is not in the Creed as a loose separate particular only, joined to its other articles in a purely outward way. It holds its place there, by virtue of its own intrinsic right to be considered a necessary part of the system of faith which is embodied in the symbol.

---

15. [For what Nevin meant by "Puritanism," see Nevin, "Nevin and Bushnell: Christian Nurture and Baptism," 60 and note 6.]

The order of this faith, the evolution of its proper organic sense, is such as imperiously to require the presence of the article just where it comes into view. The whole Creed, thus, moves in the power of the church system; all its articles have a churchly tone; and it is not possible for them to find a hearty and full response, where the Puritanic unchurchly spirit has come generally to prevail. This is the reason that it is so little popular with most of our religious sects at the present time. They can have no sympathy, as sects, with the old idea of the Church. Hence, consciously or unconsciously, their indifference, if not positive dislike, to a symbol which is felt to be mysteriously full of it from beginning to end.

It would be a curious and interesting experiment, to try what would be the effect of the Creed upon the unchurchly habit of religion, if it were brought into use again where it is now thus unhappily forgotten or disowned. Let its authority be revived in the midst of any Puritanic sect. Let earnest be made with the use of it, for the purposes of religious instruction and worship. Let its old familiar voice be heard once more, in the family and in the great congregation. Let it be publicly honored in the sanctuary, at the altar and in the pulpit. Could the unchurchly habit of religion endure any such test? We feel very sure that it could not. It would be ready in the first place, to resent it as the coming in of a spirit dangerous to the interests of evangelical religion, an insidious tendency towards Puseyism or Popery. It must be forced in the next place, should the trial still go steadily forward, to bend gradually to the new order of thought thus pressed upon it, and to give up its unchurchliness in some measure at least in favor of the opposite style of Christianity. Puritanism and the Creed can never reign in full force together. The introduction of the Creed into general use in New England would be the sure signal at once of a general revolution in its whole theological and ecclesiastical life.

[XIII. Call to Common Faith in the Creed]

Looking at things as we have seen them to be, it must seem strange certainly to find the representatives of this unchurchly Christianity—who have no power to frame their lips to a sincere pronunciation of the Apostles' Creed—boldly arrogating to themselves the highest style of evangelical orthodoxy, and denouncing as seriously in error all who refuse to be governed by their private rule and measure. What then is orthodoxy? Has the Christian world been mistaken all along, in supposing it to be rightly set forth, first of all, in the articles of the old Christian Creeds? Whatever else it may embrace in the way of true confessional development, must it start at least in this form of sound words, and grow forth from it organically as its unchanging root? Can any later Confession, Catechism, or Creed, deserve to be considered of force except as it may be taken to unfold and carry out what was here proclaimed to be the only order of faith in the beginning? Is the *Symbolum Apostolicum* to be regarded still as the primary, fundamental symbol of Christianity; or is it not? Let this question be answered.

DOCUMENT 4: "THOUGHTS ON THE CHURCH" (1858)

Let men look at it, and answer it fairly and distinctly in their own minds. Let our sects answer it to themselves, and to one another. Then we shall know all round, where we are, and what we mean. In this whole controversy concerning the Church, the first preliminary requiring to be settled would appear to meet us just here. There can be no meaning in it, if the parties in debate have no common faith in the Creed. When church principles, therefore, are called in question, or opposed in any quarter, it is but fair to ask first of all whether those who set their face against them are believers or unbelievers in Christianity as we have it defined in this primitive catholic symbol. No such unbeliever deserves to be considered respectfully in the case. What right can any one have to set himself up as a critic or judge of orthodoxy here, who is so grossly at fault in the quality of his own faith? To what can it amount, that the idea of the Church is disowned by those, who at the same time disown the idea of the Creed?

J. W. N.
Windsor Place, Lancaster co., Pa.

Thoughts on the Church: Second Article[1]

[XIV. The Creed as Regula Fidei][2]

Can a sect be *evangelical* which refuses to accept the Apostles' Creed as the fundamental symbol of its faith? The question is simple, clear, and important enough, one would suppose, to command some respectful attention. The point is not, whether other symbols may not be worthy also of regard in their place; but whether any form of belief, written or unwritten, can be considered evangelically sound and orthodox, which does not start in this plain rule, and grow forth from it as its normative ground and type. Can the Augsburg Confession,[3] for instance, or the Westminster Confession[4], or the Heidelberg Catechism,[5] be of greater symbolical authority at any point than the Creed, for the determination of the true and proper sense of Christianity; so that the last may be lawfully required to bend to any of the first, instead of its being held necessary that the order of subordination should fall the other way? In the relation, here between the older confessionalism and the confessionalism of later times, which is to be considered first and which second; which must be taken for the foundation, and which for the superstructure, of the Christian scheme of faith? And so in regard to

---

1. [J. W. N[evin], *Mercersburg Review* (July 1858) 399–426.]

2. [*Regula Fidei* means "rule of faith," early summaries of Christian belief. See *Dictionary of the Christian Church*, 1424.]

3. [The first of the great Protestant Confessions, the Augsburg Confession, Latin *Confessio Augustana,* is the confession of the Lutheran Churches presented on June 25, 1530, in German and Latin, at the Diet of Augsburg to the emperor Charles V. The principal author was the Reformer Philipp Melanchthon.]

4. [The Westminster Confession of Faith is a Reformed confession of faith in the Calvinist theological tradition drawn up by the 1646 Westminster Assembly, largely of the Church of England. It was first published in 1647 under the title *The Humble Advice of the Assembly of Divines, Now by Authority of Parliament Sitting at Westminster, Concerning a Confession of Faith: with the Quotations and Text of Scripture Annexed. Presented by Them Lately to Both Houses of Parliament.*]

5. [The Heidelberg Catechism was written in Heidelberg by Zacharius Ursinus and Caspar Olevianus at the request of Elector Frederick III, ruler of the German province, the Palatinate, from 1559 to 1576. The Catechism was adopted by a Synod in Heidelberg and published in German with a preface by Frederick III, dated January 19, 1563.]

any unwritten judgment or conception of Christianity, which may be cherished in any quarter as a favorite sectarian phase of what is counted evangelical religion, the point for consideration comes up always in the same form. Can any such conception ever be allowed rightly to take precedence of that view of Christianity which is set before us in the ancient Creed, and which was received by the whole Christian world in the beginning, as the necessary and only legitimate expression of what the Christian religion is in its first constituent principles and facts? Can any confessionalism, in one word, written or unwritten, disown the Creed, ignore the Creed, make no conscious account of the Creed practically, as the basis of its opinions and teachings, and yet be, at the same time, evangelical, that is, answerable truly to the life and spirit of the Gospel? Can a Christian teacher, or a body of Christian teachers, occupy this position of broad indifference, or full antagonism, to what was held universally to be the absolutely binding *regula fidei* in the first ages, and yet deserve to be honored, notwithstanding, as sound in the faith and biblically orthodox?

With many in this incongruous predicament, we know, a ready and convenient escape from all difficulty is felt to be ever at hand, in the trite sophism which pretends to fall back at once on the Bible as the last rule of all right Christian belief. Here all our unchurchly sects fancy themselves to be planted on impregnable ground. They find it perfectly easy to stand forward with their diversified schemes of opinion, regardless of all primitive confessions and creeds, and to challenge the respect of the world for them as evangelical, on the simple ground of their having been drawn directly from the Scriptures and from no other source. Whether their schemes may agree strictly with the Apostles' Creed, they have not felt it necessary at all carefully to inquire. They have, on the whole, a sort of instinctive apprehension that they do not; but to what can that amount, in a case which confessedly refers itself, at once, to the higher rule of the Bible, to which every rule besides, it matters not how old, must be required of course to bend and yield? If there *be* any discrepancy between their faith and the proper historical sense of the Apostles' Creed, they are sorry for it, but it cannot be helped; they at all events follow the Bible, and in such case it is plain to see that if the Creed is not with them, the Creed must be wrong. With the ordinary sect spirit, setting all logic at defiance in this transparently stupid style, the less discussion one may have the better. We write for the thoughtful only, and such surely do not need to be told that this pretended setting up of the Bible against the Creed is a hypocritical sham of the poorest order, and nothing more. The question, as one would suppose any child might be able to see, regards not at all the authority of the Bible, but wholly and exclusively the interpretation of the Bible, the true and proper construction of what is to be considered its actual sense. It is not as is sometimes shamelessly pretended: Must the Bible yield to the Creed or the Creed to the Bible? but something very different indeed, namely this: Must the sense of the Bible as outlined in the Creed be regarded as its true sense, or may some other construction, some radically different way of understanding it, be allowed at pleasure to set this outline aside, and to make it of no force as a standard of Christian faith? Whether it be pretended to supersede the authority of the symbol in this way by a new written formulary, or by an unwritten scheme of Christianity professedly drawn fresh from the Bible, signifies nothing; all comes to the same thing in the end. In either case, it is the confessionalism of the Creed contradicted and opposed by another confessionalism, another theory of the Gospel, cast in a different mould and bearing a different type; and the only point to be settled is which should be allowed to prevail over the other and to carry with it the highest authority, as a key for opening the full and proper sense of God's word. That the opposing interest should in any case affect to be ruled by no confessional authority whatever and claim to be the direct voice of the Bible, would seem not to improve its position certainly but to throw it rather into the worst possible form. A sect or party then, or it may be with just as much reason a single individual, is found setting up what, after all, can never be anything better than a mere private opinion against the testimony of the general Church spoken through ages; and gravely asking all mankind to be well assured that such private opinion is the veritable doctrine of Christ and his Apostles, which has a right therefore to be heard with implicit trust, in opposition if need be to all other professions of faith made since the world began. Simply to state the case, is to expose it. It is not easy to conceive of any pretension more outrageously absurd and yet, strange to say, the spirit of it meets us on all sides, forming, one may say, the reigning tone and temper of a very large part of our American Christianity at the present time.

Again we ask: Can any system of religion which thus sets up, not the Bible really, but its own construction of the Bible, in opposition to what is exhibited as being the true sense of the Bible in the Creed, in opposition to this form of sound words in which the Church has seen fit to express its apprehension of the fundamental truths of the Gospel from the beginning—can any such system of religion, we say, deserve to be acknowledged as evangelical and orthodox?

We have a number of religious denominations in the modern Puritan world, which arrogate to themselves the title *Evangelical* as preeminently their own, for the very reason, as it would seem, that they agree in repudiating the churchly theory of Christianity presented in the Creed, as being in their mind contrary to the proper genius of the Gospel, and choose to substitute for this another and different theory altogether, extracted immediately, they pretend, from the Bible itself. However much they may differ among themselves, on other points, they are all happily of one and the same way of thinking here. They stand on the common ground of Puritanism as opposed to the old Catholic doctrine of the Church and the entire theology of the Apostles' Creed. Over against all this, they parade what they call the authority of the Bible. In other words, a general scheme of religion which they declare with great confidence to be the only true sense of the Bible, and thus will have it, that this new rule of theirs shall be taken for the test of evangelical character the whole world over, so that whatever in any age or country is found not to agree with it, must for that very reason be condemned as contrary to true godliness and sound faith. Can any such pretension, we ask, be allowed to hold good? Most certainly not; unless we choose to turn all confessionalism into derision.

Here surely we have a right to join issue boldly with the whole system of unchurchly Puritanism, and to put it solemnly on its own apology and defence. Its points of difference within itself are indeed of only minor significance; what it needs most of all is the vindication of its general or main cause, the position namely by which it stands arrayed as a whole against the primitive faith of the Christian world. Take it, for example, in the form of some one of its manifold religious "persuasions"; let us say, the wide spread numerically powerful sect of the Baptist.[6] They reject infant baptism, a serious matter of controversy between them and other sects of like Puritanic mind, but this is not the beginning of their error, the deepest and most comprehensive form of their heterodox faith. To reach that we must go back of all such heads of sectarian dispute to what is in fact common ground for the disputing parties: their want of faith in the Church, their state of full opposition in this view to the Creed. The Baptists are heretical because they are thus at variance with the foundation symbol of Christianity. Here, first of all, they are bound to give account of themselves before the tribunal of the Christian world. Other points, so far as they are concerned mean nothing, are in truth mere impertinences and irrelevancies, till this root issue be fairly met and settled. As it is a matter of small moment what Unitarians may hold on other topics of theology while they refuse to own the doctrine of the Trinity and the proper divinity of Christ; so is it also of little consequence what may be thought of the economy of the Church at other points, its sacraments and forms of worship, its prerogatives and powers, by those who call in question, or at once deny, the very being of it as it is made an article of faith in the Apostles' Creed. Why should breath be spent in discussing the question of infant baptism where the whole conception of the Church giving it significance is quietly disowned as an antiquated superstition? Let the controversy fall back on this point, the true idea of the Church, as its proper beginning. The Baptists call themselves evangelical and orthodox, because they follow, as they tell us, the rule of the Gospel in distinction from every other rule. We charge them with heresy, and pronounce them unevangelical and unbiblical, because they follow in reality only their own arbitrary and partial interpretation of the Scriptures, and refuse to find in them the sense in which they have been read by the orthodox faith of the Church through all ages. They are in broad conflict with the original symbol of Christianity, requiring the world to receive instead of it their own spiritualistic glossary everywhere as the only sure and sufficient medium for getting at the true sense of God's word. Shall we be expected to yield to any such barefaced arrogance as this? No. The Baptists

---

6. [As noted above, the quotation marks reference Winebrenner's *History of all Religious Denominations . . . containing authentic accounts . . . of the different persuasions. . . .* This volume identifies seven different Baptist denominations and gives a brief but detailed "History of the Baptists" by Joseph Belcher, pastor of the Mount Tabor Baptist Church in Philadelphia (42–75).]

are neither evangelical nor orthodox. A main constituent of the Christian faith, one whole side indeed of the mystery of godliness as it was held by the universal Church in the beginning, finds no place in their system of belief. Their religion is not in the Bible, because it agrees not with the original *regula fidei* set before us in the Creed.

And so with Puritanism in general. Its cause here, as we have seen, is throughout the same. In discarding the old doctrine of the Church, in making Christianity to be a full and complete fact on the outside of the Church, it sets aside really the mysteries of the Church altogether; and by doing so brings in actually what must be considered a different Gospel from that which is preached by the Apostles' Creed, and which was held by the whole Church in the beginning to be the true glorious Gospel of the Lord Jesus Christ. Is this to be evangelical? Is this to be orthodox, and sound in the faith as it was once delivered to the saints? Let the representatives of unchurchly Puritanism, who are never weary of repeating their stale insipidities on the subject of the Church, look this accusation fairly in the face, and meet it with some manly and honest answer if they can. It is high time, indeed, that attention were fixed more than it has been upon what must be held to be in this whole controversy with Puritanism the grand first matter in debate. The defenders of the interest should be required, first of all, to come to some positive explanation of their own posture toward the original faith of the Christian world, as we have it expressed in the Creed. Till this be done, it is idle to talk with them on other points. Where there are no common premises, there can be of course no common conclusions, no such conclusions at least in one and the same sense. To what can it amount to argue sacramental questions, points of ecclesiastical polity, Church topics of any sort, with men who have yet to learn, or who at any rate do not feel themselves bound to acknowledge, "what be the first principles of the oracles of God,"[7] as these were supposed to be settled in past ages by the old Catholic standard of the Christian faith? If we are to have any argument at all with such men, it should be made to fall back at once to the beginning. All that we can do properly is to charge home upon them the practical heresy of their whole theological position. Let them set themselves right with the Creed, before they pretend to dogmatize in any other direction.

[XV. The Indissoluble Interconnection of the Articles of the Creed][8]

The doctrine of the Church, we have seen, is not in the Creed in any merely outward and mechanical way. It appears there as a necessary part of the general mystery of faith, being absolutely required, just where it comes into view, to carry forward the significance and power of the Christian salvation from what goes before to what follows after, being nothing less in truth than the connecting link between the mission of

---

7. [Heb 5:12.]
8. [Nevin wrote on this further in "The Unity of the Apostles' Creed" (1869), forthcoming in vol. 8 of MTSS.]

the Holy Ghost and the full course of grace subsequently in the experience of believers. In this view, the article could not be dropped from the system, nor transposed in it to any different place, without marring its organic completeness throughout, as on the other hand the article itself, so torn from its connections, could no longer retain its own proper meaning as an object of faith. So it is indeed with all the articles of the Creed. The symbol is not so much a number of separate acts of faith brought together in a common confession, as one single act rather compassing at once the whole range of the new creation from its commencement to its close. It has to do with its successive points, not as disjointed notions merely, but as concrete forces belonging to the constitution of a common living whole. Its articles are bound together thus, with indissoluble connection, from beginning to end. To believe any one part of it in its own sense is implicitly at least to believe every other part, for the truth of every part stands in its relations to the whole system in which it is comprehended, and if it be not apprehended in these relations it cannot be said to be apprehended and believed in its own proper sense at all. In this way it is that the article of the Church in the Creed is conditioned by the sense of the formulary at other points, as these other points are conditioned also by it again in their turn. There can be no true faith in the resurrection and glorification of Christ, and none in the consequent sending of the Holy Ghost, where it is not felt necessary to follow out still farther the objective progress of the mystery, and say: "I believe in the Holy Catholic Church," and so, on the other hand, there can be no true faith in the Church, where it is not perceived to be the necessary outbirth in this way of these glorious antecedents, leading on to it, and making room for it in the world. It is not any and every way of owning the Church that can be said to satisfy the requirement of the Creed, as it is not enough for it either to own in any and every way the mission of the Holy Ghost.

The whole Creed carries with it thus from beginning to end an import, which accords in full with what it makes the Church to be in the order of salvation, and its articles can be rightly uttered, therefore, only as they are taken in real correspondence with this view. In other words, the theology of the symbol is churchly throughout. Its positions all hold only in that order of grace which involves the conception of the Church as the necessary fruit of its presence in the world. Sundered from this order, they cease to be altogether the objects of faith they are made to be in the system, and become instead mere matters of speculation and opinion. Hence it is that the difficulty of Puritanism with the Creed is not confined by any means to the article of the Church itself, but extends to its universal form and structure so that even when any of its propositions may seem to be readily received, it is still always with some want of entire complacency in the particular way in which they are here articulated and spoken. Left to itself, Puritanism would choose to utter the same truths always in a different manner and with a different tone. To its reigning habit of theological thought, the organization of the Creed must ever appear to be unnatural and defective. Its own construction of Christianity may embrace to a certain extent the same christological and soteriological positions and terms, but they will be found to have not just the same meaning; there is a difference always in their drift and scope. Puritanism may lay great stress on its orthodoxy in owning the doctrine of the Trinity, the true and proper Divinity of Christ, and the Atonement wrought out by his death, and yet see no necessity whatever for carrying out all this to the issue which is ascribed to it in the Creed. It may acknowledge the Remission of Sins and the Resurrection of the Dead, and yet see no dependence of either one or the other mystery on the supernatural constitution of the Church. But this is not to hold these articles in the sense of the Creed. The confessional concord in such case is in outward sound only, and nothing more. The orthodoxy of the Creed moves, from its first article on to its last, in that method of faith which requires and implies in its proper place the presence of the Holy Catholic Church, and no point belonging to it can be held answerably to its general and only true sense, except as it is held in this way. No Gnostic apprehension of Christ's person, no merely spiritualistic view of his work of redemption, can satisfy its demands even in part. All must be taken in the form of an actual history, completing itself in the Church, "which is his body,"[9] running its course here as an order of grace in distinction from the order of nature, onto the glorious resurrection of the last day. So with all the benefits of the Christian salvation. They are, in the view of the Creed, fruits of the Spirit, which are to be found only in the Church, the home of the Spirit. The life everlasting proclaimed by the Creed is a mystery, that depends wholly on the process of the new creation in Christ, which is here exhibited as the object of the Christian faith, and in this way it has place only within the economy of the Church, and can be truly believed therefore only under such view. The remission of sins, in the same way, is regarded as holding in the Church, and not on the outside of it. Men may dream of its being elsewhere; may take it for something that is possible in the general relation of man to his Maker; may claim to be evangelical and spiritual, just because they conceive of it in this spiritualistic way, and make it independent of all sacramental forms and limitations. But no such notion of the remission of sins amounts to what the article means in the Creed. There it is a mystery conditioned by the more general mystery of the Church; it comes through the obedience of faith yielded to this heavenly constitution, and finds its proper symbol, its real signature and pledge, in the sacrament of introduction into the Church, which is for this reason also the sacrament of regeneration, serving to translate its subjects from the power of darkness into the kingdom of God's dear Son, in whom we have redemption through his blood, even the forgiveness of sins.[10] Hence the form given to the article in the Nicene Creed, "We confess one baptism for the remission of sins," adds nothing in fact to the sense of its shorter expression.[11] To believe in the remission of sins at all in the

---

9. [Eph 1:23.]

10. [Col 1:13–14.]

11. [After reviewing the historical development of the form of the Apostles' Creed, Nevin explains the priority of this ancient symbol over others, like the Nicene-Constantinopolitan, which took their

sense of the old Christian faith, is to believe that it comes through baptism as the door of entrance into the Church.

[XVI. No Confessionalism Without the Creed]

As the Creed is constructed within itself, in the way now stated, on a theological scheme which is peculiarly its own, and which determines the true sense of it at every point, requiring all its articles to be understood in one manner only and not in another; so it is easy to see, how it must in this way also draw after it a corresponding construction of all Christian doctrine beyond itself, imparting to it in like manner the power of its own principle and life. By its very conception, the formulary is archetypal and regulative for the whole world of Christian truth. It does not pretend to exhaust the necessary topics of divinity; it leaves room for a broad field of confessionalism beyond itself. But still, if it be indeed what it claims to be, a true scheme of what are to be considered the first principles of the oracles of God, it must necessarily rule the order and shape of all such additional belief throughout, in such way that no doctrine or article of faith shall deserve to be counted orthodox, except as it may stand in the bosom of the same scheme, growing forth from it, and carrying out the scope of it in a natural and regular way. All later confessionalism, to be genuine and valid, must have its genesis or birth from the Apostles' Creed, must refer itself to this as the real matrix of its growth and development. There must ever be a wide difference thus between a system of thought in which this order of faith is acknowledged and observed, and a system of thought in which it is disowned and disregarded; the theological system of the Creed and a theological system made to rest on any other basis; theology in the churchly and theology in the unchurchly form. A difference not confined to the immediate topics of the Creed itself, but extending through these to all topics; a difference not so much turning on single outward propositions (though on this also to some extent), as it is to be measured rather by the inward life of such propositions, the way in which they are understood, their spirit, their general purpose and aim. No Christian doctrine can be held under exactly the same form, within the system of the Creed, and on the outside of this system. Thus it is that the authority of the symbol reaches out to all points of faith, and pervades with its presence the whole range of evangelical truth, making it necessary for every theological article to be held in full conformity with this fundamental rule, in order that it may have a right to be considered orthodox and true.

---

final shape much earlier: "The true power and value of the symbol were felt to stand, not in a given fixed version established for its universal use, but in the divine substance of its contents, which was capable of retaining its identity under very considerable change of expression. So far as this was concerned, the christian catholic world considered itself in possession always of one and the same faith, however much freedom it might see fit to exercise with the utterance of it in different places ("The Apostles Creed," 109; forthcoming in vol. 8 of MTSS)."]

It is not enough, for example, to acknowledge the prophetical, priestly, and kingly offices of Christ, if they be set in no union with the true apprehension of his Mediatorial Person.[12] It is not enough to maintain infant baptism, if we refuse to own at the same time the relation which the sacrament is made to bear in the Creed to the remission of sins. It is not enough to confess the inspiration of the Scriptures, if it be not with faith first in the Church; as though without such an apprehension of the Christian mystery as leads immediately on from Christ's glorification and the sending of the Holy Ghost to this great fact, it might be possible for any one, leaping over it as it were and having no sense of its presence, to come in some other way altogether to firm faith in the Bible as God's infallible word and so through this afterwards to a full and complete scheme of evangelical religion. The Bible, great as it is in the scheme of Christianity, could not be substituted for the Church in the place assigned to it as an article of faith, in the Creed, without violence to the whole order and sense of the Creed. In the view of this archetypal symbol, it comes rightly for all real faith, not before the Church, but after it. It is not the principle or beginning of Christianity, though it be truly its rule. It shines as a light from heaven *in the Church,* and was never intended to be a sufficient and final light for the world, as such, on the outside of the Church. Rationalism, Naturalism, Humanitarianism, of all shapes and types, taking it in such wrong view, however much stress they may affect to lay on its authority, never receive it truly as God's word, have no power to understand it, and in their use of it make it for themselves, as a matter of course, a mere *ignis fatuus*[13], all the world over, "blind leaders of the blind."[14] It would be an appalling spectacle, only to see in fact what an amount of actual infidelity—disobedience to the faith—is sheltered in our time beneath the specious plea of honoring the Bible in this false way.

Take again the doctrine of justification by faith. It is not expressed in the Creed. This of itself makes nothing against it; for the Creed does not pretend to set forth all Christian doctrines; it is an outline simply of what Christianity is in its primary, fundamental facts; leaving room for much to follow in the way of confessional superstructure. It is enough, if the doctrine before us be in the symbol by implication. But this at once serves, as we may readily see, to limit and define at the same time its proper conception. To be true at all, the doctrine must be held in union with the general system of the Creed, and not as something independent of it, and bearing to it only an outside relation. To conceive of justification by faith as a thing having no

---

12. [Nevin was critical of the traditional Reformed formulation of the "offices of Christ": "Sartorius on the Person and Work of Christ," 20 and "The Bread of Life," 224.]

13. [Trans. foolish fire, i.e., an illusion.]

14. [Matt 5:14. Increasingly after 1860 Nevin became skeptical of the use of technology and science to ameliorate human existence. This was of a piece with his long-standing critique of "rationalistic supernaturalism," the attempt to demonstrate the truth of Christianity through reason. For a starting point, see Layman, general introduction to *Born of Water and the Spirit*, 30, and in that volume, "Nevin and Bushnell: Christian Nurture and Baptism," 76n23, and "Bread of Life," 228–29n18, 230n21, 243n55.]

connection whatever with the objective world of grace brought into view by the Creed, a thing pertaining to the general idea of man's relations to God in the order of nature, instead of being bound in any way to the mysterious organization of the Church—the common error of the Puritanic mind—is to turn the doctrine into a fiction, which contradicts the symbol and virtually sets aside its authority, bringing in indeed a new scheme of Christianity altogether. There can be no true faith, in the view of the Creed which does not begin by owning and obeying the mystery of godliness proclaimed in its own articles; no true justification, which does not come from being set thus in real communication with the objective righteousness of Jesus Christ, as the power of a new creation actually present in the Church. No wonder the theories which make justification by faith to be a mere abstraction and that also which resolves it into justification by fancy or feeling,[15] find little or no satisfaction in the old Christian confessions. *Their* theology here, most assuredly, is not the theology of the Apostles' Creed.

[XVII. The Churchly and Unchurchly Schemes Compared]

What we have said, may be sufficient to show, how deep the distinction is between the churchly and the unchurchly schemes of theology, and how far in the end it is found to run. It regards not some points only, in the case of which there may be direct and formal opposition, but serves to qualify, in a very material way, the sense of all points. No article, either of the Creed or of theology in general, can be just the same for one who owns the old Catholic idea of the Church, and for one to whom that idea has come to seem an empty fiction. Doctrines appear under different relations and so under different aspects as apprehended from the one stand-point or from the other, and even where they may seem to have the same sound are still felt some how to carry with them always a different signification and force.

Let any one compare, in this view, the theology of the old Church Fathers, with the theology of modern New England, in what is commonly regarded as its most orthodox form.[16] How the two methods vary continually from one another, hardly ever presenting the same topics in the same way! The Trinity, the Incarnation, all Christ's offices and acts, the authority of the Scriptures, Baptism and the Lord's Supper, regeneration, justification, and sanctification, faith, hope, charity, the resurrection, and the life to come—all are made to have a meaning in the one case, which is not just what they are felt to mean in the other. The two schemes are not strung on the same key, and they sound accordingly no note in common. Each has its own christology, its own

---

15. [Evans, *Imputation and Impartation*, 169–75 contrasts Nevin's doctrine of justification to alternative theories.]

16. [Perhaps a reference to the Old or Moderate Calvinists, like Jedediah Morse (1761–1826), who formed a coalition to establish Andover Seminary (1807), the first seminary in America. The direct impetus for the establishment of Andover "by the orthodox Congregationalists," was the Unitarian "take-over" at Harvard. In 1809, Boston's Park Street Church was also organized as a bastion of "orthodoxy" (Noll, *History of Christianity*, 229–31; Naylor, "The Theological Seminary," 19–20).]

soteriology, its own eschatology; in one word, its own whole atmosphere of thought and habit of faith, so sharply defined and strongly marked, that it is impossible to avoid some sense of embarrassment, some feeling of strangeness, in passing out of one into the other. For one brought up in the Puritan habit of religion, it requires a new education, to be able either to understand or appreciate properly the Christianity of the ancient Fathers; as on the other hand we may be very sure, that any one of these returning to the earth would need to undergo a full revolution of thought, before he could feel himself at all at home in the bosom of Puritanism or find in it any aliment whatever for faith and piety. We have in the case, in fact, two Christianities, two radically different schemes of religion, two whole systems of divinity that never move in exactly the same line.

So much hinges on this great question of the Church, which to the view of many seems so far away from the true-central life of the Gospel. In comparison with it, as we have said before, the ordinary points of denominational controversy, the shibboleths that divide one unchurchly sect from another are only of partial, superficial interest. Such sectarian confessionalism, with all its differences, holds notwithstanding for the most part in a common system or scheme of faith, and rests in substantially the same general conception of Christianity. To pass over from one branch of it to another involves no violent revolution. It is simply to go out of one compartment of a wide and spacious mansion into another. The mansion remains the same. But the question: Church or no Church in the old Catholic sense is of a widely different nature, having to do with the very consciousness of religion itself and determining its universal order, method, and form. Its home is in the depths of Christianity, far down beneath the issues from which spring the ordinary divisions of denominations and sects.

[XVIII. What is the Root of the Difference Between the Two Systems?]

In view of such a generic difference holding between the two systems, the churchly scheme of Christianity and the unchurchly, the theology of the Creed and its opposite—a difference which lies so deep and reaches so far—it becomes a matter of peculiar interest to determine precisely what its whole character signifies and means. In one case, as we have seen, the Church is taken to be an essential constituent of the mystery of godliness, while in the other it is considered an arrangement belonging to it only in an outward adventitious way. Here we get back to the last sense of the Church Question; which is found to be at the same time strangely implicated with the right construction of the Creed, conditioning in truth the way in which all its articles are to be understood. For not only does the Creed affirm the doctrine of the Church, making it a necessary part of Christianity, and so a necessary object of faith, but it throws the entire scheme of Christianity into such a shape and form, from first to last, as imperatively requires the doctrine in this sense, and cannot be satisfied without it. The Creed is constructed throughout, both in its antecedent and consequent articles, on that view of Christianity which involves the idea of the Church in the form now stated, and makes it necessary for it to come into view just where it does in the onward flow of that good confession. This does not imply, however, that the Creed starts from the idea of the Church as its own proper principle. That which is the first question in regard to the doctrine of the Church itself, namely, what place is to be ascribed to it in the conception of Christianity, is not just the first question in regard to the theological system in which it is comprehended as a necessary article of faith. When we have said, therefore, that the Church is made in the Creed to be of the essence of Christianity, and that all the articles of the symbol are so framed as to shut faith up to this conclusion, and that it leads on thus to an entire theology of answerable form and complexion throughout—it remains still to ask: What then is that peculiarity of doctrine in the Creed, that distinguishing quality of faith, back of its doctrine of the Church, which calls this forth in its order, gives to it all its force, and imparts what we call a churchly character to the universal scheme of religion into which it enters as an organic part? What is the root or beginning of the broad difference, which reigns between the Catholic Christianity of the first ages and the Puritanic Christianity of modern times, between the theology which breathes the spirit of the Creed and the theology which breathes a different spirit between the churchly construction of the Gospel and the unchurchly? It is not easy to conceive of a theological inquiry more interesting than this, or more worthy of being followed out with right study to a right answer.

[XIX. The Spirit of the Creed: Salvation is Supernatural and therefore Historical]

Were we called upon to give in a word the distinguishing peculiarity of the Creed, in the view suggested by the inquiry, we should place it in the *historical* character it assigns to the Christian salvation, regarded as a supernatural process of grace, in opposition to every scheme which resolves it into a matter of more speculative thought. Its doctrine of the Church falls back on its doctrine of Christ, and this is made to include, from first to last, the conception of a real union between the divine and the human, the life of God and the life of man, in the person of the Mediator, carrying along with it the work of redemption, as the process of a new creation in the bosom of the old, onward to the end of time.

In the Creed, as in the New Testament, Christianity has its last ground in the mystery of the Ever Blessed and Glorious Trinity, which is exhibited as an object for faith, however, not so much in the light of a doctrine, as in the light of a fact, opening the way for the revelation which God has been pleased to make of himself through the mystery of the Incarnation. This forms, accordingly, an act of self-manifestation on the part of God, by which he is to be regarded as coming into the world in a sense in which he had not been in it before, for the purpose of redeeming and saving men from their sins. The Word became flesh. That is the beginning of the Gospel of Jesus Christ, and power to own and confess it, not as a dogma merely but as a simple historical fact, is the beginning of all faith in the proper evangelical sense of the term. The beginning of all heresy, on the other hand, lies in the open or virtual denial of this great mystery. Hence, St. John's memorable touch-stone for distinguishing true Christianity from that which is spurious and false. "Every spirit that confesseth that Jesus Christ is come in the flesh," he tells us, "is of God; and every spirit that confesseth not that Jesus Christ is come in the flesh, is not of God, and this is that spirit of antichrist, whereof ye have heard that it should come; and even now already is it in the world."[17] The spirit of antichrist, in this way, is the rationalistic temper of the natural mind which substitutes for the mystery of the incarnation in its proper form a mere notional construction of Christ's person, in which, after all, no real historical union of the divine nature with the human is allowed to have place, setting up thus in opposition to the true Christ a false shadowy image, a mere spiritualistic phantom, which is made to counterfeit his name and usurp his place. Over against all such rationalistic spiritualism, the Creed makes full earnest with the criterion of St. John. It takes up and carries out in its own simple, historical way, that notable confession of Peter, "Thou art the Christ, the Son of the Living God," in reference to which our Saviour said, "Blessed art thou, Simon Bar-jona; for flesh and blood hath not revealed it unto thee, but my Father which is in heaven."[18] The merit of Peter's faith stood in its power to break over the natural order of the world so as to see and acknowledge in the person of Christ, there actually before him, the presence of a new and higher form of existence, joining the nature of God with the nature of man in a way transcending all common understanding and thought. Thou, Jesus of Nazareth, it could say—whom we know to be in all respects a real man like ourselves, and no spirit merely in human show—Thou, the Son of Mary, art at the same time the Son of the Most High God, and as such the Messiah, the true Saviour of the world. Such precisely is the confession, which forms the burden of the Apostles' Creed. Its theme may be said to be throughout, "Christ come in the flesh." In that fact, the objective mystery of godliness (1 Tim. 3:16), it sees the whole fulness of salvation, the entire economy of redemption; and it lays itself out, accordingly, to set it forth in its necessary conditions and consequences, under a purely historical view, as the proper substance of Christianity, the one grand object of all true Christian faith. So apprehended, the Gospel is in no sense theoretical, but supremely practical. It is the presence of a supernatural fact in the world, confronting men under an outward form, carrying in itself objectively the powers of the world to come, and challenging actual submission to its claims in such view as the only way in which it is possible to be saved. Faith has to do in the case, first of all, not with any doctrines which may be supposed to flow from the fact, but with the fact itself as a simple matter of history; the history being, however, at the same time supernatural, out of the whole ordinary course of things in the world, and requiring, therefore, a very different kind of belief

---

17. [1 John 4:2–3; the scriptural text of *Antichrist* in Nevin, *One, Holy, Catholic, and Apostolic, Tome 1*.]

18. [Matt 16:16–17.]

from that which is needed to take up the facts of history in its common human form. It is a great thing—too great for the reach of mere natural thought—to believe truly that Christ has come in the flesh, that Jesus was no mere man attended by the extraordinary inspiration of the Almighty, according to the old Ebionitic view, and yet no mere shadow either, according to any of the old Gnostic theories, but that in him the Word became actually and enduringly incarnate for us men and for our salvation.

On this supernatural fact, the Creed fastens its whole attention, referring it to its necessary origin, and following it out steadily to its necessary results, all in the way of simple historical apprehension and conception. Christ, the Son of God, we are required to believe, came down from heaven, and was incarnate by the Holy Ghost of the Virgin Mary and was made man. He suffered, died, descended into hades. But it was not possible that he should be held under the power of death. He rose again; he ascended on high, leading captivity captive, and having all power given unto him in heaven and in earth. All this served only to prepare the way for his kingdom in the world through the mission of the Holy Ghost, his great ascension gift and the constitution of the Church, which is declared by St. Paul to be his body, the fulness of him that filleth all in all, and with which he has himself promised to be present always to the end of time. In the Church, accordingly, as distinguished from the natural constitution of the world, the new order of grace brought to pass by the victory of Christ over sin, death, and hell, runs its course from age to age, in the salvation of all true believers. "We confess one baptism for the remission of sins; we look for the resurrection of the dead, and the life of the world to come."

The peculiarity of the old Christian Creeds is their way of grasping and following out the historical realness of the mystery of the incarnation, so as to make full earnest with the objective, continually enduring character of the new order of life it has served to bring into the world. In this respect, it falls in with what appears to have been the reigning tone of the Apostolic preaching, as we are made acquainted with it in the Acts of the Apostles. The same peculiarity runs through all the theological literature of the Ancient Church, as it entered also into its universal life. The object of faith is made to be always Christ in the flesh, Christ coming into the world, working, dying, rising again, conquering, reigning, carrying forward his kingdom in the most real way to the end of time. The whole Gospel is regarded as being in this way a *mystery,* not in the sense of an unfathomable, incomprehensible doctrine merely, but in the light of a fact not resolvable into the ordinary constitution of the world, which has nevertheless at a certain time entered into it, from the depths of eternity, under the most actual form, serving to bring out the inmost purpose of God in reference to man, the "mystery of godliness" (1 Tim. 3:16); the mystery hid from ages and generations, but now manifested to the saints (Col. 1:26); the mystery which from the beginning of the world was hid in God, who created all things by Jesus Christ, to the intent that now unto the principalities and powers in heavenly places might be known by the Church the manifold wisdom of God, according to the eternal purpose which he purposed in Christ

Jesus our Lord (Eph. 3:9–11); the mystery of grace which was given us by God's purpose in Christ Jesus before the world began but is now "made manifest"—the purpose having passed into supernatural act—by the "appearing" of our Saviour Jesus Christ, who hath abolished death, and hath brought life and immortality to light through the Gospel, which in such view is nothing more nor less than his own glorious advent into the world creating and bringing to pass what it serves thus to reveal (2 Tim. 1:9–10). Such an apprehension of the Gospel involves and draws after it necessarily the old Catholic idea of the Church as it is presented to us in the Creed.

[XX. Unchurchly Christianity and the Incarnation]

All heresy, so far as Christianity is concerned, starts in the form of unbelieving opposition to this mystery, refusing to see and acknowledge in Christ the objective, abiding presence of the new creation—the world of grace in full parallel with the world of nature—under its own proper historical character and form. Wherever it may end, it is sure to begin always, consciously or unconsciously, in a wrong view of the Incarnation. It does not lay hold of the fact with any just sense of its terms and conditions, so as to be borne along by the outward authority of it in its own direction—the only true conception of faith; but turns it rather into a mere matter of speculative contemplation, by which it comes to be at last nothing more in truth than a thought or notion in the mind itself, substituted for the fact it pretends to believe. The mind thus does not pass over really into the objective sphere of the christological revelation, as it is in its own nature, but remains rationalistically bound all the time to its simply natural order of existence, fetching the mystery down to this, as it were, instead of rising above it by its means. The result is such a separation of the natural from the supernatural in Christ, and so in Christianity throughout, as will not allow them to come to any organic, abiding, and truly historical union whatever. Broad exemplifications of this false way of thinking we have in the strange dreamings of the old Gnostics, and afterwards again in the more subtle errors of Nestorius and Eutyches,[19] by the coming round in opposite directions to the same end—such a sublimation of Christ's divinity, as left no room for the conception of his true and proper humanity in one and the same person, and served thus to transfer the entire mystery from the region of real outward history to the region of unreal inward imagination and fancy. These ancient heresies have been long since surmounted and condemned by the orthodox theology of the Church. But the spirit that gave birth to them, which is nothing else than the natural indisposition of the human mind to confess that "Christ is come in the flesh," still lives, we may be sure, and will continue to do so, and to make itself felt as a "false spirit," to the end of time. It is a spirit too which may be readily recognized always by

---

19. [*Dictionary of the Christian Church*, 577, 1105, 1138–9, provides background on Nestorius and Eutyches. Nevin discussed these alleged errors in *Antichrist*, in *One, Holy, Catholic, and Apostolic*, Tome 1.]

being brought into comparison with what we have just found to be the true spirit of Christianity as it breathes in the Creed. The distinguishing peculiarity of the Creed is its sense of the actual, the objective, the outwardly historical, in the mystery of the Word made flesh, the regard it has throughout to the enduring realness of the new creation brought to pass in the world by Christ Jesus. Any system, then, which refuses to conform inwardly to this rule of faith must be distinguished in the nature of the case by the opposite principle, a tendency, namely, to look away from the objective realness of the new creation in Christ, and to substitute for this a mere theoretical apprehension by which the mystery is lifted out of its own necessary historical conditions and made to resolve itself at last, more or less, into a scheme of doctrinal abstractions.

In this way, we reach what must be considered the fundamental difference, between the churchly and the unchurchly schemes of Christianity, the Catholic order of faith and the Puritanic, the theology of the Creed and all theology besides.

[Conclusion]

Here it is then, that the full theological significance of the doctrine of the Church comes finally into view. Entering as it does organically into the construction of the Creed, it becomes necessarily a test or criterion by which to determine the quality of all Christian belief, as either corresponding or not corresponding with the proper sense of this symbol. The idea of the Church presented in the Creed is inseparably joined with its general conception of the historical nature of Christianity, proceeds with necessary development, we may say, from its way of looking at Christ's person and work. Not to see the force of the idea, then, and to have no sense of its necessity, is to stand as a matter of course, not in this habit or method of faith at all, but in some other form of belief altogether which, in such case, cannot fail to labor under the general christological defect that is found to characterise necessarily any theological system bearing a different type from the Creed. An unchurchly spirit, in other words, is in reference to Christianity always to a greater or less extent, a Gnostic spirit, tending to sublimate the true historical character of the Gospel into a spiritualistic abstraction and causing it to become thus a doctrine or theory rather than the presence of a perpetual fact, a subject of opinion rather than an object of faith. The charge, we are aware, is serious, but it is not made lightly or at random; the truth of it is easily established, we think, both from the nature of the case itself, properly understood, and from actual observation.

It matters not, that those who are under the power of this spirit may profess and believe themselves really to hold sound christological views according to the standard of the Creed, rejecting and condemning the heresies which struck at the true constitution of Christ's person in the first Christian ages. The soul of an error is not so much bound to its first outward forms that it must necessarily die and pass away when these come to an end. It may migrate into new bodies and thus walk the earth as before. Particularly must this be the case with the error now before us, which St. John declares to be the root or salient point of all contradiction to the great mystery of godliness revealed in Christ, and which cannot fail in such view, therefore, to make itself felt as long as this contradiction shall last, counterfeiting the mystery and setting up its own mock image (the "mystery of iniquity"[20] shall we call it?) in its room and place. Conquered in one form, it may be expected to appear still again in some other form, more refined it may be and plausible, but involving always in the end the same sense. It is not enough to confess that Christ has come in the flesh, in the terms of the Creed— "conceived by the Holy Ghost and born of the Virgin Mary"—if the confession break down afterwards with any part of what necessarily follows from this fact, as we have it carried out in the same rule of faith. For the objective realness of any fact includes its necessary connections, its historical antecedents and consequents, no less than the naked fact itself; and to be believed at all truly—to be apprehended as a reality and not as a mere dream or fancy—it must be so believed that these shall be owned and acknowledged at the same time. To deny the supernatural birth of Christ on the one hand, or to call in question the truth of his resurrection on the other, would be to turn the whole mystery of the Incarnation into a myth, though it were pretended never so strongly in the same breath to accept it as true. And so with the points that follow in the Creed, if indeed they *do* follow in the actual order of the mystery itself, as they are made to stand forth consecutively here in the order of faith. They must be believed in order that there may be any full historical faith in the advent of Jesus Christ into the world; and not to believe them, is virtually to make such faith null by turning its object into a Gnostic fiction, whatever pains may be taken to use at the same time, as far as they go, the old orthodox terms in reference to Christ's person. In the system of the Creed, the article of the Church is made to stand prominent among these points, and the assumption is, of course, that the coming of Christ in the flesh, regarded in its proper historical view, leads on to this in the way of necessary consequence, just as really as it draws after it his glorification at the right of God and the mission of the Holy Ghost. Not to have faith in the Church then—not to have any sense of its historical necessity in the general mystery of Christianity—as it implies in the first place a different conception of the Gospel from that which is presented in the Creed, involves also, in the second place necessarily, a want of harmony to the same extent with what we have seen to be the distinguishing peculiarity of this old rule of faith, the stress namely, which it lays throughout on the historical realness of the Incarnation. As the christology of the Creed, the way in which it looks at Christ's person and confesses his coming in the flesh involves in the end the idea of the Church, it follows as a matter of course that those who can feel their faith complete, their religious system round and full without it, must have the mystery of the Incarnation before their minds in some different way. From the nature of the case, thus, the unchurchly spirit, not falling in fully with the sound christological sense of the Creed, is found to carry with it always some portion of the leaven of Gnosticism.

20. [2 Thess 2:7; widely interpreted throughout the history of Christian belief as the Antichrist.]

Document 4: "Thoughts on the Church" (1858)

It requires only small observation to verify this conclusion in actual life. The unchurchly spirit prevails largely in the religious world at the present time, under all imaginable varieties of form; and it is easy enough to see, that just in proportion to its power, it is everywhere a spirit unfavorable to a sound and just apprehension of the mystery of the Incarnation, regarded in the historical light of the Creed. Its tendency is universally towards such a spiritualism here, as goes finally to remand the mystery from the world of fact into the world of fancy, causing it to dissolve thus into thin air. In one direction, this amounts in fact to an open giving up of the higher nature of Christ altogether, as among Socinians and Unitarians; in which case, it is especially worthy of notice, how completely the idea of the Church is made to perish at the same time. Infidelity in such form may pretend still to honor Christianity and to make high account of the Bible, but it can never be churchly. There is an inward contradiction, plainly, between its rationalistic doctrine of Christ and the old Catholic doctrine of the Church. The first does not lead over in any way to the last (as in the Creed), but excludes it, showing that there is a natural affinity thus between the want of faith in the Church and the want of faith in Christ. But the spiritualism which is opposed to a just view to Christ's person may take another form, not denying his higher nature but, on the contrary, so exalting this in thought as to sink out of sight, more or less, the historical verity of his lower nature; and it is in this character more particularly, that it claims attention and observation, as going hand in hand with the unchurchly spirit in the modern religious world.

Of this we have a striking example in the history of the Quakers. Their Christianity was from the start unchurchly in the lowest degree—owning no dependence on outward ministrations, outward sacraments, outward ordinances and arrangements of any kind. It repudiated in fact the universal conception of the Church in the old Catholic sense; while it professed, notwithstanding, the highest veneration for Christ, and affected to make more of his supernatural presence and power than the whole Christian world besides. But it is easy enough now to see, that this pretension was vain; and that what the system honored in such view was not so much the real historical Christ of the Gospel, as a Gnostic fiction rather made to bear his name. With the progress of time, the error has worked itself out more and more into view—its sublimated conception of Christ resolving itself into the "inward light" of mere natural reason—until it seems ready now at last to fall over into the arms of open infidelity.

In the case of other unchurchly sects, the want of a sound historical sense of the mystery of the Incarnation is no less certain, although it may not be so immediately and broadly apparent. One general evidence of it is found in the simple fact itself, before noticed, that they have so little complacency in the Creed, as feeling it to be in some way opposed to their own habit of thought, not merely in its doctrine of the Church, but in its whole theological construction. The symbol has for them a certain peculiarity throughout which is felt to be mysteriously interwoven with the presence of this article in its place, and, for this reason, it is not to their taste. But what this peculiarity is we have now seen. It is nothing more nor less than the objective, historical light in which the fact of Christ's coming in the flesh is made to stand in this ancient rule of faith, imparting a corresponding character to its whole conception of Christianity. Out of this way of believing in the Incarnation grows forth its doctrine of the Church, and also its general churchly bearing and tone. Want of sympathy, thus, with the ecclesiastical spirit of the Creed is in truth want of sympathy at last with its christological spirit. In having no taste for the formulary then, those unchurchly sects show themselves in full proportion to their unchurchliness, estranged from its historical apprehension of the Christian mystery, and so under the power of a faith which must ever be as differing from this, more or less Gnostically spiritualistic in its character. This is the true secret at bottom of their silent prejudice against the Creed, as it serves to explain also the true nature of their bad understanding generally with the Christianity of the first ages.

Still farther practical proof, ample and full, of the charge here preferred against the unchurchly spirit, as it reigns among Puritanic sects of the better class, is to be found in the prevailing character of their entire theology and religious life. The Church system of the Creed, we have already seen, not only rules the sense of its own articles throughout but reaches through these to all Christian doctrine and practice, producing a style of Christianity which is very different from all that may exist under any other form. The principle of this difference it now appears, is not just the doctrine of the Church itself in the form in which it is here made to be a necessary part of the Christian faith, but the Christology which lies behind it—the peculiar way in which the coming of Christ in the flesh is here apprehended and confessed. This it is—this historical apprehension of the great fact of the Incarnation in distinction from all Gnostic spiritualism—that calls out the article of the Church, among other mysteries, in its place, and communicates a churchly spirit at the same time to the whole symbol, and to the universal religious system also into which the symbol naturally runs. It follows therefore, that all religious thinking which is not ruled by this spirit must stand, so far as that is the case, in a view of the Incarnation which fails to make full earnest with the objective historical realness of the fact in the way of the Creed; the result of which must be a certain tinge of Gnosticism, extending in the end to its whole scheme of faith. The peculiar genius of the unchurchly system of Christianity in this way, as distinguished from the theological spirit of the Creed, will be found on examination to penetrate every part of its doctrinal and practical life. Any such examination, however, would amount to a comparison of the system in its details with the opposite form of Christianity, a comparative view of the Catholic and Puritanic schemes of religion in particulars, such as we have no mind to enter upon at the present time.

J. W. N.
Lancaster, Pa.

Bibliography

WORKS INCLUDED IN THIS TOME:

Nevin, John Williamson. "Catholicism." *The Mercersburg Review* 3 (1851) 1–26.
———. "The Christian Ministry." *The Mercersburg Review* 7 (1855) 68–115. Reprinted as *The Christian Ministry*. Chambersburg, PA: M. Kiefer, 1855.
———. "Hodge on the Ephesians." *The Mercersburg Review* 9 (1857) 46–83, 192–245. Reprinted as *A review of A Commentary on the Epistle to the Ephesians by Charles Hodge, D.D., Professor in the Theological Seminary, Princeton, N.J.* New York: Robert Carter & Brothers, 1856.
———. "Thoughts on the Church." *The Mercersburg Review* 10 (1858) 169–198, 399–426.

WORKS CONSULTED IN THIS TOME:

Acts and Proceedings of the Synod of the German Reformed Church in the United States at Harrisburg, Dauphin Co., Pa., October, 1859. Chambersburg, PA: M. Keiffer, 1859.
"American Peace Society Records, 1828–1947." Swarthmore College Peace Collection. http://www.swarthmore.edu/library/peace/DG001-025/DG003APS.htm.
Appel, Theodore. *The Life and Work of John Williamson Nevin*. Philadelphia: Reformed Church Publication House, 1889.
Avis, Paul D. L. *The Church in the Theology of the Reformers*. New Foundations Theological Library. Atlanta: John Knox, 1981.
Bavinck, Herman. *Reformed Dogmatics*. Vol. 4: Holy Spirit, Church, and New Creation. Edited by John Bolt. Translated by John Vriend. Grand Rapids, MI: Baker Academic, 2008.
Bigler, Robert M. *The Politics of German Protestantism: The Rise of the Protestant Church Elite in Prussia,* 1815–1848. Los Angeles: The University of California Press, 1972.
Borneman, Adam S. *Church, Sacrament, and American Democracy: The Social and Political Dimension of John Williamson Nevin's Theology of Incarnation*. Eugene, OR: Wipf & Stock, 2011.
Calvin, John. *A Treatise on the Eternal Predestination of God*. Translated by Henry P. Cole. London: Wertheim and Macintosh, 1856.

BIBLIOGRAPHY

Chandler, David. Introduction to *William Taylor of Norwich: A Study of the Influence of Modern German Literature in England (1897)*. By Georg Herzfeld. Translated by Astrid Wind. http://www.rc.umd.edu/sites/default/files/chandler_herzfeld.pdf.

Conser Jr., Walter H. *Church and Confession: Conservative Theologians in Germany, England, and America, 1815–1866*. Macon, GA: Mercer University Press, 1984.

Crouse, Robert D. "Problems of Ecclesiology: Patristic Perspectives." Conference report of the Atlantic Theological Conference. In *The Idea of the Church in Historical Development*, edited by D. A. Petley. Charlottetown, PE: St. Peter Publications, 1995. http://www.stpeter.org/crouse/writings/ecclesiology.htm.

DeBie, Linden J. Biographical Essay in *Coena Mystica: Debating Reformed Eucharistic Theology*. By John Williamson Nevin and Charles Hodge. Edited by Linden J. DeBie. Mercersburg Theology Study Series, vol. 2. Eugene, OR: Wipf & Stock, 2013.

———. Editor's Introduction to *The Mystical Presence and the Doctrine of the Reformed Church on the Lord's Supper*. By John Williamson Nevin. Edited by Linden J. DeBie. Mercersburg Theology Study Series, vol. 1. Eugene, OR: Wipf & Stock, 2012.

———. *Speculative Theology and Common-Sense Religion: Mercersburg and the Conservative Roots of American Religion*. Eugene, OR: Wipf & Stock, 2008.

Dictionary of the Christian Church. Edited by F. L. Cross and E. A. Livingstone. 3rd ed. Oxford: Oxford University Press, 1997.

DiPuccio, William. *The Interior Sense of Scripture: The Sacred Hermeneutics of John Williamson Nevin*. Macon, Georgia: Mercer University Press, 1998.

———. "Nevin's Idealistic Philosophy." In *Reformed Confessionalism in Nineteenth-Century America: Essays on the Thought of John Williamson Nevin*, edited by Sam Hamstra, Jr. and Arie J. Griffioen, 43–67. Lanham: Scarecrow, 1995.

Drummond, Lewis. *Spurgeon: Prince of Preachers*. Grand Rapids, MI: Kregel, 1992.

England, John. *A View of Arminianism Compared to Moderate Calvinism: Wherein is showed the Dangerous Tendency of Arminian Doctrine Compared to Moderate Calvinism*. London: T. Parkhurst, J. Clark, and J. Miller, 1707.

Evans, William B. *Imputation and Impartation: Union with Christ in American Reformed Theology*. Eugene, Oregon: Wipf & Stock, 2009.

Forbes, John. "Christ the Head of the Church." In *Lectures on the Headship of Christ, Embodied in the Constitution and Illustrated in the History of the Church of Scotland*, 1–26. Glasgow: William Collins, 1840.

Gerrish, Brian A. *Tradition and the Modern World: Reformed Theology in the Nineteenth Century*. Chicago: University of Chicago Press, 1978.

Gockel, Matthias. "New Perspectives on an Old Debate: Friedrich Schleiermacher's Essay on Election." *International Journal of Systematic Theology* 6, no. 3 (July 2004) 301–318.

Hatch, Nathan O. *Democratization of American Christianity*. New Haven: Yale University Press, 1991.

Hall, Charles. *An Oration Delivered at Plymouth December 22, 1824*. Boston: Cummings, Hollard, 1825.

Hamstra Jr., Sam. General Introduction to *One, Holy, Catholic, and Apostolic, Tome 1: Nevin's Writings on Ecclesiology (1844–1849)*. By John Williamson Nevin. Edited by Sam Hamstra Jr. Mercersburg Theology Study Series, vol. 5. Eugene, OR: Wipf & Stock, 2017.

———. "Nevin on the Pastoral Office." In *Reformed Confessionalism in Nineteenth-Century America: Essays on the Thought of John Williamson Nevin*, edited by Sam Hamstra Jr. and Arie J. Griffioen, 169–191. Lanham: Scarecrow, 1995.

———, ed. *The Reformed Pastor: Lectures on Pastoral Theology by John Williamson Nevin.* Princeton Theological Monograph Series. Eugene, OR: Wipf & Stock, 2006.

Hart, Darryl G. *John Williamson Nevin: High Church Calvinist.* Phillipsburg, NJ: Presbyterian and Reformed, 2005.

Hirsch, Emanuel. *Geschichte der neuern evangelischen Theologie im Zusammenhang mit den allgemeinen Bewegungen des europäischen Denkens.* Funfter Band. 4. Auflage. Gütersloh: C. Bertelsmann, 1951, 1968.

Hodge, Charles. "Idea of the Church." *The Biblical Repertory and Princeton Review* (April 1853) 249–90; (July 1853) 339–89.

Hoffecker, W. Andrew. *Piety and the Princeton Theologians: Archibald Alexander, Charles Hodge, and Benjamin Warfield.* Grand Rapids, MI: Baker, 1981.

Kremer, Abner R. *A Biographical Sketch of John Williamson Nevin.* Reading, PA: Daniel Miller, 1890.

Layman, David W. General Introduction to *Born of Water and the Spirit: Essays on the Sacraments and Christian Formation.* By John Williamson Nevin, Philip Schaff, and Emanuel V. Gerhart. Edited by David W. Layman. Mercersburg Theology Study Series, vol. 6. Eugene, OR: Wipf & Stock, 2016.

———. "Revelation in the Praxis of the Liturgical Community: A Jewish-Christian Dialogue, with Special Reference to the Work of John Williamson Nevin and Franz Rosenzweig." PhD diss., Temple University, 1994.

Littlejohn, W. Bradford. *The Mercersburg Theology and the Quest for Reformed Catholicity.* Eugene, OR: Wipf & Stock, 2009.

———. "Sectarianism and the Search for Visible Catholicity: Lessons from John Nevin and Richard Hooker." *Theology Today* 71 (2015) 404–415.

———. Series Introduction to *The Mystical Presence and the Doctrine of the Reformed Church on the Lord's Supper.* By John Williamson Nevin. Edited by Linden J. DeBie. Mercersburg Theology Study Series, vol. 1. Eugene, OR: Wipf & Stock, 2012.

Loetscher, Lefferts A. *Facing the Enlightenment and Pietism: Archibald Alexander and the Founding of Princeton Theological Seminary.* Contributions to the Study of Religion, no. 8. Westport, CT: Greenwood, 1983.

Maxwell, Jack Martin. *Worship and Reformed Theology: The Liturgical Lessons of Mercersburg.* Pittsburgh Theological Monograph Series, no. 10. Pittsburgh: Pickwick, 1976.

Mulsow, Martin and Jan Rohls, ed. *Socinianism and Arminianism: Antitrinitarians, Calvinists and Cultural Exchange in Seventeenth-Century England.* Leiden, Netherlands: Brill, 2005.

Murray, Iain H. *Revival and Revivalism: The Making and Marring of American Evangelicalism 1750–1858.* Carlisle, PA: Banner of Truth Trust, 1994.

Naidu, Ashish J. "Reading and Interpretation of Scriptures in the Early Church." In *Transformed in Christ: Christology and the Christian Life in John Chrysostom*, 18–82. Eugene, OR: Wipf & Stock, 2012.

Naylor, Natalie A. "The Theological Seminary in the Configuration of American Higher Education: The Ante-Bellum Years." *History of Education Quarterly* 17, no. 1 (Spring, 1977) 17–30.

Nevin, John Williamson. *The Ambassador of God: or the True Spirit of the Christian Ministry as Represented in Jesus Christ.* A Sermon Preached in the Ger. Ref. Church, Chambersburg, Pa., July 10, 1842; at the Ordination and Installation of the Rev. W. Wilson Bonnell, as Pastor of Said Congregation. Chambersburg, PA: German Reformed Church, 1842.

———. "The Anglican Crisis." *Mercersburg Review* 3 (1851) 359–98.

———. "The Apostles' Creed." *Mercersburg Review* 1 (1849) 105–127.

———. "The Bread of Life: A Communion Sermon." In *Born of Water and the Spirit: Essays on the Sacraments and Christian Formation*, 214–44. By John Williamson Nevin, Philip Schaff, and Emanuel V. Gerhart. Edited by David W. Layman. Mercersburg Theology Study Series, vol. 6. Eugene, OR: Wipf & Stock, 2016.

———. "Cyprian." *Mercersburg Review* 4 (1852) 259–77, 335–87, 417–52, 513–63.

———. "Early Christianity." *Mercersburg Review* 3 (1851) 461–90, 513–62, [vol. 4] 1–54. Reprinted in *Catholic and Reformed: Selected Theological Writings of John Williamson Nevin*, edited by Charles Yrigoyen Jr. and George H. Bricker, 177–310. Pittsburgh Original Texts and Translations, no. 3. Pittsburgh: Pickwick, 1978.

———. "Election Not Contrary to a Free Gospel." *Presbyterian Preacher* 1 & 2 (1832–1834) 209–24.

———. "Faith, Freedom, and Reverence." *Mercersburg Review* 2 (1850) 97–116. Reprinted in *The Mercersburg Theology*, edited by James Hastings Nichols, 286–306. New York: Oxford University Press, 1966.

———. "Human Freedom." *American Review: A Whig Journal Devoted to Politics and Literature*, n.s., 1, no. 4 (1848) 406–18. Reprinted in *Human Freedom, and A Plea for Philosophy: Two Essays*. Mercersburg, PA: P. A. Rice, 1850.

———. "Inaugural Address of Professor Nevin." In *Addresses Delivered at the Inauguration of Rev. J. W. Nevin, D.D., as Professor of Theology in the Theological Seminary of the German Reformed Church, Mercersburg, PA., May 20th, 1840*, 13–28. Chambersburg, Pa.: German Reformed Church, 1840.

———. "The Internal Sense of Holy Scripture." *Reformed Quarterly Review* 30 (1883) 5–39.

———. "Jesus and the Resurrection." In *The Incarnate Word: Selected Writings on Christology*, 139–161. By John Williamson Nevin, Philip Schaff, and Daniel Gans. Edited by William B. Evans. Mercersburg Theology Study Series, vol. 4. Eugene, OR: Wipf & Stock, 2014.

———. Letter to J. A. McMasters, February 26, 1853. Lancastriana Collection. Philip Schaff Library, Lancaster, PA. Microfilm of originals in the Brownson Archives, Notre Dame University Library.

———. "Nature and Grace." *Mercersburg Review* 19 (1872) 485–509.

———. "New Creation in Christ." In *The Incarnate Word: Selected Writings on Christology*, 32–45. By John Williamson Nevin, Philip Schaff, and Daniel Gans. Edited by William B. Evans. Mercersburg Theology Study Series, vol. 4. Eugene, OR: Wipf & Stock, 2014.

———. "Nevin and Bushnell: Christian Nurture and Baptism." In *Born of Water and the Spirit: Essays on the Sacraments and Christian Formation*, 34–77. By John Williamson Nevin, Philip Schaff, and Emanuel V. Gerhart. Edited by David W. Layman. Mercersburg Theology Study Series, vol. 6. Eugene, OR: Wipf & Stock, 2016.

———. "Noel on Baptism." In *Born of Water and the Spirit: Essays on the Sacraments and Christian Formation*, 78–115. By John Williamson Nevin, Philip Schaff, and Emanuel V. Gerhart. Edited by David W. Layman. Mercersburg Theology Study Series, vol. 6. Eugene, OR: Wipf & Stock, 2016.

———. "The Old Doctrine of Christian Baptism." In *Born of Water and the Spirit: Essays on the Sacraments and Christian Formation*, 196–213. By John Williamson Nevin, Philip Schaff, and Emanuel V. Gerhart. Edited by David W. Layman. Mercersburg Theology Study Series, vol. 6. Eugene, OR: Wipf & Stock, 2016.

———. "Once for All." *Mercersburg Review* 17 (1870) 100–124.

———. *One, Holy, Catholic, and Apostolic, Tome 1: Nevin's Writings on Ecclesiology (1844–1849)*. Edited by Sam Hamstra Jr. Mercersburg Theology Study Series, vol. 5. Eugene, OR: Wipf & Stock, 2017.

———. *Personal Holiness: A Lecture Delivered, June, 1837, at the Opening of the Summer Term in the Western Theological Seminary*. Pittsburgh, PA: William Allinder, 1837.

———. "Puritanism and the Creed." *Mercersburg Review* 1 (1849) 585–607.

———. "Sartorius on the Person and Work of Christ." In *The Incarnate Word: Selected Writings on Christology*, 4–28. By John Williamson Nevin, Philip Schaff, and Daniel Gans. Edited by William B. Evans. Mercersburg Theology Study Series, vol. 4. Eugene, OR: Wipf & Stock, 2014.

———. "The Unity of the Apostles' Creed." *Mercersburg Review* 16 (1869) 313–317.

———. "Wilberforce on the Eucharist." In *Born of Water and the Spirit: Essays on the Sacraments and Christian Formation*, 134–155. By John Williamson Nevin, Philip Schaff, and Emanuel V. Gerhart. Edited by David W. Layman. Mercersburg Theology Study Series, vol. 6. Eugene, OR: Wipf & Stock, 2016.

———. "Wilberforce on the Incarnation." In *The Incarnate Word: Selected Writings on Christology*, 49–86. By John Williamson Nevin, Philip Schaff, and Daniel Gans. Edited by William B. Evans. Mercersburg Theology Study Series, vol. 4. Eugene, OR: Wipf & Stock, 2014.

Nevin, John Williamson, and Charles Hodge. *Coena Mystica: Debating Reformed Eucharistic Theology*. Edited by Linden J. DeBie. Mercersburg Theology Study Series, vol. 2. Eugene, OR: Wipf & Stock, 2013.

Nesti, Donald S. "Early Quaker Ecclesiology." *Quaker Religious Thought* 47 (1978) 4–34. http://digitalcommons.georgefox.edu/qrt/vol47/iss1/4.

Nichols, James Hastings, ed. *Mercersburg Theology*. New York: Oxford University Press, 1966. Reprint, Eugene, OR: Wipf & Stock, 2007.

———. *Romanticism in American Theology: Nevin and Schaff at Mercersburg*. University of Chicago Press, 1961. Reprint, Eugene, OR: Wipf & Stock, 2006.

Nikolajsen, Jeppe Bach. *The Distinctive Identity of the Church: A Constructive Study of the Post-Christendom Theologies of Lesslie Newbigin and John Howard Yoder*. Eugene, OR: Pickwick, 2015.

Noll, Mark A. *A History of Christianity in the United States and Canada*. Grand Rapids, MI: Eerdmans, 1992.

OED Online. June 2016. Oxford: Oxford University Press.

Paley, William. *Horce Paulince; or the Truth of the Scripture History of St. Paul evinced, by a Comparison of the Epistles which bear his name with the Acts of the Apostles and with one another*. London: n. p., 1790.

Payne, John B. "Schaff and Nevin, Colleagues at Mercersburg: The Church Question." *Church History* 61, no. 2 (June 1992) 169–190.

Peck, T. E. *Notes on Ecclesiology*. Second Edition. Richmond, VA.: Presbyterian Committee, 1892.

Pelikan, Jaroslav. *The Emergence of the Catholic Tradition (100–600)*. Chicago and London: The University of Chicago Press, 1971.

Pétrement, Simone. *A Separate God: The Christian Origins of Gnosticism*. Translated by Carol Harrison. New York: HarperCollins, 1990.

Ramsey, Michael. *The Gospel and the Catholic Church*. London: Longmans, Green, 1936.

Rauch, Frederick A. "Ecclesiastical Historiography in Germany." *American Biblical Repository* 10 (1837) 297–317. Reprinted in *Reformed Church Review* 9 (1905) 380–402.

———. *Psychology; or, A View of the Human Soul*. New York: M. W. Dodd, 1840. 4th ed., rev. and imp., 1846.

Sailhamer, John. "John August Ernesti: The Role of History in Biblical Interpretation." *Journal of the Evangelical Theological Society* 44 (June 2001) 193–206.

Schaff, Philip. *History of the Creeds of Christendom*. Three Volumes. New York: Harper & Brothers, 1877.

———. *The Principle of Protestantism*. In *The Development of the Church: "The Principle of Protestantism" and other Historical Writings of Philip Schaff*, 35–205. Translated by John W. Nevin. Edited by David R. Bains and Theodore Louis Trost. Mercersburg Theology Study Series, vol. 3. Eugene, OR: Wipf & Stock, 2016.

———. *What is Church History? A Vindication of the Idea of Historical Development*. In *The Development of the Church: "The Principle of Protestantism" and other Historical Writings of Philip Schaff*, 232–316. Edited by David R. Bains and Theodore Louis Trost. Mercersburg Theology Study Series, vol. 3. Eugene, OR: Wipf & Stock, 2016.

Scott, Donald. "For the Purpose of Mutual Improvement: Lyceums, Debating Societies and Popular Entertainment." Old Sturbridge Village, Sturbridge, MA. http://resources.osv.org/explore_learn/document_viewer.php?DocID=1015.

Shantz, Douglas H. *An Introduction to German Pietism: Protestant Renewal at the Dawn of Modern Europe*. Baltimore: John Hopkins University Press, 2013.

Stewart, John W. "Mediating the Center: Charles Hodge on American Science, Language, Literature, and Politics." *Studies in Reformed Theology and History* 3, no. 1 (Winter 1995) 1–114.

Sykes, Norman. *Old Priest and New Presbyter*. Cambridge: Cambridge University Press, 1956.

Thompson, Bard, and George H. Bricker. Editors' preface to *The Mystical Presence and Other Writings on the Eucharist*. Lancaster Series on the Mercersburg Theology, vol. 4. Philadelphia: United Church, 1966.

Trost, Theodore Louis, Lee Barrett, and David Bains. General Introduction to *The Development of the Church: "The Principle of Protestantism" and other Historical Writings of Philip Schaff*. By Philip Schaff. Edited by David R. Bains and Theodore Louis Trost. Mercersburg Theology Study Series, vol. 3. Eugene, OR: Wipf & Stock, 2016.

Turretin, Francisco. *Institutio Theologiae Elencticae*. Pars Tertia Et Ultima. Geneva: Samuelem de Tournes, 1686.

Wallace, Peter J. "The Defense of the Forgotten Center: Charles Hodge and the Enigma of Emancipation in Antebellum America." *Journal of Presbyterian History* 75 (Fall 1997) 165–77.

———. "History and Sacrament: John Williamson Nevin and Charles Hodge on the Lord's Supper." *Mid-America Journal of Theology* 11 (2000) 171–201.

Wentz, Richard E. *John Williamson Nevin: American Theologian*. New York: Oxford University Press, 1997.

Yrigoyen Jr., Charles and George H. Bricker, ed. *Catholic and Reformed: Selected Theological Writings of John Williamson Nevin*. Pittsburgh Original Texts and Translations, no. 3. Pittsburgh: Pickwick, 1978.

WORKS CITED IN THE ORIGINAL

[where possible, the edition likely used by Nevin is provided; otherwise, either the original edition or a more modern edition is given]

Calvin, John. *Institutes of the Christian Religion,* 2 vols. Translated by Ford Lewis Battles, edited by John T. McNeill. Philadelphia: Westminster, 1960.

"The Church—Its Perpetuity." *Biblical Repertory and Princeton Review* (October 1856) 689–715.

Griffin, Edward Dorr. *Sermons Not Before Published on Various Practical Subjects.* New York: M. W. Dodd, 1844.

Hodge, Charles. *A Commentary on the Epistle to the Ephesians.* New York: Robert Carter & Brothers, 1856.

Nevin, John Williamson. *The Mystical Presence and the Doctrine of the Reformed Church on the Lord's Supper.* Edited by Linden J. DeBie. Mercersburg Theology Study Series, vol. 1. Eugene, OR: Wipf & Stock, 2012.

Paley, William. *Works of William Paley.* Philadelphia: Woodward, 1835.

Winebrenner, John, ed. *History of All the Religious Denominations in the United States: Containing Authentic Accounts of the Rise and Progress, Faith and Practice, Localities and Statistics, of the Different Persuasions: Written Expressly for the Work by Fifty-Three Eminent Authors, Belonging to the Respective Denominations.* Second, Improved and Portrait Edition. Harrisburg: John Winebrenner, 1848.

Subject and Author Index

Act of Supremacy, 45
Adam, 25, 90, 99, 100–101, 106, 115
Ambassador of God, 36
American Bible Society, 143
American Tract Society, 143
American Peace Society, 31
Annihilationism, 25
Antichrist, 4, 55–56, 165
Anxious Bench, 1–2
Appel, Theodore, 60, 129–30
Apostles' Creed, 3, 9, 11–12, 31–32, 41, 45, 53, 77, 91, 99–100, 102–3, 111–12, 123–24, 130, 140
    as *regula fidei*, 153–57
    common faith of, 151–52
    interconnection of the articles of, 157–60
    no confessionalism without, 160–62
    spirit of, 164–67
Apostolic Succession, 48, 54–55, 118, 137n, 145
Arminianism, 71–72, 78, 87, 89, 91, 94–95, 102, 134, 138
Augsburg Confession, 153
Augustine, 103, 137, 149

Baptists, 134, 142, 145–46, 150, 156
Baxter, Richard, 2
Book of Common Prayer, 129

Calvin, John, 44, 61, 73, 82, 91–93, 103, 118
Calvinism, 60, 79, 81–82, 86, 89–90, 134
    and Arminianism *see* Arminianism
Catholic Apostolic Liturgy, 129
children, 9, 28–29n, 135, 140
China, 21, 24, 28
Christ
    ascension, 38, 40–45, 99, 112, 118, 123, 148, 166
    incarnation, 4, 10–11, 17, 26, 39, 55, 72, 74, 99, 101, 109, 113, 162–71
    reign of, 17n, 18, 24, 42, 44, 74, 100–101, 117
    Second Adam, 26

Christianity
    mission of, 16–21, 24
    new creation, 18, 23, 39, 41–42, 56, 63, 88, 95, 97, 99–102, 106, 108, 116–17, 158–59, 162–67
    redemption, 18, 26
    wholeness of, 25, 26, 50, 54, 115 *see also* Church, wholeness of
Chrysostom, John, 121n, 137
Church, 98–101
    Actual and Ideal, 3
    Churchly and unchurchly compared, 162–64
    development of, 3
    dualism, 77
    idea of, 143–46, 150–51
    living constitution, 50, 141–42
    marks of, 9–10
    missionary nature, 15–16, 21
    as power of Christianity, 142–43
    supernatural, 44
    and State, 22, 24, 45
    Thoughts on, 131–33
    as invisible, 60, 75–78, 80–81, 110, 146n
    as visible, 16, 37, 111, 146n
    wholeness of, 2, 10, 14–15, 29, 32
Church of England, 139
Church Question
    accusers of, 138–41
    answered, 148–50
    controversy over, 146–47
    essence of, 147–48
    judgment of the ages on, 136–38
    person asking, 134–36
    primacy and unity of, 132–33
    significance of, 133–34
Conser, Walter, 139n
Cyprian, 103, 149
    Nevin's articles on, 5–6, 59

DeBie, Linden, 59
Docetism, 4, 87

SUBJECT AND AUTHOR INDEX

Economy, 74, 89, 99–100, 109
    Christian, 96
    of grace, 116
    of redemption, 39, 56, 60, 104, 111, 113, 117, 165
    of salvation, 102, 146
    of the Church, 71, 108, 156, 159
    of the gospel, 52, 74, 88
    of the pastoral office, 44
    of the spirit, 48
    of the world, 24
    of our present life, 43
Ebionism, 4, 87
Election and Predestination, 71–73, 78–87, 93–97, 102–4 *see also* Nevin, John Williamson, doctrine of election
Episcopacy, 132, 144–45
Ernesti, Johann, 63
experimental religion, 16–17
Eutychianism, 4

Freedom, doctrine of, 21–22

German Reformed Church, 1, 30, 36, 59, 129
Griffin, Edward, 138n
Grotius, Hugo, 114–15

Hegelianism, 3–4, 5n, 22n
Heidelberg Catechism, 153
Hirsch, Emanuel, 37
Hodge, Charles, 18n, 59–60, 61n, 62, 72–79, 92–93, 122–23, 146n
Holy Spirit, 16, 40, 44, 166
    economy of, 48
    gift, 39, 41
    mission of, 39, 73, 123, 147, 157–58, 166, 169
    sending of, 148–49, 158, 161

Inaugural Address, 35

Jerome, 137
Judaism, 28

Kingdom of God, 15, 17, 19–20, 22, 31, 67, 77, 79, 159
    catholic, 15, 26
    progressive nature of, 23
    mysteries of, 52–53

Ladd, William, 31n
Layman, David, 104n
Lectures on Pastoral Theology, 36
Littlejohn, Brad, 10, 37n

Löhe, Johann, 37
Lutheranism and Lutheran theology, 30, 37

Manichaeanism, 4, 20
Marshall College, 59
Mayer Liturgy, 129
Mercersburg Seminary, 35, 59
Methodism, 31
Millennium, 17, 24, 27
Mohammedanism, 15, 27

Nestorius and Nestorianism, 4, 167
Nevin, John Williamson
    doctrine of election, 18, 25–26, 60, 61n, 107n
    high-church Calvinist, 1, 10
    organicism of, 2
    predestination according to, 108n
    pastoral ministry, 34–37
    pastoral office, 36–37
Nicene–Constantinopolitan Creed, 9, 159n
Nichols, James, 37, 59

Order of Worship (1866), 36, 129
Olshausen, Hermann, 120
Origen, 137
Osiander, Andreas, 37

Paganism, 27, 135–36
Paley, William, 96, 100n
Pelagianism, 4, 95
Personal Holiness, 35
predestination *see* election and predestination
Presbyterianism, 1, 31, 145
Princeton *and* Princeton Theology, 1n, 73n, 111
private judgment, 5, 31, 35
Procrustes, 93
Provisional Liturgy (1857), 36, 129
Prussia, Evangelical Church of, 45
pseudo-catholicism, 32
Puritanism, 150–51, 155–59, 163

Quakers, 143, 145–46, 170

Rauch, Frederick, 3, 13n, 51n,
Romanism, 21, 30

Schaff, Phillip, 1, 3–5, 9, 37, 129
science, 19–22, 24, 28, 42, 161n
Sectarianism, 3–5, 10, 29–31, 142–43, 163
Socinianism, 102n
Spener, Jacob, 130
Spurgeon, Charles, 137
Supralapsarianism, 73, 90

Taylor, William, 96
Tertullian, 137, 140, 149n

Unitarianism, 95
Universalism, 25

Village Lyceum, 143
Visser 't Hooft, William, 9

Wentz, Richard, 10
Western Theological Seminary, 35, 61n
Westminster Confession, 60, 110n, 153
Winebrenner, John, 4, 156
world, evangelization of, 16

Yoder, John Howard, 9
Young Men's Association, 143

www.ingramcontent.com/pod-product-compliance
Lightning Source LLC
Chambersburg PA
CBHW080411230426
43662CB00016B/2376